WITH CHRIST THROUGH THE YEAR

VIDI AQUAM

ALLELUIA

With Christ Through the Year

The Liturgical Year in Word and Symbols

By

Rev. Bernard Strasser, O.S.B.

Illustrated by
Sister M. A. Justina Knapp, O.S.B.

AROUCA
PRESS

ISBN: 978-1-990685-20-0

Arouca Press
PO Box 55003
Bridgeport PO
Waterloo, ON N2J 3G0
Canada
www.aroucapress.com
Send inquiries to info@aroucapress.com

PREFACE

In that intimate discourse which our Blessed Lord had with His disciples the evening before He went to His death He said to them: "I will not now call you servants, for the servant knoweth not what his lord doth. But I have called you friends, because all things whatsoever I have heard from my Father, I have made known to you" (John 15:15).

It may be said that the purpose of this book is to continue this work of Christ in behalf of those who are faithful to Him, that love and devotion for Him may grow in their hearts. The liturgy has been called "the life of the Church." The life of the Church is itself a mystical re-presentation of the life of Christ. Therefore, whoever enters into a more loving appreciation of the life of the Church, as it is brought before us in the course of the liturgical year, will arrive at a better understanding of "what his lord doth."

While seeking to bring a better understanding of the liturgical year than the mere use of the missal can give to one who is not trained to analysis and meditation, the author avoids the abundance of instruction found in some works of like purpose. His one great aim is to lead the faithful to live on a higher plane — the plane on which Christ lived His earthly life, in union with and in submission to the will of the Father — by living in union with His

Mystical Body and daily offering themselves with Him in the sacrifice of the Mass as a holocaust to the Father.

A truly sublime aim! Who but God can foresee what the results will be for the individual, for the Church, for the world at large, if many are won over, by the use of this book, to live the Christ-life, to which it gives inspiration and guidance? May the Spirit of God fill the hearts of those who follow its teachings with peace and joy to sweeten life in this vale of sorrows, a foretaste and pledge of life everlasting, to which we are called but which we so often lose sight of in the trials and temptations of the present.

✠ ALCUIN DEUTSCH, O.S.B.

Abbot

St. John's Abbey
Collegeville, Minnesota

FOREWORD TO THE AMERICAN EDITION

In his *Motu Proprio* on sacred music, issued November 22, 1903, the saintly Pope Pius X, with strong emphasis on the value of public divine worship, urged a deeper understanding and an "active participation in the most holy mysteries and in the public and solemn prayer of the Church."

In response to this wish of the Vicar of Jesus Christ and to meet the growing need for an intelligent and intimate living with the Church and her liturgy, the original of this book was written and published in 1938 at the Abbey of Clervaux in the Grand Duchy of Luxemburg, a renowned center of liturgical life and prayer.

In its scope this book occupies a position between the more detailed works of those champions of the liturgical movement in Europe, Dom Prosper Guéranger and Pius Parsch, and the somewhat condensed introductions found in most editions of the missal. The author's aim has been to present simply and clearly the historical and grace-giving significance of the liturgy with its holy feasts and seasons and in this way assist the faithful to appreciate its riches and beauty.

For this edition, the original has been revised and adapted to American needs and conditions with the help of American confreres at St. John's Abbey, Collegeville, Minnesota, and the Sisters of St. Benedict's Convent, St. Joseph, Minnesota.

The illustrations, originally drawn by Dom Pirmin Fox of Clervaux, have been supplied by Sister M. A. Justina Knapp of St. Benedict's Convent, author of *Christian Symbols* (Milwaukee: The Bruce Publishing Co., 1935).

Both to his confreres at St. John's Abbey and to the Sisters at St. Benedict's the author gratefully acknowledges their generous assistance.

May this American edition help the faithful to live more fully the liturgical life of the Church, which is the primary and indispensable source of the true Christian spirit.

BERNARD STRASSER, O.S.B.
St. Michael's Abbey
Metten, Bavaria

St. John's Abbey
Collegeville, Minnesota
Easter, 1945

CONTENTS

TEMPORAL CYCLES: THE PROPER OF THE TIME

LIST OF ILLUSTRATIONS

WITH CHRIST THROUGH THE YEAR

INTRODUCTORY

The Liturgy: What It Is

The word *liturgy* is of Greek origin and means public work or service. Greeks of the pre-Christian era used the term for the service rendered to the State by government officials and for whatever service the individual citizen might render to the same authority. Referred to a mere citizen, the term was generally used to designate his contribution to the public welfare in time of war, whether by way of equipping some unit of the army or navy or by some less spectacular means.

In the language of the Christian Church, *liturgy* also means a public service. It is that service or worship which we, as Christians, members of the Mystical Body baptized in the name of Christ our Saviour, owe to the Triune God, our Creator, Redeemer, and Sanctifier.

1. *Liturgy is service.* It is neither play nor recreation nor artistic enjoyment. It is not something which is meant to please or displease us, nor is it a subjective act which we may watch or listen to with complete sympathy or utter apathy, depending on our mood at the moment. Service is not a matter of caprice or frame of mind, or of free choice; it is a matter of duty. The official, the laborer, the working girl, each

and every human being exists not for his own sake but primarily for the honor and glory of almighty God, to whom he is in duty bound.

The primary consideration, therefore, is not that one may get something from liturgical worship; rather the primary consideration is God and His glory. The important thing is not whether a man is in the right mood or humor for the liturgy, for Sunday Mass, for instance, but that he fulfill his duty to God, as St. Benedict says, "that God may be glorified."

2. *Liturgy is the service of God.* It is that service or worship which God desires and can demand as Lord, Creator, and Judge of mankind. The Lord, and not the servant, determines *how* this service must be rendered, *what* must be done, and *when* and *where* it is to be done. How wrong, therefore, are those who say, "I pray in the woods, on the mountaintop; I worship God in the quiet of my room, out in God's free nature." Such prayer, of course, may be good. But the notion that it fulfills man's obligation to worship God is obviously false. The right to make decisions belongs to the master, not to the servant; not the children but their parents make final decisions. Similarly, it is for God, and not His creatures, to decide on the type of service men are to render Him.

As Christians we are in the happy position of having God Himself actually determine our way of worship. The only-begotten Son of God, Jesus Christ, came down to earth from heaven to show us what we owe to God. Through His holy life, His teaching and prayer, through His suffering, sacrifice, and death, He offered that service to God which our first parents in their pride and disobedience denied Him. By means of that sublime and holy service Christ redeemed mankind and reconciled us with God.

Because this divine service of Christ was all powerful in bringing salvation to the world, the Church in her liturgy has added nothing new to it. She merely continues the redemptive activity of Christ, her Divine Founder, for the honor of God and the salvation of souls. And she does this primarily in the holy sacrifice of the Mass because it is the sacrifice of Christ, the center and the starting point of all liturgy. In the Mass the Church prays, teaches, and offers as Christ has taught her to do; and in her other liturgical acts, particularly the sacraments, instituted and entrusted to her by Christ, she continues the work of our Redeemer. For that reason we can rightly say that in the Catholic Church Christ continues to live. He lives in His sacrifice, in His sacraments, and in all other acts or prayers which stem from these vital sources and confer grace on men. Together these acts make up our divine service, the liturgy of the Church.

3. *The Catholic Church is a body,* an assembly, a community of the baptized; it is the family of Christians, God's children. Her divine services are, therefore, social or communal. Man is not an isolated unit; hence he should not pray alone. The priest does not offer sacrifice alone; all Christians, the entire Mystical Body of Christ, the entire Communion of Saints, pray and offer together, and Christ Himself offers and prays with them.

The most complete expression of this social aspect of divine service is the parochial or parish Mass on Sundays and feast days. There the priest and the faithful, the pastor and the parish, without distinction of wealth or poverty, age or youth, fulfill their divine service to God. Together they sing and pray; together they hear the word of God as it is preached to them; and together they offer sacrifice and receive the Bread of Life.

"The Catholic liturgy is, therefore, the most sublime thing on earth. It is the very heart of the Catholic Church. In the liturgy God is praised, and the fruits of the redemption are applied to us in an ever growing measure. In the liturgy God comes to us, and we approach God. God comes to us through His Son with His word, with His life, and with His Holy Spirit. We approach God with our thanks, with our praise, and with our petitions through Christ, our Lord and Redeemer. In the liturgy the entire 'Our Father' is realized. The name of the Father is hallowed. His kingdom comes. His will is done. He gives us the daily bread of our souls, and all the rest shall be given besides. He forgives us our sins. He helps us overcome temptation and delivers us from evil. Hence, the holy martyr-bishop Ignatius, a disciple of the apostle John, could write: 'See to it that you meet more frequently for the Eucharistic sacrifice and give praise to God. For if you meet frequently, the power of Satan will be broken and his pernicious influence will be annihilated through the perfect unity of your faith.' "[1]

[1] P. Ettensperger, O.S.B., *Das Ministrantenbuch* (Freiburg: Herder, 1937), p. 11.

Of course, Christ did not determine minutely every detail of the liturgy. For the most part, He indicated only the essentials. He said, for instance, "Do this for a commemoration of me" (Luke 22:19). With these words He commanded His apostles and their successors to celebrate the sacrifice of the Mass unto the end of time, thus continuing and re-presenting His sacrifice on the cross. Again, He said: "Going therefore, teach ye all nations, baptizing them in the name of the Father, and of the Son, and of the Holy Ghost, teaching them . . ." (Matt. 28:19). Here He gave them their apostolate, commissioning them to evangelize the world and to administer Baptism and the other sacraments. Previously He had said: "Thus therefore shall you pray: 'Our Father . . . give us this day our daily bread . . .'" (Matt. 6:9 ff.). These words stress the significant fact that liturgical prayer is not for personal needs but rather for God's glory and the welfare of His Church.

But the Saviour desired that all divine service be performed worthily, with dignity and beauty, so that the greatness and majesty of the infinitely holy God might be fittingly honored and glorified. For that reason Christ sent the Holy Ghost upon His apostles and the Church. With His help they were to nurture and develop the Christian way of worship, the essentials of which He had entrusted to them. Thus in the early days of the Church, the apostles and their successors throughout the centuries have prescribed in detail how priests should celebrate Mass, administer the sacraments and sacramentals, and

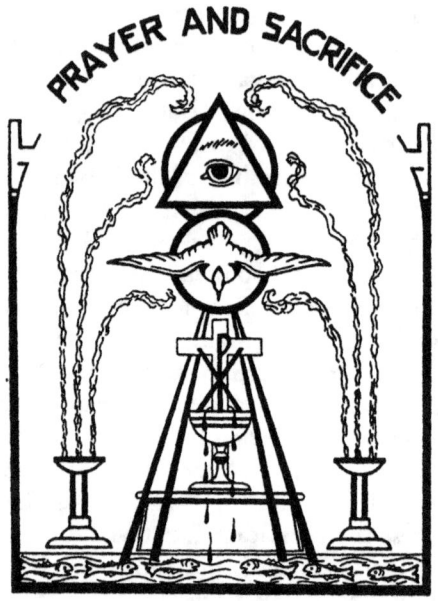

This illustration expresses the ideal and purpose of all liturgy. Liturgy, the service of God, comprises the prayer and sacrifice (*incense*) which we, as members of the community of the redeemed must give to the Triune God in adoration and praise, in thanksgiving, propitiation, and petition. Through the Holy Ghost, the Sanctifier (*dove*), the Triune God (*triangle*) distributes to us the redeeming merits of Christ's death on the cross. The graces of Christ (*rays*) come to us principally through the sacrifice of the Mass (*chalice, altar*). From the inexhaustible stream of the Church's graces we receive, like *fish* in a stream, grace and strength for a holy life and a happy death. The illustration also represents the liturgical prayers of the priest at a solemn High Mass when, after blessing the *incense* (the symbol of our prayer and sacrifice), he incenses the offerings, and says: "May this incense, which Thou hast blessed, O Lord, ascend to Thee, and may Thy mercy descend upon us."

observe the feasts and seasons of the Church year. All this belongs to the liturgy of the Church.

In summary: *Liturgy is the Church's official service of God and everything directly pertaining to that service.* The entire liturgy has a twofold aim: the honor and glory of God, and the sanctification of souls.

The Liturgical Community

Our Divine Saviour said: "Where there are two or three gathered together in my name, there am I in the midst of them" (Matt. 18:20). Where, therefore, two or three pray together in the name and for the sake of Jesus, there is a liturgical community in the broadest sense of the term.

1. The *Christian family* is the first and most important liturgical community. It is founded on the sacraments of Baptism and Matrimony, sustained and strengthened through participation in divine services and the reception of the sacraments, through family prayer, through labor, love, and in obedience to the commandments, through the Christian education of children, and through a life lived in the spirit of the Church, a life in conformity with the liturgy and the liturgical year.

The Christian family is in the spiritual sense a true house of God, built up by God through the sacrament of Matrimony on the pillars of unity, sanctity, and indissolubility, and furnished with the treasures of His grace. As such its prayer life is a corporate one: the members pray together in the morning, before and after meals, and in the evening. The old custom of family prayers at night should be revived. It is especially desirable and of truly inestimable spiritual value. Prayers are followed by a short reading from Sacred Scripture (appropriate to the season) or the reading of some other commendable spiritual book.

It will be natural then, for a family altar or shrine to have an honored place, decorated according to the respective season of the Church year, to stimulate genuine Christian piety. These things will lead to a more solemn and Christian celebration of family feasts and anniversaries: wedding anniversaries of parents, name days, baptismal and First Communion days of the entire family. There is abundant opportunity for a more complete understanding of the spiritual significance of these occasions, and the fitting celebration of them would do much to restore to our American homes true family joy and unity.[2] Of such families it could be said in truth, "Where there is prayer, there is faith; where there is faith, there is love; where there is love, there is peace; where there is peace, there is God; and where God is, there is no need or grief."

2. The next and larger liturgical community is the *parish,* frequently and significantly called the parish family. This is made up of the families belonging to a definite parish church. As the house of God, the parish church is their communal, paternal home. Here among His children dwells the eternal God as the infallible teacher of truth, as the generous dispenser of graces, as the infinitely powerful bringer of peace.

---

[2] Cf. Terese Mueller, *Family Life in Christ* (Collegeville, Minn.: The Liturgical Press, 1942).

Every part of His house, the parish church, has but one purpose: to unite us more closely to Him. The tower points an inviting finger to heaven, the ideal and goal of our life and labors. This same tower contains the blessed bells which sound in our hearts over and over the *Sursum Corda* (lift up your hearts). In this parish church is the baptismal font where we were introduced to supernatural life and made children of God. Here is the confessional where repeatedly we have received the remission of our sins from an all-merciful Father. Here is the Communion rail at which we have often knelt to receive the Bread of Heaven. Most prominent of all is the altar representing Christ, on which He daily makes the supreme oblation of Himself to His Father. At its steps we received the sacrament of Confirmation from the hands of the bishop, and before it our parents in holy Matrimony pledged eternal fidelity to one another. Not far away stands the pulpit from which God's truth and commandments are preached to us by His representative, our pastor. Here, too, are the cross and the Way of the Cross, symbols teaching us the meaning of the love of Christ for man, and asking us to love Him in return and to carry courageously our own cross in times of pain and sorrow. Finally, there are pictures and statues of saints which depict their Christian life and death, and seem to say to us: "What we have accomplished, you, too, can do. Follow us on the road to heaven."

In the parish church liturgical and communal life finds its most complete expression in the parochial solemn High Mass of Sundays and holydays. Here the pastor, the parish father, who is the consecrated mediator between God and man, offers the sacrifice of the Mass for his parishioners. In this act, father and children, pastor and people are one; they are united in love and loyalty to a common Father. In the parish church the members of the parish family pray during the parochial Mass, not individually, but jointly with one another. They become a sacrifice-offering community, a worshiping community, a banquet-sharing community in the Offertory, Consecration, and Communion of the Mass. As one body they pray that God may be glorified in their parish church, that a pure and acceptable sacrifice may be offered to Him, and that, having destroyed the power of the evil one, Christ may reign forever. Their prayer at Mass is never a private one; rather they pray the Mass with the priest, the official representative of the invisible divine High Priest, Jesus Christ.

This communal worship is necessary if the parish family is to live the life of the Church and to share fully in Christ's sacrifice on the cross, re-presented to us in each Mass. In his Apostolic Constitution, *Divini Cultus,* Pope Pius XI writes: "The faithful come to church in order to derive piety from its chief source, by taking an active part in the venerated mysteries and public solemn prayers of the Church. It is most important that the faithful should not assist at the sacred ceremonies merely as detached and silent spectators, but, filled with a deep sense of the beauty of the liturgy, they should sing alternately with the clergy or the choir. . . ."

Today pastors are profoundly disturbed by the lack

of interest on the part of the parishioners in the parochial High Mass. In large cities for the most part it is meagerly attended. There are many reasons which may account for this: the custom of having a children's Mass, the demands of sports, leisure-time activities, vacations, excursions, the desire to attend the shortest Mass possible (which is likely to be the earliest or the latest), and, in general, the soul-killing pagan spirit of today. The suggestions of Pius XI, quoted above, if they were carried out, would help to restore the parochial High Mass to its own position of prominence. He says, for instance, that the faithful should participate more actively in divine worship by singing Gregorian chant, especially the parts definitely assigned to the people. The wise pontiff believed that this could be "best effected by teaching chant in schools, pious confraternities, and similar associations." The faithful, imbued with a better understanding and appreciation of High Mass, would no longer be idle spectators nor silent bystanders, but active co-offerers, co-worshipers, and co-partakers in the Holy Sacrifice.

The average parish, like the normal American family, has many other activities of a social or semi-social nature, such as community gatherings and clubs of various kinds. Important as these may be in the sphere of Catholic Action, they are never a substitute for the official parish worship. Our parishes should strive to recapture the spirit of the early Christians, united as they were in a common brotherhood whose most sublime act always was the communal celebration of the parish Mass. Then truly realized in the parish church would be the words used at the Mass of the Dedication of a Church. "Awe inspiring is this place: it is the House of God and Gate of heaven."[3]

3. *The diocese*[4] is the next largest liturgical community, since it is composed of a number of parishes. A diocese is often called a bishopric, for at its head is the bishop as father and spiritual overseer. Successor to the apostles, the bishop has the power to ordain priests as his helpers. On Holy Thursday he consecrates for all his parish churches the holy oils (oil of catechumens, chrism, and oil of the sick) to be used in the administration of the sacraments of Baptism, Confirmation, Holy Orders, and Extreme Unction as well as in various blessings and consecrations (blessing of bells, blessing of baptismal water, consecration of a church, etc.).

The bishop's church, known as the *cathedral,* is the mother church of the diocese. If it has been consecrated, the annual commemoration of its dedication is observed in all parishes of the diocese. The bishop must from time to time visit every parish in his diocese to administer Confirmation. As marks of his dignity he wears the pectoral cross, the miter, the crozier, symbolizing the pastoral solicitude he has for his flock. The ring on his right hand is a symbol of the union existing between him and the faithful of his diocese; to him it is a symbol of the love and

---

[3] Cf. "The Parish as a Supernatural Reality," by Dom Maurier Schurr, O.S.B.; *Orate Fratres,* Vol. XII, Apr. to Aug., 1938.

[4] The word *diocese,* derived from the Greek, means literally the surrounding countryside. The Church uses the term, however, to denote the territory under the jurisdiction of a bishop.

care he owes his people, and to them it is a symbol of the love, obedience, and respect they owe their shepherd.

In the direction and government of the diocese, the bishop is assisted by the vicar-general, the chancellor, various officials, and especially by the consultors and deans.

That there is such a thing as diocesan family-consciousness is evidenced by the second prayer of the Canon of the Mass, in which the priest prays daily for the bishop of the diocese and for the faithful entrusted to his care.

4. *The Holy Catholic Church* as the universal Church includes the entire liturgical communion, the great Catholic world-family. Its head is the pope or Holy Father. As bishop of Rome he is the direct successor of St. Peter, the first bishop of Rome. For this reason the Catholic Church is also called the Roman Church, that is, the church which recognizes the bishop of Rome as its head and representative of Christ, its Divine Founder. To this great world-family belong all who have been validly baptized "in the name of the Father and of the Son and of the Holy Ghost." In the administration, guidance, and ruling of this large family, the Holy Father is assisted by the cardinals and various Congregations.

In the Canon of every Mass the celebrant prays for the pope. Anniversaries of the dedication of the principal (papal) churches of Rome are feast days for the entire Church.[5]

Every Christian is obliged to love this Catholic

[5] See Chapter on Feasts of the Dedication of a Church, page 315 ff.

world-family just as he loves his own parish or diocese. Nor may he remain indifferent when the Church is being persecuted or oppressed in other lands. As a member of this family, he must be concerned with the welfare of all the other members; their sufferings and their happiness are a matter of vital interest to him.

Divisions of the Liturgy

Every good act performed with the right intention and for the love of God is a service of God, and therefore, in a certain sense, divine service. The divine service, however, to which the term *liturgy* specifically applies is the official, communal cult in which external acts are performed by ordained and duly authorized ministers (liturgists) for the honor of God and the salvation of souls. The liturgy was instituted in part by Christ Himself and in part by the Church under the guidance of the Holy Spirit. Most of the liturgical functions, at least in their essentials, date back to the early Christian era; others developed in the course of centuries, for the liturgy is not rigid and dead, but living and flexible, subject to continual development, yet always unchanged in its basic and dogmatic elements. Moreover, in a society as large and as well organized as the Church, the liturgy is not performed at the whim of the individual minister; rather, the Church determines who may validly enact the liturgy, and how, when, and where this is to be done.

Since the liturgy includes and influences so vast a range of persons and things, it will be well to consider its various elements one by one. For that purpose they are taken up in the following order:

1. *Holy Seasons:* Every Catholic knows that if he misses Mass on Sunday or a holyday of obligation without sufficient reason, that is, if he neglects to be present at the principal parts of Mass, he commits a grievous sin. The Church celebrates Mass on weekdays too, though generally with less solemnity. In fact, in the manner of the celebration she makes a definite distinction between weekdays and Sundays. Even the individual weeks and seasons of the year differ in festive character, and are wonderfully arranged according to the significance of the redemptive mysteries which they commemorate. All these, the days, weeks, and feast-day periods, are *holy seasons.*

2. *Sacred Places:* The liturgy of the Church, especially the holy sacrifice of the Mass and the sacraments, may not be celebrated or administered in just any place regardless of its character. We have, therefore, churches and chapels solemnly dedicated and blessed for that purpose. Only by way of exception is the liturgy performed elsewhere, like in the open or in private homes. Catholic cemeteries and the individual graves in which the bodies of Christians are buried, are blessed. All these places, which have been dedicated and blessed, are called *sacred places.*

3. *Sacred Things:* In the celebration of the liturgy, the Church uses a uniform language, Latin; in the sung parts, the use of Gregorian chant has been consistently urged by the supreme pontiffs. As

ministers of the liturgy, priests wear special garments, called vestments; there are also sacred vessels reserved for liturgical rites: chalice, paten, monstrance, etc., and sacred linens: corporal, purificator, pall, etc. In our churches and chapels, the altar, which represents Christ, occupies the central place; there are also other furnishings such as the baptismal font, the pulpit, confessionals, Communion rail, stations, etc. Many of these receive their own particular blessing, and accordingly are called *sacred things*.[6]

4. *Sacred Persons:* As was previously said, the Church has laid down requirements for those who are to initiate and to enact official divine service. Only a regularly ordained Catholic priest has the power to change bread and wine into the Body and Blood of Christ or to remit sin; he receives both of these sacred powers in the sacrament of Holy Orders. From among the priests are chosen the bishops, cardinals, and pope. They direct the liturgy of the Church and prescribe, in minutest detail, everything concerning its celebration. The pope, bishops, and priests together make up the *hierarchy*[7] and rule the Church of

---

[6] By special indult various Eastern rites, while professing the same faith and acknowledging the jurisdiction of the pope, use their own language (Greek, Armenian, Syriac, Chaldean, etc.) as well as their own ceremonies, vestments, and prayers, which differ from the familiar Latin rite. These are the Eastern Catholic Churches and are to be distinguished from the schismatic so-called Orthodox Eastern Churches which do not belong to the Roman Catholic Church. Thus as many as ten different languages are used in liturgical functions.

[7] *Hierarchy* is a word derived from the Greek meaning sacred government, that is, "the totality of powers established in the Church for the guiding of men to their eternal salvation, but divided into various orders or grades, in which the inferior are subject to and yield obedience to the higher ones" (*The Catholic Encyclopedia*, Ed. 1910, Vol. VII, p. 322, A. Van Hove).

Christ in the exercise of their duties as teachers, priests, and shepherds.

Members of various religious orders who, through their profession of vows, have consecrated themselves to the service of God and the Church are also called *sacred persons.*

5. *Sacred Functions:* Under the previous divisions we have presented the things which are needed or employed in the liturgy and the persons who enact the liturgical functions. These functions consist primarily of the holy sacrifice of the Mass and the administration of the sacraments. Included also are the sacramentals such as the blessings and consecration of a church, blessing of bells, graves, candles, water, ashes, etc. The recitation of the Divine Office, as given in the breviary, is also considered a liturgical act.

These, in summary, are the five divisions in the liturgy:

1. Holy seasons: day, week, church year, feasts of Christ and of the saints.
2. Sacred places: churches, chapels, cemeteries.
3. Sacred things: language and chant; vestments, vessels, linens, and books; furnishings of the church.
4. Sacred persons: hierarchy — pope, cardinals, bishops, priests, religious.
5. Sacred functions: Mass, sacraments, sacramentals.

The Lord's Day: Sunday

To sincere Christians every day is holy, for it measures out a portion of the time which God gives us to work for His honor and for our salvation. Knowing the fickleness and forgetfulness of men, God ordained that certain days be set aside and dedicated to His service; in the Old Law it was the Sabbath; in the New Law, it is the Sunday.[8] In the first pages of Sacred Scripture we read that God created heaven and earth and all things in six days. On the seventh day He rested from His labors; He blessed and sanctified that day, and called it the Sabbath, the day of rest. People used to abstain from all work on that day and serve God in prayer and sacrifice; hence, the Sabbath became for the Jews the great day of rest, of prayer, and of sacrifice. On that day they commemorated the greatness of God's deeds and blessings, His wonderful guidance of the people of Israel, and they offered to Him sacrifices of praise, thanks, petition, and propitiation. God's command, "Remember thou keep holy the Sabbath," had been clear and stern. Transgression of this command was punished with death.

In the New Law the apostles themselves made the first day of the week a holyday, "the Lord's day," to be devoted to the worship of God and the care of one's soul. They had substantial reasons for this change. On the first day, God the Father created light; hence that day was known as the day of light, the day of the sun, Sunday. Furthermore, Christ's resurrection took place on a Sunday. All four Evangelists bear witness to this. The day is considered the holiest and most sacred of the Church year. Christ,

---

[8] In the liturgy the word *dominica* is used for Sunday (e.g., *dies dominica,* the Lord's day). Cf. Apoc. 1:10.

the Light of the World, shone brightest on this His resurrection day, a fact which is symbolized by the beautiful paschal candle, solemnly blessed on Holy Saturday. By His resurrection Christ dignified and elevated the first day of the week in a particular and special manner. And it was on Pentecost Sunday that the Holy Ghost, in the form of fiery tongues, descended upon the apostles to enlighten and strengthen them for their pentecostal work of evangelizing the Jews and Gentiles.

Sunday is truly the Lord's Day, the day of the Blessed Trinity, the day of the Father, the Son, and the Holy Spirit. In her liturgy and especially in the preface of the Holy Trinity the Church calls our attention to the creative, redemptive, and sanctifying operations of the Trinity, inviting us to meditate on these sublime truths. Each Sunday is a miniature Easter, a postcelebration of the most significant Sunday in the life of Christ and in the life of the Church. Just as Easter is the pivotal point of the ecclesiastical year, so Sunday is the pivotal point of the week. From it flow blessings or curses upon our work of the week, upon our lifetime work. "As your Sunday, so the day of your death."

Each Sunday, then, is a day for thanking God for all His goodness to mankind and for His guidance and providence in our own lives. It is also a day to be set aside for the care of our souls that we may realize in them Christ's redemption. For this reason the day must be one of personal resurrection from sin and indifference. Nor is Sunday to be spent for ourselves alone; it should be a day of holy, pentecostal labor for our fellow men. In the commandments of the Church, God asks that one seventh of our lives be directed exclusively to His service and to the care of our souls — how little to give in exchange for the treasures of heaven!

The apostles carried out their divine service every Sunday with readings, singing, preaching, and the celebration of the Eucharist. After Constantine gave freedom to the Church in the year 313, the Sunday rest was prescribed by law. Thereupon, the ecclesiastical celebration of Sunday spread rapidly, and the development of a more elaborate liturgical celebration followed quite naturally. The people were not satisfied with assembling only for the sacrifice of the Mass, but met also for an early morning service (Lauds) and an evening service (Vespers). Sunday thus became more and more what it was intended to be: a day of prayer on which the Holy Sacrifice was offered; a day of recollection set apart from the secular cares of the other days of the week; a day dedicated to the Holy Trinity.

The heart of Sunday is the re-presentation of the sacrifice of Christ through which we were redeemed. God's commandment to keep the day holy is most perfectly fulfilled, therefore, by the parish High Mass with sermon and with the communal, sacrificial banquet, Holy Communion, partaking of which in the early Christian centuries was a matter of course to all who were present.

Sanctified Weekday

Sunday is not the only holyday; every day is holy. And so the Church celebrates Mass daily, and daily invites the faithful to participate, for it is at Mass and in Holy Communion that Christ makes present to us His sacrifice on Calvary and distributes the graces there merited for us.

Each day priests, clerics in major orders, and religious with solemn vows are obliged by the command of the Church to perform in her name, that is, in the name of the entire Mystical Body of Christ, the *Canonical Hours.*[9] These contain the official praise, thanksgiving, propitiation, and petition of the Church and constitute the prayer of Christ, living, praying, and working in her. In some communities of secular clergy and in many regular religious communities, this Divine Office is solemnly prayed or chanted at various hours of the day and night. In Benedictine monasteries it is performed with special solemnity, for St. Benedict specifically commanded his monks "to prefer nothing whatsoever to the work of God" (the Divine Office).

The breviary is divided into eight parts: *Matins* and *Lauds,* the midnight prayer; *Prime, Tierce, Sext, None* (prayers to be said at the first, third, sixth, and ninth hours of the day), *Vespers* (the objective evening prayer),[10] and *Compline* (the final night prayer).

It is a source of consolation and joy to know that at every hour of the day and night, Holy Mass is

---

[9] From the short index of rubrics, *breviarium,* the book (or books) containing these *hours* received the name *breviary.*

[10] *Vespers* is the Church's official song of praise at the end of the day; as such it is objective in contrast to *Compline* which reflects to a great extent the personal feelings of the individual soul as he seeks God's protection for the night, and, symbolically, for the moment of death.

being celebrated somewhere in the great Catholic world, and that the prayer of the breviary constantly rises up to God for each individual Christian and for all collectively. It is possible for Christians all over the world to unite themselves daily, at least in spirit, with this uninterrupted service of sacrifice and prayer. In this way, every day, even every hour takes on a deeper significance, and we can truly speak of a holy weekday, sanctified as it is by liturgical prayer and sacrifice.

Sanctified Week

The Church in her liturgy does not reckon the year according to months, but according to weeks. Every week derives its meaning from the preceding Sunday, which is the beginning and focal point of the week. Thus we understand the expressions *week in Advent, week in Lent, Easter week,* etc. In the liturgy the days of the week are designated with reference to the Sunday, which, as the Lord's Day, *dies dominica,* is considered the first day. Monday, the second day of the week, is called *feria secunda;* Tuesday, the third day, *feria tertia;* the other weekdays are similarly treated, with the exception of Saturday which still retains its ancient name of *Sabbath.*

The votive Masses (Masses of special devotion promised for certain reasons), which the priest may celebrate on weekdays when there is no feast of rank, give a hint of how the Church wants us to sanctify the week. The glory of God and the veneration of His Blessed Mother and the saints all have their place in weekday divine service.

The following votive Masses are suggested in the liturgy as particularly appropriate:

Monday: Mass of the Blessed Trinity (refrain of Sunday); Tuesday: Mass of the Angels; Wednesday: Mass of St. Joseph (or of Sts. Peter and Paul or of the Common of the Apostles); Thursday: Mass of the Holy Ghost or of the Blessed Sacrament; Friday: Mass of the Holy Cross or of the Passion; Saturday: Mass of the Blessed Virgin (according to the season).

THE WEEK SANCTIFIED BY PRAYER LABOR AND SUFFERING

This sketch illustrates what the liturgy means by a sanctified week. Sunday, dedicated to the Blessed Trinity (symbolized by the *triangle*), holds the central position, and the graces of its Mass (represented by the *streams* flowing from the *chalice*) inundate and supernaturalize the entire week, though the votive intentions of each weekday Mass may vary, as has been pointed out. A life consisting of weeks and days so sanctified will surely end in an eternal Sunday in the enjoyment of the beatific vision of the Triune God.

Sanctified Year

The civil calendar is altogether a prosaic and monotonous thing, presenting month after month, day after day with numerical accuracy, but with no variation except a possible change of color to mark red-letter days like Sundays and holidays. In contrast, the liturgical calendar of the Church is rich and beautiful. Sensitive to the joy or gravity of each season, its color corresponds to the mood of the various feasts and fasts. To be sure, this calendar, too, is a succession of days and weeks and months. But they are not cold and lifeless; they have been impregnated with warmth and vitality, and are concerned with the deepest mysteries and truths of our redemption — guilt and atonement, sin and grace, life and death, resurrection and eternal life.

In fact, the theme of the Church year is none other than Christ Himself: His life, His teachings, His miracles, His death and victory. The redemption He won for mankind is further portrayed in the lives of the saints (in whom redemption has been effective) who are presented to us in the course of the Church year as models and intercessors. The Church's purpose in her liturgical year is to keep before us the mysteries of Christ's life and the glorious achievements of His saints, so that by meditating on these and understanding them more fully we may become faithful imitators of Him and thus share more completely in the graces He is so ready to dispense to us. But the Church year is more than a memorial. From Christ it has received the very power to sanctify

THE SANCTIFIED YEAR

The significance of the Church year is clearly indicated in the accompanying illustration. Everything emanates from the Triune God (represented by the *triangle* above), the beginning and end of all things. Into this world was sent the only-begotten Son of God, Christ (signified by the *Chi-Rho* symbol), our Redeemer, the beginning and end of all Christian life (suggested by the use of *Alpha* and *Omega,* the first and last letters of the Greek alphabet). His life and work are re-presented to us by Mother Church in her liturgical seasons, the Christmas and Easter cycles of the Church year. In the illustration, the *inner circle* symbolizes the Christmas cycle which celebrates the mystery of the Incarnation. It is divided into three sections referring to (1) the time of preparation, (2) the celebration, culminating in the feasts of Christmas and Epiphany, and (3) the prolongation, consisting of the Sundays after Epiphany. The *outer circle* represents the Easter cycle which commemorates the mystery of the redemption. It, too, has three sections: (1) the preparation, consisting of Pre-Lent, Lent, and Passiontide, (2) the culmination of the season in Easter and Pentecost, and (3) the prolongation of the cycle in the Sundays after Pentecost. The two encircling *arrows* indicate that these mysteries proceed from God and lead back to God.

us, to re-enact in us at each season the mystery peculiar to it, and to confer its grace upon us, thus giving the divine nourishment we need to live our days and months in union with Christ.

Experience teaches that our knowledge of Christ and His mysteries and our love for Him and His saints would be sadly limited were not these facts recurrently put before us each year. As Pius XI said in the encyclical *Quas primas,* on instituting the Feast of Christ the King: "For people are instructed in the truths of faith and are brought to appreciate the inner joys of religion far more effectually by the annual celebration of our sacred mysteries than by any official pronouncements of the teaching of the Church. . . . Man is composed of body and soul, and he needs these external festivities so that the sacred rites, in all their beauty and variety, may stimulate him to drink more deeply of the fountain of God's teaching, that he may make it a part of himself and use it with profit for his spiritual life." The late holy father reinforces the truth of the statement: "to live the liturgical year is a most sure way to sanctity and perfection."

From God, with God, to God through Jesus Christ — these words express the spirit of the ecclesiastical year, the purpose of the entire liturgy, and the end of all Christian living.

Sanctified Life

The life of every Christian is to be a sanctified life, for such is the will of God: "Be holy because I am holy" (Lev. 11:44). At Baptism, the sponsors promise holiness of life in the name of the child, and God, in turn, says to the newly baptized soul: "Thou art my son" (Ps. 2:7). These baptismal promises are often repeated: at first Holy Communion, at Confirmation, and on other solemn occasions, when the Christian says before God and the assembled faithful: "Yes, I do promise to live and die a Catholic. I do renounce the devil and all his works. I do renounce his pomps. I do believe in God . . . in Jesus Christ . . . in the Holy Ghost . . . in the Holy Catholic Church."

Each call to divine service on Sundays and feast days, each ringing of the Angelus bell, each joy and each sorrow sent to us by God is an admonition: "Walk before me and be perfect" (Gen. 17:1). But especially by her holy liturgy, with the Eucharist as its center, Mother Church constantly reminds us to lead a holy life. Not only does she urge us to do so, but she also shows us the way. She supplies us with the grace to sanctify each hour, each week, each season, each year, in fact, our whole lives from the cradle to the grave. She even accompanies us beyond the grave into eternity, where by means of her prayers and offerings she secures for us eternal peace and rest.

Of this Christian life Christ is the beginning, the center, and the end. He, the only-begotten Son of God, our eternal King and Redeemer, through His atoning death on the cross reunited God and man. In Him we were baptized into a new life, into the Communion of Saints (suffering, militant, and triumphant), and into a close union with Christ, for we were engrafted onto the vine which is Christ, incorporated into the Mystical Body of which He is the

Christ who is the source of all sanctity normally dispenses His graces to us through the sacraments. His *Chi-Rho* symbol, therefore, occupies a central position in this illustration. The symbols for the sacraments of *Holy Orders* and *Matrimony* are within the inner circle near the source of the Christ-life, for these sacraments have been instituted primarily to perpetuate, safeguard, and foster, each in its own way, the supernatural and natural life of man, and thus have become the foundation stones of the Church and the home.

In the symbol for Holy Orders, the *fiery tongue* signifies ordination (the descent of the Holy Ghost); the *chalice* signifies the holy sacrifice of the Mass; and the *stole*, priestly power. In Matrimony, the *two rings* closely interlocked about the *Chi-Rho* indicate the indissolubility of the sacrament and also the fact that in marriage the contracting parties have entered into a closer union with Christ.

In the outer circle are the sacraments necessary for all Christians: *Baptism* gives us supernatural life (the *fish* is a symbol

Head. St. Paul repeatedly refers to this union between Christ and the baptized: "Now you are the body of Christ, and members of member" (1 Cor. 12:27); and "So we being many, are one body in Christ" (Rom. 12:5). Christ Himself compares this living union with that of the vine and the branches: "I am the vine, you are the branches" (John 15:5).

The visible community on earth which symbolizes the invisible, grace-giving, spiritual relationship of Christ and His members is the Church. She has in her treasury His inexhaustible supply of grace which she lavishly pours out on His members in the seven sacraments, instituted by Christ Himself.

Every Christian who is conscientious about his baptismal promises and who wishes to attain to his eternal goal realizes that it is his duty to lead a sanctified life. This means living the liturgical life of the Church with the Church, which entails above all an earnest and devout participation in the Eucharistic sacrifice

---

of the soul, the *candle* of life-in-Christ); *Confirmation* brings this life to adult status and makes us soldiers of Christ (the insignia are the *sword* and the *shield*); *Holy Eucharist,* as sacrifice (Holy Mass) and sacrificial meal (Holy Communion), has the highest position because it is the greatest and holiest of all the sacraments toward which all the others tend as to their goal and end; *Penance* reunites us to fellowship with Christ whenever sin has destroyed our union with Him (the *keys* suggest the binding and loosing power of the sacrament and the *scourge* denotes penance); *Extreme Unction* anoints and strengthens us for our passage into the fellowship of the saints in heaven (indicated by the *oil-stock* and the *olive branch,* a sign of victory).

The symbols of the different sacraments are linked together by those of the four ember seasons: *flowers* for spring, *spikes of grain* for summer, *grapes* for autumn, and the *olive branch* for winter. For further explanation, see page 37.

and sacrificial banquet. It means, too, the reception of the other sacraments according to his state of life and daily steadfastness in carrying out whatever particular work or duties God has entrusted to him.

Sundays and Feast Days

Besides Sundays, there are many feasts which the Church celebrates in the course of the year, feasts of our Lord, of His Blessed Mother, and of the saints. The greatest feast days are usually holydays of obligation.

1. *Not all Sundays and feast days are of equal rank.* Whoever examines a missal or a liturgical calendar will find listed for almost every day a feast either of our Lord or of a saint together with its rank. He will note that not all feasts of our Lord or of our Lady are of equal order, their rank depends upon their relative importance to the mystery of the redemption. Feasts of the saints also vary as to rank depending upon the importance of the role played by the saint in the history of the Church. The same principle applies to Sundays, their rank and significance depend almost entirely upon their incidental position in the Church year.[11]

2. Sundays may be classified as (*a*) Sundays of the first class, (*b*) Sundays of the second class, and (*c*) ordinary Sundays.

a) The following are Sundays of the first class: the first Sunday of Advent, the four Sundays of Lent, Passion Sunday, Palm Sunday, Easter Sunday, Low

---

[11] The Sunday on which the Feast of Christ the King is celebrated is an exception to this rule.

Sunday, and Pentecost Sunday. These Sundays take
precedence over every other feast.

b) The following are Sundays of the second class:
the second, third, and fourth Sundays of Advent, and
the three Sundays immediately before Lent (Septuagesima, Sexagesima, and Quinquagesima).

c) All the other Sundays of the Church year are
ordinary Sundays: the Sundays after Epiphany, the
Sundays after Low Sunday, and the Sundays after
Pentecost.

3. In her differentiation of feasts, the Church has
classified them in six groups according to the solemnity with which they are celebrated. They are:

a) Doubles of the first class: These are so designated, first, because they have two Vespers, one on the
eve of the feast and the second on the feast itself; and
second, because the antiphons are doubled, that is, the
entire antiphon is said both at the beginning and at
the end of each psalm, whereas on lesser feasts[12] the
antiphons, having been merely intoned at the beginning of the psalm, are said in their entirety only at
the end of the psalm. This class includes about thirty
feasts: first, feasts of our Lord, Christmas, Epiphany,
Maundy Thursday, Good Friday, Holy Saturday, Easter Sunday, Easter Monday and Tuesday, Ascension,
Pentecost, Pentecost Monday and Tuesday, Trinity
Sunday, Corpus Christi, feasts of the Sacred Heart
and of Christ the King; second, some feasts of our
Lady and of the saints: Immaculate Conception (December 8), Annunciation (March 25), Assumption of
the Blessed Virgin (August 15), Dedication of St.

---

[12] See (*d*) and (*e*).

Michael the Archangel (September 29), Nativity of St. John the Baptist (June 24), St. Joseph (March 19), Solemnity of St. Joseph (third Wednesday after Easter), Sts. Peter and Paul (June 29), All Saints (November 1), the Precious Blood (July 1). Included also in this class are feasts of the dedication of the parish church and the dedication of the cathedral of the diocese, feasts of the patron of the parish church, the patron of the diocese, the patron of the country, of the founder of a religious order, etc. Some of these feasts are holydays of obligation, and many of them have a vigil and an octave.[13]

b) *Doubles of the second class:* Under this category there are about thirty feasts. For the most part they are feasts of our Lord and of the Blessed Virgin not included in the doubles of the first class. The feasts of the apostles (with the exception of Sts. Peter and Paul and St. Barnabas) are found here as are those of other saints such as St. Stephen, St. Lawrence, etc.

c) *Greater doubles:* To this class belong about forty feasts, among which are the Presentation of the Blessed Virgin, Seven Dolors, Our Lady of Mount Carmel, the Holy Guardian Angels, and the feasts of a number of major saints: Augustine, Benedict, Ignatius, Dominic, Francis of Assisi, Francis Xavier, Alphonsus de Liguori, etc.[14] Octaves of doubles of the first or second class also fall in this group.

d) *Doubles:* Belonging to this group are the feasts of many saints of lesser prominence.

---

[13] See page 39 ff., on octaves.
[14] The feasts of these founders of religious orders are celebrated as first-class feasts in their respective orders.

e) Semidoubles: They are so called because, though they have both a first and second Vespers, the entire antiphon is said only at the end of each psalm, its first words having been intoned at the beginning. Most of the feasts of the saints fall within this classification. It is to be noted that there are always at least three orations at Masses of this class.

f) Simple feasts: These feasts have only one Vespers, celebrated on the eve of the feast.

4. *Privileged weekdays:* Those weekdays are considered specially privileged which take precedence over a feast happening to fall on that day. Such weekdays are Ash Wednesday, and Monday, Tuesday, and Wednesday of Holy Week.

5. *Simultaneous occurrence of feasts:* This simultaneous occurrence happens when, due to the varying date of Easter, some movable feast falls on the same day as a set feast or a Sunday. For example, the Feast of the Assumption of the Blessed Virgin (August 15) may occur on a Sunday after Pentecost; the same thing may happen to the Feast of St. Michael the Archangel (September 29). A question often asked is: Which Mass is to be said, that of the feast or that of the Sunday? If the Mass of the feast is said, is the Mass of the Sunday to be transferred, completely displaced, or merely commemorated? The precise regulations of the Church for each individual occurrence of this kind are to be found in the *Ordo,*[15] but the

---

[15] Many diocesan papers carry an English translation of the *Ordo* for the week, and the same information can be obtained from liturgical calendars such as Puetter's *Christian Life Calendar* (Milwaukee: The Bruce Publishing Co.), and *The Mass Year* (St. Meinrad, Ind.: The Grail Press).

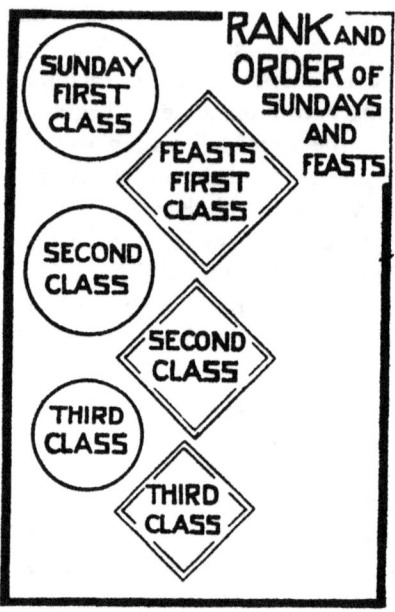

This illustration summarizes the principles which determine the rank of a feast or Sunday. The Sundays of the various classes, represented by the *circles* at the left are placed above the corresponding types of feasts, represented as *squares* at the right. The Sundays of the first, second, and third class are higher in rank than the corresponding feasts of the same degree; hence, they suppress them. The illustration shows, too, that feasts of the first class rank higher than Sundays of the second class; in this case, then, the Sunday is suppressed in favor of the feast. The proper order is now clearly seen to be as follows: Sundays of the first class, feasts (doubles) of the first class, Sundays of the second class, feasts (doubles) of the second class, etc.

Material for more intensive study of this problem may be found in the introduction to the daily missal as well as in the liturgical calendars previously recommended on page 33.

general rule is as follows: When feast days or feast days and Sundays occur simultaneously, the rank or degree of each is the decisive factor, and the lesser gives place to the greater. Thus a minor feast gives precedence to a major Sunday, and a major feast takes precedence over an ordinary Sunday. If the days have the same ranking, they share the Vespers. In the examples cited, the Feasts of the Assumption and of St. Michael, the feasts are celebrated and the proper Sunday Masses are transferred to the first free day of the following week.[16] If the Sunday enjoys a higher rank, e.g., if a first-class feast should occur on a first-class Sunday, the Sunday takes precedence and the feast is postponed. A case in point is the Feast of the Annunciation (March 25) when it occurs on a Sunday in Lent or during Holy Week or Easter Week.

Ember Days

While man's prayer is often entirely a petition, liturgical prayer is primarily praise, thanksgiving, and adoration. A typical example is the *Gloria* of the Mass in which we note the gradual rise of praise of God until it reaches a wonderful climax: *"Laudamus te. Benedicimus te. Adoramus te. Gratias agimus tibi propter magnam gloriam tuam"* (We praise Thee. We bless Thee. We adore Thee. We give Thee thanks for Thy great glory). In her official liturgical prayers the Church constantly exhorts us to praise, adore, glorify, and thank God. Moreover, she has set aside special seasons to offer special prayers of gratitude for

---

[16] Then the *Gloria* and *Credo* are usually omitted in the Mass.

the gifts of God. This happens four times a year on Wednesday, Friday, and Saturday of the ember weeks which fall at the beginning of the four seasons of the year.

Ember days and ember weeks originated in early Christian days, and were first celebrated in Rome. Early in summer, in Pentecost week, the wheat was harvested. In order to thank God for this harvest, at the Offertory of the Mass a part (a so-called tithe, a tenth part) was offered for the benefit of the Church, the priests, and the poor. In like manner, it was customary to offer tithes of the other harvests in their respective seasons. When the grapes were harvested in September, there was another week of thanks, and similar offerings were made in December when the olive crop was gathered. The fruits of those harvests, wheat, wine, and oil, have been put to the highest possible use in the liturgy of the Church, for she uses them sacramentally, that is, as external signs of the inner grace imparted through her sacraments. She uses bread and wine at the holy sacrifice of the Mass and at Holy Communion; she uses oil at Baptism, Confirmation, Holy Orders, Extreme Unction, and for many of her sacramentals (baptismal water, blessing of bells, churches, chalices, etc.). Later, a fourth week of thanksgiving was added in the spring, when it is but natural for man to thank God for the awakening of nature, the budding of the first flowers, and the lengthened hours of daylight.[17] Thus there was apportioned to each season of the year a week of

[17] The gift of light is important to the Church both because of its symbolism and its use in various liturgical ceremonies.

thanksgiving for the gifts of nature with which God has so generously enriched the world:

1. In spring, during the week after Ash Wednesday, to give thanks for the rebirth of nature and for the gift of light.

2. In summer, within the octave of Pentecost, to give thanks for the wheat crop.

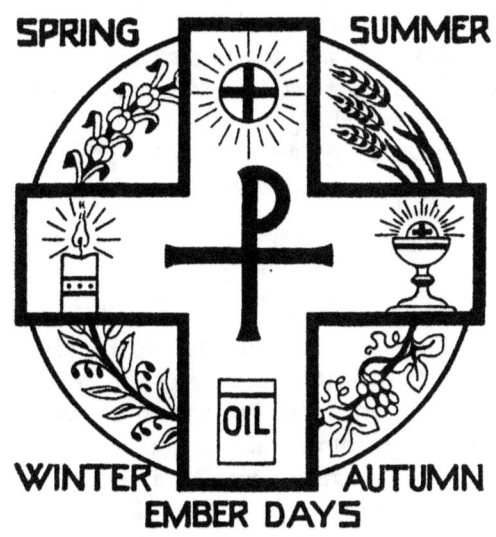

This illustration shows, to a certain extent, how the ember days resemble our own lives. In the springtime we receive supernatural life through Baptism (represented by the *baptismal candle*); throughout the summer and autumn of our lives our souls are nourished by the Body (the *host* has been made from the kernels of *wheat*) and the Blood (the *chalice*) of our Lord. In the winter we reap the harvest of our good works as we begin our journey into eternity, fortified by Holy Viaticum and the sacrament of Extreme Unction (*oil*).

3. In autumn, beginning on the Wednesday immediately after the Feast of the Exaltation of the Holy Cross (September 14), to give thanks for the grape harvest.

4. In winter, within the week following the Feast of St. Lucy (December 13), during the third week of Advent, to give thanks for the olive crop.

On ember days we thank God four times a year for all the gifts of nature, especially for those used by the Church in her sacraments and sacramentals. We also thank Him for the sacraments, administered to us under the external signs of these gifts of nature. Finally, on these days we pray for the priests, usually ordained at this time, who administer the sacraments to us.

Vigils

Everyone is familiar with the term Christmas Eve, as it is commonly used to refer to the day before Christmas. But, in the language of the liturgy there is a day of preparation or anticipation not only before Christmas, but before each major feast, generally spoken of as its vigil. Essentially, a vigil is a day of preparation. Just as we have a good house cleaning before any family celebration, so does the Church want our souls to be house cleaned on the day before a feast.

The word *vigil* is derived from the Latin, *vigilia,* meaning a night watch, that is, a period during which the Roman soldiers took their turn at duty. The word was appropriated by the early Christians and used to refer to the eve of major feasts when they used to gather in their churches and keep watch throughout the night with prayer and sacred song. Although in later centuries the preparation for the feast was transferred from the evening to the morning of that same day, and centered around the holy sacrifice of the Mass, lengthened, however, by additional readings and prayers, the name *vigil* still remained. The vigil day was generally, and is often now, a day of fast and abstinence, on which only one full meal is permitted, and meat is not allowed.

Octaves

Just as each Sunday is followed by six weekdays, so also every major feast day is followed by an octave during which the mysteries of the feast, its joys, and its graces are commemorated and allowed to become more deeply impressed upon our souls. *Octave* means an eight-day celebration, that is, the prolongation of a feast to the eighth day (*dies octava*) inclusive. The feast itself is considered the first day, and it is followed by six days called "days within the octave." The eighth or octave day is kept with greater solemnity than the "days within the octave."

The Jews celebrated their highest feasts, especially that of the Passover, for a period of eight days. Easter and Epiphany were the first feasts to acquire an octave among the Christians. Under the emperor Constantine the major dedication feasts of the churches of Rome were celebrated with octaves. Among the saints, the feasts that were the first to have octaves were those of Sts. Peter and Paul, St. Lawrence, and St. Agatha.

Not all octaves are alike in their festal character.

There is a difference in their solemnity according to the respective rank of the feast. They may be classified as:

1. *Privileged Octaves,* commemorating the feast each day in the Mass and Divine Office, and permitting no votive Mass. These may be further divided into three groups.

> *a*) Two octaves of the *first order,* Easter and Pentecost, during which no other feast may be celebrated; it may only be commemorated by its proper Collect.
>
> *b*) Two octaves of the *second order,* Epiphany and Corpus Christi, during which only feasts of the first class or the octave day of a first class feast may be celebrated; the octave itself, however, is always commemorated.
>
> *c*) To the *third order* belong the octaves of Christmas, Ascension, and the Sacred Heart of Jesus, during which all feasts greater than a simple may be celebrated. On the octave day itself only feasts of the first and second class may be celebrated; the octave day is always commemorated.

2. *Common octaves* are comparable to the *third order* of the privileged octaves in that they permit the celebration of any feast greater than a simple, and that the octave day itself gives place to feasts of the first and second class. A commemoration of the octave is made except on doubles of the first and second class. To this group belong the Octaves of the Immaculate Conception, the Assumption, All

Saints, the dedication of churches, patronal feasts, etc.

3. *Simple octaves* commemorate feasts of the second class only on the eighth day with the rite of a simple feast. Examples are St. John the Evangelist, St. Stephen, etc.

The Easter Season

Because Easter is the greatest feast of the Church, this Sunday ranks highest within the Church year. Not only is our whole faith based upon Christ's resurrection on that first Easter morning in Jerusalem, but the course and the divisions of the ecclesiastical year are almost entirely determined by the date on which Easter falls. In the liturgical calendar there is a distinction of feasts; some are movable, others are immovable. The latter are those celebrated each year on a determined date,[18] for example, Christmas always falls on December 25, Epiphany on January 6, All Saints on November 1, the Assumption on August 15, etc. Easter, however, and all the feasts dependent on it (e.g., Ascension, Pentecost, Corpus Christi, etc.) are movable feasts, that is, they do not fall on the same date each year. In fact, there will be a great diversity of dates for Easter; one year it may be at the end of March, another at the beginning, the middle, or even the end of April.

If Easter is early, then the preparation for Easter begins early; only a few of the Sundays after Epiphany are celebrated and the others are postponed until after the twenty-third Sunday after Pentecost. If Easter is late, then Septuagesima and Pentecost are

---

[18] For possible exceptions see page 33 ff.

late, and the Sundays after Epiphany can be celebrated in their regular season. So the question arises: How does it happen that Easter is sometimes early and sometimes late? How is its date determined? The rule is this: *Easter is always on the Sunday which follows the first full moon after the spring equinox, which is March 21.*[19] The extreme dates on which Easter may fall are March 22 and April 25. The Church has determined the date of Easter according to these principles since the time of the apostles. The actual working out of the rule may be more clearly illustrated by the following diagram:

Spring Equinox	*Full Moon*	*Date of Easter*
March 21	On March 21, but after the equinox (exactly calculated), if this day happens to be Saturday.	March 22 — the earliest date for Easter.
March 21	On April 1; it was Wednesday of Holy Week.	April 5 — occurred in 1942.
March 21	Full moon occurred on March 21; it was, however, *after* the exactly calculated time of the equinox. Hence, the first full moon *after* the equinox is April 18, and since this is on a Sunday, Easter falls on the following Sunday, April 25.	April 25 — the latest possible date for Easter; occurred in 1943.

---

[19] The equinox occasionally falls on March 22.

Alleluia

The *Alleluia* (Praise the Lord) is frequently used by the Church in prayer and song. Among the Jews the word was a cry of joy and as such the Church has taken it over into her liturgy. It is a cry of joy — a short, joyful hymn of thanks for our redemption, the graces of which, through the liturgy and especially through the sacrifice of the Mass and the sacraments, are poured out on all the baptized.

More frequently than ever and with greater solemnity the Alleluia resounded during the Eastertide as an exclamation of joy over the completion of the redemption. Already on Holy Saturday, when the Easter-night Mass is anticipated, it re-echoes jubilantly after the mournful stillness of Lent and Holy Week. On Easter Sunday the joy and gratitude of the Church know no bounds. "Christ is risen! Alleluia! Alleluia!" Thus we all sing with the Church, for this is the most significant and exalted feast of our redemption. It commemorates the greatest miracle of our Saviour, the one which offers the most convincing proof of His divinity and divine Sonship. Easter is the oldest and most important feast of the Church; the apostles themselves celebrated it. This Sunday is supreme among all the other Sundays of the year, for as the pivot of the Church year it determines almost the entire liturgical calendar.

The joyful Alleluia during the greater part of the year is a refrain of the Easter Alleluia; the Church continually gives expression to her joy by interpolating this exclamation in her liturgical texts. In the

early centuries of the Church the Christians lived
intimately with her liturgy. They saw in the holy
sacrifice of the Mass, and in Holy Communion received during the Mass, the renewal of their redemption. Returning home, they took the Alleluia, the
symbol of their joy at having been redeemed, into
their daily life and labor; with this exclamation they
consecrated their daily work so that it became an act
of divine worship.

The deep and earnest piety of the Middle Ages did
not permit the use of the joyful Alleluia during Lent;
for that reason at the beginning of this season, it was
laid aside with impressive ceremonies.[20] Today we
have strayed so far away from the inner spirit of the
Church that we are not truly conscious of the omis-
sion of the Alleluia during Lent. In fact, there remains
only a single ceremony at the beginning of the pre-
Lenten period reminiscent of the old liturgical custom
of saying farewell to the Alleluia. This occurs on the
Saturday before Septuagesima when according to the
rubrics of the season, two solemn Alleluias are added
to the *Benedicamus Domino* and to the *Deo Gratias*
at Vespers. Then follow the Alleluia-less days of pre-
Lent and Lent which bring before our eyes the suffering and death of our Saviour, and so prepare our
hearts for Easter with its glad and blessed Alleluias.

---

[20] It was called the "Burial of the Alleluia." In some localities
they even had burial services; e.g., in the fifteenth century in
Toul, France, choir boys bore a picture representing the Alleluia,
and the procession of clergy and altar boys with candles, incense,
and holy water, followed to the burial place.

Christian Symbols

As a medium for expressing abstract ideas symbols have a decided advantage over realistic representations. Whereas these are apt to recall to the mind pre-eminently sense perceptions, rousing the imagination to re-create a situation, symbols make a strong appeal upon the intellect, presenting to it spiritual truth in such a manner that the interrelationship of realities is manifest at one glance. For instance, being acquainted with the ordinary symbols used to refer to the Deity, to the human soul, to the Church, to prayer and grace, enables the mind to interpret a symbolic representation by observing the combination or the juxtaposition of the individual symbols. Thus the relationship between God and man becomes evident when the grace-giving and grace-receiving process is shown by the fountain of living waters at which the deer slake their thirst (cf. Psalm 41). Similarly rays of light or streams issuing forth from a cross, the sign of salvation, or from any symbol of the Deity, indicate the transmission of the Christ-life to humanity (illustration No. 1, page 6). On the other hand, there are symbols indicating the activity of creatures in respect to God, such as prayer and thanksgiving represented by the rising clouds of incense, the sacrifice of the martyrs by a palm branch or by the instrument of torture, purity or virginity by a lily, and the joy and tribute of angelic beings by wings.

Symbolism is not limited like painting or plastic art to portraying only things which coexist at one given moment. It can transcend the moment and, like the art of poetry, show a succession of events. An example of this is the illustration of the Christmas and Easter Mountain (page 56). Here the entire cycle of the year with its seasons, feasts, and Sundays is shown in an orderly sequence. Another example is the illustration on page 52, the symbol of the Redemption. With one glance there is flashed before the mind a picture of time that extends from the fall in paradise to the end of the world. And not only that — it emphasizes the Incarnation, the most significant event that ever happened in that span of time, indicating its cause and its effect. These are also excellent examples showing how a simple design can serve to summarize graphically the substance gathered from pages of printed matter. Symbols, therefore, can clinch an idea.

Accordingly, in order to interpret more easily the illustrations in this book, it may be well to give the meaning of a few essential symbols that are used more frequently.

Foremost is the *Chi-Rho* monogram, the *X* and *P*, which are the first two letters of the word Christ in Greek. The significance of Christ's mediatorship is brought to the fore by the fact that this symbol occurs more than seventy times in this book and in more than half of the illustrations.

In connection with the *Chi-Rho* there is often a circle or the Greek letters, *alpha* and *omega*. The circle, having no beginning and no end, signifies that God is eternal; the Greek letters, that Christ is divine.

The dove may also represent the human soul, the temple of the Holy Spirit.

Christ, the Light of the World, is sometimes represented by the paschal candle (illustrations, pp. 104, 136, 162). According to St. Anselm the wax represents Christ's virginal flesh, the wick His soul, and the flame His divinity.

A candle also symbolizes sanctifying grace which is the Christ-life within the human soul (illustrations, pp. 104, 114, 136).

A fish is one of the most ancient symbols for Christ, because each letter of the Greek word for fish, "*I-ch-th-u-s*," stands for the initial letters of "Jesus Christ, God's Son, Saviour" (*Iesous Christos, Theou Uios, Soter*).[21] By means of this symbol the early Christians eluded their persecutors who mistook the sign for an announcement of a pagan funeral banquet. At the same time it guided their fellow-Christians to the place where the Divine Banquet was held.

Fish swimming in water are also a symbol for the faithful, the baptized souls submerged in the saving stream of the Precious Blood of the Redeemer.

---

[21] The symbol *IHS* is often popularly taken for the abbreviation for *Iesus Hominum Salvator* (Jesus, Saviour of men); in reality it is the abbreviation for the name of Jesus as written in Greek (IHSOUS) which was the language of the Church in the West for the first two and a half centuries of our era.

THE CHURCH YEAR

In General

Among the most cherished memories of life are those of excursions into regions or districts of great natural beauty. Artists of every nation and of every age bear witness to this in their works, in which they extol the beauty of nature, the product of God's creative hand. Especially is this joy experienced by the mountain climber who dares to scale the highest peaks. Only after strenuous exertion does he reach the heights where the pure air, the warm sunshine, and the widespread panorama below afford intensive satisfaction and repay him for his arduous climb. Years later in the humdrum of daily life, the memory of such an experience, often awakened by a casual glance at a collection of snapshots or pictures, is strong enough to revive his flagging spirit and to arouse again some of the joy of the original adventure.

Man's life may well be compared to the experiences of the mountain climber. His path is an upward one that ultimately leads to God. The ascent is not easy. There are stones and boulders in the way, crevices and pitfalls to be avoided, and crags that seem unsurmountable. Alone he can never reach the top, but with a competent guide there is every probability of his safe arrival. For the Catholic there is the supreme joy of being sure that he has just such a guide in his holy mother, the Catholic Church. The way along which she leads him is none other than the Church year, the liturgical year in which she annually directs his steps up mountainous peaks, and thus eventually, after a lifetime of such climbing, brings him to the pure, unadulterated air of God's heaven.

In the beginning of time, centuries ago, God created heaven and earth and all things in them. And upon His greatest masterpiece, man, in the persons of Adam and Eve, He poured out His blessings in superabundant measure. Our first parents failed to co-operate with God's plan; in their pride and disobedience, they sinned and sinned grievously. Of themselves they were incapable of offering satisfaction; only God could make adequate reparation for an offense against God. And so it happened that the Divine Son of God, the Second Person of the Blessed Trinity, offered to make atonement for the sin of our first parents. The Father accepted His Son's offering, and after centuries of waiting and expectation during which His chosen people were prepared little by little for the coming of the Redeemer, He sent His only-begotten Son to earth to redeem man. He came not, as many of His people anticipated, as a royal Messias, but as a tiny, weak man-child, poor, unknown, and persecuted, even in the days of His infancy. Later this same Christ spent three years teaching His people, announcing to them · His doctrine of truth and love. To prove His divinity

He worked miracles, and He ended His mission by dying as our Saviour on the cross. Three days later He arose from the dead and, after another brief stay on earth, returned to His Father in heaven. Before His departure, however, He founded His Church, and after His ascension He sent down His Holy Spirit to strengthen, guide, and govern it until the end of time.

The Church which Christ founded has no other purpose than that which our Saviour had during His days on earth: the glory of His Father and the salvation of the souls of men through the grace He won for them by His passion and death on the cross. Since our first parents lost their primitive grace, man's days of grace began anew the first Christmas night,[1] they continued throughout Christ's sojourn on earth, throughout the centuries that have intervened since His ascension into heaven, and they will continue until the end of time. Hence, the history of man's redemption must include the entire period of time in which Christ's redemptive grace is, has been, and will be active. It is this tremendous span of time that the Church asks us to relive in our own lives during each liturgical year.

But the Church year is not primarily a commemoration of the history of our redemption, a recalling of the past. Nor is it a mere anticipation of the joys of our future life in eternity. Rather, the liturgical year is the opportune *present*. It is the day on which, as our Lord says, we are to work out our salvation (John

---

[1] Cf. St. Paul, *Titus*, 2:11–15, used as the Epistle at Midnight Mass on Christmas.

9:4), the grace-laden present which alone belongs to us since the past is irrevocably gone and the future quite uncertain. Therefore, in the ecclesiastical year, the Church does not simply narrate or commemorate the acts and events of our Lord's life that played a large part in our redemption. Rather, she re-presents these acts and events to us so that they may be a means of nourishment to our supernatural life, a means whereby the life of grace may develop and be strengthened in the soul of each individual member of the Mystical Body of Christ. As each mystery is commemorated, Christ, our eternal High Priest, places at our disposal the graces He won for us by that particular work of His. Thus the whole Church year is like a channel, through which the inexhaustible stream of the graces Christ merited for us flows out upon all those who are ready and willing to receive them.[2]

Viewed in this way, the liturgical year is no longer something apart or entirely accidental to the life of a Christian, for it is seen in its true light as the school of sanctity in which we learn how to receive the merits Christ distributes to us in the sacred cycles of the year. In this school, the supernatural, divine life we received at Baptism is nourished and strengthened and readily grows to maturity under the healthful influence of the sacred seasons. Each year, to a certain extent, we begin anew, and each year there should be a corresponding growth and power secured by a frequent participation in the holy sacrifice of the Mass and by the reception of the sacraments, especially Holy

[2] See frontispiece.

THE NEW TESTAMENT TIME OF

CONSUMMATION

GRACE TO GROW TO RIPEN

THE OLD TESTAMENT ADVENT

REDEMPTION

LONGING FOR THE REDEEMER

PAX

ADAM EVE

CREATION

This illustration, with its three *circles,* depicts the history of the redemption. The *lower* circle represents the creation and the fall of man; the *intermediate* one, the principal events of the redemption: the birth of Christ, His death, His resurrection, and the descent of the Holy Spirit (Christmas, Good Friday, Easter, and Pentecost); the *third* circle, the eternal peace and beatific joy of the heavenly city of Jerusalem. Between the events symbolized by the lower and intermediate circles, that is, between the fall of man and the redemption of Christ, there is a long period of expectation and preparation, the time of the Old Testament, now commemorated by Advent. Between the redemption (*middle circle*) and its fulfillment in eternal glory (*upper circle*), there is another long period of grace, in which Christ's kingdom develops and matures. It is the era of the New Testament, to last until the end of the world where the perfect fulfillment (*third circle*) of Christ's kingdom in heaven will begin.

Communion. And the more intimately we are living the Church year, the mysteries of which are vividly presented to us in the proper of the Mass, the more perfect will be our celebration of the holy sacrifice. As a result we will be more abundantly enriched with grace and will more perfectly realize in ourselves the whole work of redemption. As we scale the mountains of each liturgical year, we will climb a little closer to heaven, a little nearer to our final glory in Christ, the King of glory. Thus lived and used, the Church year is a truly *holy year,* the "year of salvation," for as the apostle says, "We all, beholding the glory of the Lord with open face, are transformed into the same image from glory to glory, as by the Spirit of the Lord" (2 Cor. 3:18).

Faithful co-operation with the mind and spirit of the liturgical year will acquaint us more familiarly, too, with the life, works, suffering, and death of Christ, and thus help us to center our life more completely in His and so live in closer conformity with His divine ideals. Our Christ-life, ever growing more perfect under the beneficent influence of each liturgical year, will help us to achieve even within ourselves the primary purpose of the Church, that is, the glory of God and the sanctification of souls.

Beginning of the Church Year

Unlike the civil year which is divided into twelve months and always begins on January 1 regardless of the day on which this date falls, the Church year is divided into weeks and always begins on the first Sunday of Advent. Since the Church depicts the his-

tory of our redemption, the first mystery to be commemorated is the birth of our divine Saviour in the
stable at Bethlehem. But the whole period of the
Old Testament, thousands of years of waiting and
expectation, preceded the Incarnation. Similarly,
there is in the church calendar before Christmas a
preliminary period of preparation which always
extends over four Sundays.[3] The first Sunday of
Advent is the Church's New Year's Day.

Division of the Church Year

We have already discussed on page 38 ff., the manner in which the Church celebrates her greater
feasts. There is always a preparatory period (the
vigil), then the feast itself, and after that a subsequent period of eight days (the octave), in which the
Church draws out the celebration so as to enter more
fully into the mysteries and graces of the feast. The
whole liturgical year is based on this same principle.
For the greatest feasts there are weeks, not days, of
preparation, and after the feast has been solemnized
on the day and throughout the octave, there is a
prolongation of the dominant theme of the feast
over a long period of time so that the faithful may
imbibe, in repeated draughts, the special graces
proper to the mystery.

The four greatest feasts of the year fall quite naturally into two pairs so that in each case two of them
rivet attention on the same mystery. Christmas and
Epiphany are centered about the Incarnation; Easter

---

[3] Christmas thus regularly falls within the week following the
fourth Sunday of Advent.

and Pentecost are concerned with Christ's redemption of man. Accordingly, the liturgical year is divided into two great cycles which, taking their name from the first of the feasts named in each cycle, are called Christmastide and Eastertide.[4]

The life of a Christian has already been compared to mountain climbing because the ascent to the heights of heaven is usually a slow and tedious one. In like manner, the two great cycles of the Church year may be represented as two mountains because they are, indeed, a path, an ascent, a way of journeying heavenward.

He who has climbed a high mountain knows that it demands hours of exertion to arrive at the summit. But having attained that objective, he rejoices in the lofty heights, the pure air, the magnificent view before him. To tarry and rest a while in such a spot is such sheer delight that it more than compensates for the arduous efforts expended in the climb. Where possible, the mountain climber wanders from ledge to ledge, from one peak to another. But finally he must return to the uninteresting cares and duties of his everyday life. With new vigor he retraces his footsteps down the mountainside, gazing back again and again as if to recapture and take home with him some of the joy he experienced on the summit. And absorbed though he may be in monotonous occupations in the days that follow, when a chance word or thought revives or recalls his visit to the mountaintop, nostalgia

---

[4] For a recent and enlightening discussion of the division of the liturgical year into two cycles, see "How Many Cycles Has the Liturgical Year?" by H. A. Reinhold, *Orate Fratres*, Vol. XVII (1943), pp. 102–110.

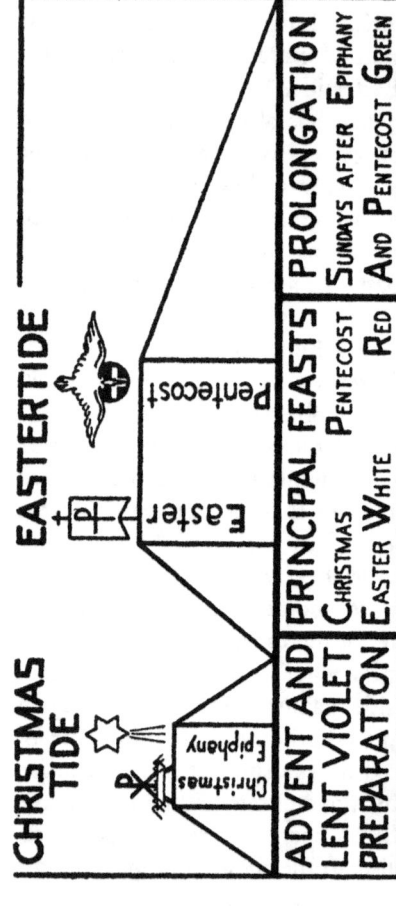

Of these two mountains, the Easter mountain is the higher and the more extensive, requiring a proportionate expanse for ascent and descent. This is because Easter is the Church's highest and most important feast. With its period of preparation (beginning properly on Septuagesima Sunday) and its prolongation (the Sundays after Pentecost), it takes approximately three times longer than the Christmas cycle. Here, too, can be noted the color the Church uses in each period: violet in Advent and Lent (as in most vigils), indicating the spirit of penance and seriousness then prevailing; white and red in the feasts proper, expressive of joy and love; and green in the prolongation periods (Sundays after Epiphany and Pentecost) to show hope and growth in God's grace.

touches his soul and arouses within him the hope of finding like pleasure in another ascent.

Such an experience is almost an exact counterpart of the liturgical year, for in it the Church annually leads the faithful up two heights, the Christmas mountain and the Easter mountain. Before each is an ascent, Advent and Lent, the preparatory periods for Christmas and Easter, paved with privations and difficulties; on the summit, spiritual joy and special graces await him who has been successful in his climb. This period of happiness, in which he drinks in copious draughts of grace peculiar to the season, continues not just for a few short hours, but for weeks — it is the happy, blessed wandering on the heights from Christmas to Epiphany, from Easter to Pentecost. Deeply enriched, the Christian then descends. The immediate joys of the feast are past, but the fruits remain. They ripen and bear fruitful seed or are preserved for the great harvest day on which their owner will reap from them abundant reward. This time of ripening is the season in which occur the Sundays immediately following Easter and Pentecost.

Each liturgical year the Church leads us to the summit of these two mountains where we receive graces and blessings for our lives. With each ascent our personal understanding of Christ's redemptive activity, portrayed so effectively in the Church year, grows and takes on a fuller meaning. And it is the desire for redemption, the desire to receive the fullness of redemptive grace here and its crown in heaven, that urges us to become proficient spiritual mountain climbers. Life thus becomes a series of literal ups and downs from the supernatural point of view, without, however, there ever being any danger of monotony; for each time we traverse the path of the liturgical year we perceive sights unnoticed previously, we experience joys of whose existence we were hardly aware the year before. Our annual journey through the liturgical year is not a mere retracing of the same road, but an ever higher mounting on a spiral, and an ever deeper penetration into the glorious mysteries of our faith.

TEMPORAL CYCLES: THE PROPER OF THE TIME

I. The Christmas Cycle

Before a traveler, especially a mountain climber, begins a trip, he studies photographic views, detailed descriptions of the road, maps of the route, in fact, everything that pertains to the proposed journey. The Christian would do well to make a comparable survey of the ecclesiastical year before entering upon it.

Preparation: Advent

Advent, from the Latin *adventus,* meaning *coming* or *arrival,* is the name given to the period of preparation for Christmas, for the coming of the Christ-Child. In our Christmas mountain this is the time during which the path ascends. It means a period of exertion, for the season is not an idle one for the good Christian. Fundamentally, the idea of preparation implies purification. No matter what the preparation is for, it will include a cleansing, a removal of all things that would be an obstacle to what we are going to receive. This principle becomes all the more evident when we stop to consider that in Advent we prepare for the coming of the Son of God. The season, therefore, is a serious one in which we try, as the first

Christmas Mountain, Part 1: The way leads upward; it is the ascent, the preparatory period for the coming of the Redeemer, known as Advent. It consists of three full weeks and four Sundays; within the week following the fourth Sunday Christmas is celebrated. In the illustration the *four circles* represent the four Sundays; the *first* circle is doubled to indicate that the first Sunday of Advent, the beginning of the ecclesiastical year, has a higher rank than the other Sundays of the same season. The Feast of the Immaculate Conception, kept invariably on December 8, is symbolized by the *M* between the second and third Sunday, where it usually falls. The *fish,* following the fourth Sunday, represents the vigil of Christmas (Christmas Eve), which is regularly a fast day, unless it falls on Sunday.

CELEBRATION

CHRISTMAS MOUNTAIN PART 2

Christmas Mountain, Part 2: On the summit of the mountain, two feasts, Christmas and Epiphany, overtower all the others, as is indicated respectively by the *crib* and the *gifts* of the three Magi. The Christmas season proper is a joyful journey from one feast to the other, our attention on the way being diverted by the galaxy of lesser feasts that intervene. They are: St. Stephen (December 26), the protomartyr, who was stoned to death (*stones* and *palm*); St. John (December 27) the Evangelist, the beloved disciple (*eagle*); the Holy Innocents (December 28), who were infant martyrs for Christ as the *sword* and *palm* signify; the Sunday within the octave, indicated by the encircled *Chi-Rho;* the Feast of the Circumcision (January 1), when the first drops of Christ's blood were shed, as is represented by the *chalice* and *knife,* and on which day the Church also commemorates the Octave of Christmas; the symbol *IHS* signifies the Feast of the Holy Name of Jesus; and, finally, the Feast of Epiphany itself (January 6), the climax of the Christmas cycle which is always preceded by a vigil. The Church's joy at the summit of the Christmas cycle is visibly expressed in the prayers and chants of the Mass as well as in the color of the vestments. White and gold prevail. On the Feast of St. Stephen the red of martyrdom is worn, while on the Feast of the Holy Innocents the violet of mourning is used out of deference to the sorrow of the mothers, unless the feast occurs on Sunday when red is substituted.

Christmas Mountain, Part 3: This is the prolongation of the Christmas cycle. The way descends, and we carry the fruits of the feasts down into our everyday life where they gradually grow to maturity and become a part of our souls. On the first Sunday after Epiphany, that is, the Sunday within the octave, the Feast of the Holy Family of recent institution may be celebrated; hence, the symbols for *Jesus, Mary,* and *Joseph.* The five following Sundays are represented by *circles,* and constitute the maximum number of Sundays which can be interpolated before Septuagesima Sunday. Actually, the number varies each year according to the date of Easter, two Sundays being the minimum. On the feast of the Holy Family white is worn; otherwise, green, the color of hope and growth, is used throughout the season to signify that increase in grace which is the result of living intimately the life of the Church. *Candlemas,* or the Feast of the Purification, closes the Christmas cycle proper.

step in our spiritual house cleaning, to rid ourselves of sin, which cannot abide in the presence of God, and try, too, to make satisfaction for our past sins and the sins of others. That the Church regards Advent as a time of penance is clear from the fact that she clothes her ministers with the violet vestments.[1] In this same spirit she omits the *Gloria* from the Mass and the *Te Deum* of Matins, silences the organ, and does not decorate the altars in her churches. She forbids the solemnization of marriages, urges her people to refrain from superfluous or spectacular amusements, and in some cases approves the custom among her religious communities of observing a strict fast.

But the preparation for the coming of Christ, which is the dominant feature of Advent, involves more than this negative aspect of ridding ourselves of sin; it has a positive side, too. It invites us to seek for the real meaning of Advent, and having found it, to enter more deeply into the mind of the Church as she prepares for the coming of our Redeemer. In reality, Advent is a preparation for the threefold coming of Christ; that is, it is commemorative of His historical coming in time, it prepares for His mystical coming into the hearts of men *now,* in the immediate present, and it looks forward to His final coming in the general judgment at the end of the world.

In its commemorative phase, Advent reminds us of the time before the birth of Christ, that long period in which sinful man waited expectantly for the often-promised Messias. Those centuries are symbolized by the four Sundays of Advent which

---

[1] The one exception is violet or rose on *Gaudete* Sunday.

represent the four ages of the Old Law: (1) the time from Adam to Noe, (2) from Noe to Abraham, (3) from Abraham to Moses, and (4) from Moses to Christ. In this sense Advent is a reminder of two great truths; first, of a grievous misfortune, the sin of Adam and Eve which left that taint of original sin on all their descendants; and second, of an inestimable blessing, the coming of the Son of God to atone for the sin of our first parents and to make redemption possible for every man until the end of time.

In anticipation, Advent looks toward and prepares for the final coming of Christ in the general judgment at the end of the world. In the liturgy the Church frequently anticipates this Second Coming, the *Parousia* or "Presence" of Christ on the last day.[2] Both St. Matthew's vivid account of the end of the world in the Gospel for the last Sunday after Pentecost and St. Luke's description of the coming of the Son of Man "in a cloud with great power and majesty" on the first Sunday of Advent impress upon the faithful the full reality of Christ's second coming, and act as a warning to so welcome the Christ-Child now that His final coming may hold no terrors for them.

But there is another coming of Christ, His coming into our hearts on Christmas Day. In fact, Christmas will be a bleak one unless we are ready to receive Him with pure souls, filled with love and gratitude.

---

[2] *Parousia* is a Greek word meaning *presence;* for the meaning of the term in the liturgy, see H. A. Reinhold, "Parousia, 1943," *The Commonweal,* Vol. XXXVII (1943), pp. 318–320.

If we were to depend on ourselves alone, we would be hard put to find ways and means of extending a proper welcome to the infinite majesty and dignity of Christ. So the Church in her never failing goodness gives us substantial assistance in the person of three eminent characters, each of whom is superlatively qualified to teach us how to make ready for Christ's advent. Our helpers are the prophet Isaias, who is the spokesman and representative of the people of the Old Law; John the Baptist, the immediate precursor of the Redeemer; and the Blessed Virgin Mary, the mother of Jesus, the supreme exemplar of the purity and love with which the Divine Infant is to be received.

Isaias, who was active as a prophet between 740–700 B.C., probably realized more intensely than any other man of the Old Law how utterly dejected unredeemed mankind was. Consequently he was all the more vehement in expressing the urgent longing and need of his people for a Redeemer. In prophetic vision he saw the wonderful majesty of the coming Saviour and revealed it in glowing colors in his prophecies. It is these divinely inspired pages, read in the lessons of Matins in the Divine Office and selected as part of the scriptural reading at Mass, that the Church puts before her children to develop and nourish in them the proper Advent spirit, that is, to arouse within them an ardent longing for the graces and blessings of the Redeemer. In his opening chapters Isaias complains in no uncertain terms of the sins of his generation. With all the vigor at his command he urges the people to do penance and to return to God. In fact, the passages are so universal in their appeal that they have as direct a message for our age as they had for the inhabitants of Juda and Jerusalem in the eighth century before Christ. But the highpoint of his prophecy is reached in the seventh chapter where we read the words realized in Christ's Incarnation, "Behold a virgin shall conceive and bear a son, and his name shall be called Emmanuel" (Isa. 7:14). The prophet foretells, too, the joy and peace that will prevail during the reign of the mighty Child. "His empire shall be multiplied and there shall be no end of peace" (*ibid.*, 9:7). And he predicts the power and titles He will possess, "For a *Child is born* to us, and a son is given to us, and the government is upon his shoulder; and his name shall be called, Wonderful, Counsellor, God the Mighty, the Father of the World to come, the Prince of Peace." From Isaias, too, comes that beautiful refrain, *Rorate Caeli,* "Drop down dew, ye heavens, from above, and let the clouds rain the just: let the earth be opened and bud forth a Saviour."[3] Thus the prophet taught his people to petition heaven for the Messias. With these same words the Church today attempts to arouse within the hearts of her twentieth-century children the same longing for the Redeemer. Again and again during Advent, she uses the vehement entreaty of Isaias, "Come, O Lord, delay no longer; come, and free us of all sin. Stir up, O Lord thy

---

[3] Cf. "Rorate Caeli," Therese Mueller, *Orate Fratres,* Vol. XVI, pp. 22–24, as well as the complete text which is given in both Latin and English with musical notes.

might, and come to save us. Permit us to see thy
countenance and save us."

St. John the Baptist, our second helper, is the immediate precursor of Christ. His insistence on proper
preparation is marked, therefore, by all the more
urgency. There is no time to be lost. He is not trying
to arouse a lethargic people to welcome a far-distant
Saviour. He wants instantaneous action, preparation
here and now for a Saviour who is nigh. "Be ye
converted! the kingdom of heaven is near!" His
message contains more than a general plea; it asks
for a specific, concrete response. "Make straight the
way of the Lord." It will not be straight as long as
sin and passion dominate our lives. "Fill up the
valleys!" They are empty, but they can be filled with
works of penance and contrition. "Mountains and
hills are to be leveled," by removing the peaks and
ledges of pride and arrogance, self-seeking and sloth.
Everything "crooked" is to be eliminated by a complete weeding out of all that is not honest, whether
it be blatant hypocrisy or petty deceitfulness. The
"rough" spots in our lives are to be made smooth;
to do this, rudeness, ingratitude, and quarrelsomeness
may have to be eliminated. Possibly, straightness
will be achieved only by the patient endurance of
suffering.

Such is the program St. John the Baptist proposes
for Advent. It is an arduous one that can be summed
up in the one word *penance*. It calls for amendment
of our ways, for a renewed effort in our living of the
Christ-life, for all that will make of our hearts a

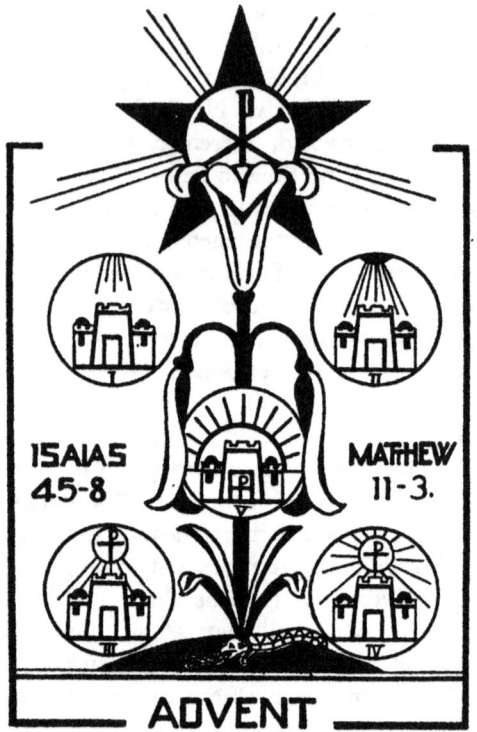

This illustration graphically depicts the meaning of Advent. Again and again Christ is portrayed in the liturgy as the rising *Sun*. The comparison is a good one, for there is nothing that can quite equal the power of the sun's rays to quicken, warm, and bless. Man, whether considered individually or collectively, is represented by the *city of Jerusalem* (to which he is often compared), which awaits its Redeemer and will reach the zenith of its development only on His arrival. The Sundays in Advent, commemorating the long centuries of the Old Testament in which the coming of the Redeemer gradually becomes more and more imminent, are indicated by the increased growth of the *sun's rays* which attain their fullness on the fourth Sunday (IV), and take

worthy dwelling place, a fitting crib, on Christmas morning.

Our most effective patron during Advent, however, is *Mary*, Christ's mother. She awaited the day of His birth with more eagerness than any other human being. Her preparation was complete in every respect, for the resting place that she had to offer Him was an immaculate heart. Recognizing this, the Church has us implore her aid daily during Advent in the second Oration of the Mass; with its corresponding Secret and Postcommunion, it is rich in content, stressing belief in her divine motherhood and assuring us of her assistance. As we come closer to Christmas, the Church puts Mary before us more frequently. In the *Rorate* Mass of Ember Wednesday,[4] we hear both God's message to her through the angel Gabriel and the beautiful reply in which she expressed her willingness to be "the handmaid of the Lord." On Ember Friday, we listen to her first glad *Magnificat* in answer to Elizabeth's joyous greeting, and with the last days of Advent we draw nearer to Mary, whose intimacy with her Divine Son typifies the union with Him to which we aspire on Christmas morning.

---

possession of the city of Jerusalem in all their effulgence on Christmas Day (V). Mary is represented as the *lily* because of her Immaculate Conception, as the *morning star* out of which rises the Sun of Justice, and as the one who crushes the head of the *serpent* (Gen. 3:15). The scriptural references to *Isaias* and *Matthew* remind us of the roles of Isaias and the Baptist, there narrated.

[4] In many places in Europe the *Rorate* votive Mass in honor of the Blessed Virgin is celebrated throughout Advent.

The spirit of Advent, then, is one of longing for our Saviour, for His grace and His love, for all that He won for us in the redemption. This longing is accompanied by a penitential spirit that prompts us to make reparation for our sins and the sins of others. The sincerity of our longing is further attested by the extent to which we enter into a spiritual house cleaning so that all may be in readiness for "the-long-expected-of-nations." And to crown our preparation we borrow something of Mary's prayerfulness, something of her purity, something of her wholehearted submission to God's will.

As we strive to emulate the longing of Isaias, the penance of St. John, and the purity of Mary, the predominant mood in our own souls is joy; it is that joy, anticipated on Gaudete Sunday, which St. Paul was trying to arouse when he said, "Rejoice in the Lord always; again I say, rejoice . . . for the Lord is nigh" (Phil. 4:4).

The Advent Wreath

The Christmas tree is universally known and used, though its real significance is often overlooked. The advent wreath, on the other hand, conveys its message more effectively, especially during the preparatory season of Christmas. It is made by winding twigs of evergreen, pine, cedar, or holly around a wire or wood hoop to which have been affixed four candle-holders (or holes in which to insert the candles). The wreath may then be suspended with four ribbons, or placed flat to form the centerpiece on the dining-room table. The candles may be red or white and the ribbons of any harmonizing colors.

It is suggested that the Advent wreath be hung on the eve of the first Sunday of Advent in the presence of the whole family. One candle is lighted and the prayer for the blessing may be read by the father. The following prayer may be used:[5]

> Father: Our help is in the name of the Lord.
> All: Who hath made heaven and earth.
> Father: Let us pray: O God, by whose word all things are sanctified, pour forth Thy blessing upon this wreath and grant that we who use it may prepare our hearts for the coming of Christ and may receive from Thee abundant graces. Through Christ our Lord.
> All: Amen.
> (The father sprinkles the wreath with holy water.)

This may be followed by the oration of the Sunday, to be repeated each day of the first week as the family gathers around the wreath for prayer in common. On the second Saturday evening, two of the candles are lighted; on the third Saturday, three, and on the fourth Saturday, all four of them; the Orations proper to the Sunday are used each week. The lighting of the candles is a privilege to be granted to various members of the family as circumstances permit.

The Greater Antiphons (O–Antiphons)

On the last seven days before Christmas, beginning with December 17, the Church chants and recites solemnly at Vespers the Greater Magnificat Anti-

---

[5] This prayer is taken from the leaflet "Advent Wreath," published by the Altar and Home Press, Conception, Mo.

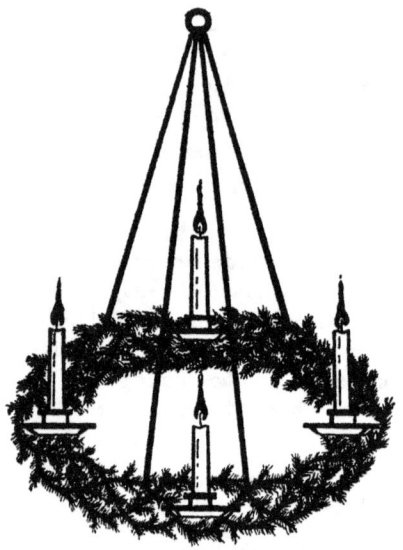

The *evergreen circle* in this illustration represents the unceasing flow of time; the *candles* divide it into the four eras, designated by the four Sundays of Advent (cf. p. 59 ff.) during which the world waited for the coming of Christ. The *lighted candle* is symbolic of Christ "the splendor of eternal light" who comes "to enlighten them that sit in darkness."

phons. They are usually called *O-Antiphons* because each one begins with a prayerful *O*. In monastic churches, the abbot, vested in robes of dignity, intones the first of these, while the solemnity of the moment is further expressed by the ringing of the church bells. On succeeding days, these antiphons are solemnly intoned by the religious, in the order of their seniority, vested in cope and assisted by ministers bearing lighted candles.

The O-Antiphons express the Church's longing and expectation for the Messias, her startled wonderment at the fullness of grace which the Christ-Child is about to bestow on the world. Their theme is the majesty of the Saviour, His wisdom, His faithfulness and sanctity, His justice and mercy, His covenant with His chosen people, who in their ingratitude broke faith with Him. They are concerned with His power and love as King and Redeemer of the world, His relation to every soul as Emmanuel, God-with-us.

December 17: *O Sapientia:* O Wisdom, who comest out of the mouth of the Most High, reaching from end to end, and ordering all things mightily and sweetly: come and teach us the way of prudence.

December 18: *O Adonai:* O Adonai, and Leader of the house of Israel, who didst appear to Moses in the burning bush, and didst give him the law on Sinai: come and redeem us with Thy outstretched arm.

December 19: *O Radix Jesse:* O Root of Jesse, who standest for an ensign of the people, before whom kings shall keep silence, and to whom the Gentiles shall pray: come to deliver us, and tarry now no more.

December 20: *O Clavis David:* O Key of David, and Scepter of the house of Israel, who openest and no man shutteth; who shuttest and no man openeth: come and lead the captive from the prison-house, him that sitteth in darkness and in the shadow of death.

December 21: *O Oriens:* O Orient, brightness of eternal life, and Sun of Justice: come and enlighten them that sit in darkness and in the shadow of death.

December 22: *O Rex Gentium:* O King of the Gentiles, and their Desire, thou cornerstone that makest both one: come and deliver man whom thou didst form out of the dust of the earth.

December 23: *O Emmanuel:* O Emmanuel, our King and Lawgiver, the Expectation of the nations and their Saviour: come to save us, O Lord our God.

If we try to make our own the thought of these antiphons on their proper days, letting their ardent aspirations dominate our prayer-life, our minds and hearts will surely be more closely attuned to the mind and heart of the Church as she prepares for the coming of her King.

NATIVITY

The Nativity of Our Lord and Saviour Jesus Christ

The liturgy of the Church is exultant in announcing the birth of its Redeemer. Joyfully it cries out, "Christ is born! Come, let us adore Him" (Invitatory of Matins). "The goodness and kindness of God our Saviour appeared" (Tit. 3:4; Epistle of the Mass at dawn); "A Child is born to us, and a Son is given to us: whose government is upon his shoulder: and his name shall be called the Angel of great counsel" (Isa. 9:6; Introit of the third Mass); "Let the heavens rejoice, and let the earth be glad before the face of the Lord: because he cometh" (Ps. 95: 11, 13; Offertory of the Midnight Mass).

The birth of Christ is the greatest event in the whole history of the human race. It was God's answer to the prayers and aspirations of the patriarchs and prophets of the Old Testament. It is the fulfillment of all the longing and anticipation the Church gives utterance to in her beautiful liturgy of Advent. In the Christ-Child we see the Saviour whose coming Isaias foretold, whose way John the Baptist made straight, whose birth His Immaculate Mother awaited with eager joy. The aspirations of heaven and earth have been realized; Jesus Christ, the Saviour of the world, true God and true man, has appeared. This Child, weak and frail, is the Son of God. By His own free will He has come down from heaven in order to atone to His Father for the sin of our first parents, and in order, too, to restore to man the supernatural life of grace which he forfeited through Adam's sin.

Adam and Eve had been God's children, children of the King. But they were dissatisfied; they wished to become like God. Instead, they became beggars and slaves against whom the gates of heaven were closed. By His coming, Christ restored man to his position as a child of God and opened for him the gates of heaven. By His death on the cross, He made complete satisfaction for man's disobedience, and thus gained for all men "power of becoming sons of God" (John 1:12).

Thinking over the profound meaning of Christmas, we begin to understand that antiphon of the liturgy which so beautifully summarizes this mystery, "O wonderful exchange! The Creator of man, having assumed a living body, deigned to be born of a Virgin, and having become man without man's aid, enriched us with His divinity."[6] Then we begin to see the feast in all its aspects as the Feast of the Incarnation of the Son of God, the feast of the redemption of man, the feast of the merciful love of the Father. From whatever standpoint it is viewed, Christmas remains a mystery of the love, wisdom, omnipotence, justice, and mercy of God.

The human mind is utterly helpless in its attempt to understand the mystery. This little Child is our great God. This Babe in Bethlehem is our eternal King. The Church, in her liturgy, kneels in awe and adoration at His crib. With her, we offer Him our worship. It is important to realize that Christmas is not a mere commemoration of the event that occurred historically two thousand years ago, but that it actually re-presents to us the birth of Christ. Our church becomes another Bethlehem, our altar is the crib on which the miracle of the first Christmas is repeated. Then Christ came with His divinity concealed under the frail exterior of His babyhood; now it lies hid under the lowly form of bread. At every Holy Communion this "wondrous exchange" is effected for which we pray in the Secret of the first Mass of the

---

[6] From First Vespers of the Feast of the Circumcision.

day when we ask that "we may, through this sacred intercourse, be found conformed to Him, in whom our substance is united to Thee." Every Holy Mass gives us a "new birth in Christ," a pledge and guarantee of that happiness promised by the angels to "men of good will."

History of the Feast of Christmas

The significance of Christmas in the mind of the Church is clearly indicated by the age of the feast and by the reverence and enthusiasm with which it has always been celebrated.

Easter and Pentecost have their prototypes in the Old Testament Pasch and Pentecost, though these feasts acquired a new and deeper meaning through the resurrection of Christ and the descent of the Holy Ghost on the apostles. Christmas, on the other hand, is a feast of purely Christian origin.

For the apostolic Christians there was just one feast to celebrate Christ's coming, the Epiphany, the central thought of which was the manifestation of His divinity to man in the persons of the three Magi. The feast was also used to commemorate His baptism in the Jordan and the first miracle at the wedding feast of Cana, for both of these events clearly revealed His divine Sonship. Christ's appearance at Bethlehem had been but the first of the manifestations, and was probably superseded by these other events to such an extent that the day of His birth was not commemorated at all. In the third century though, the practice gradually arose of observing the day of His birth as a feast. It was kept at that time at Antioch and

Cyprus, but it was probably observed most enthusiastically at Rome as a timely bulwark against the Arian attempts to discredit the humanity of Christ. From Rome it spread to Constantinople and, ultimately, in the fifth century, was accepted and came into use in Jerusalem. The East, however, continued to solemnize the Feast of the Epiphany; later it was adopted by the West with the result that both feasts are now kept by the universal Church.

The date, December 25, is quite surely not the day of Christ's birth. That this day was chosen is undoubtedly due to the fact that it was the feast of the Roman sun-god, honored as *Sol invictus.* To Christians, Christ was the Sun of Justice, and it was natural to supplant the pagan feast with the birthday of "the light of the world."

In very early times Christmas had attained a unique liturgical eminence in that the holy sacrifice of the Mass was offered three times on that day. This practice, known to Gregory the Great in the sixth century, was probably far older and in all likelihood came to Rome from Jerusalem. There on the vigil of Christmas it was customary to make a pilgrimage from the city to the grotto of the Nativity in Bethlehem where, at midnight, Mass was celebrated. Then the pilgrims returned to Jerusalem and, at dawn, offered the Holy Sacrifice again in the Church of the Resurrection; later during the day the faithful assembled in the main church to celebrate the principal liturgy of the feast.

Similar services took place in Rome. In the Nativity Chapel of the basilica of St. Mary Major, which contains a large portion of the original crib, divine services were carried out at night. As early as the fifth century the second Mass took place in the church dedicated to the popular martyr-saint of the Greeks, St. Anastasia, probably because this was the palace church of the Greeks resident in Rome, and because the name was similar in meaning to that of the Resurrection Church in Jerusalem where the Mass at dawn was celebrated.[7] The principal service took place later in the day at St. Peter's. At first only the popes had the right to celebrate three Masses (on other days, too, they were permitted to celebrate oftener); later all priests were granted the same privilege.

It is possible to see a further interior meaning in these three Masses, for it has often been pointed out that they signify the threefold birth of Christ: His eternal birth of the Father, His temporal birth in the stable at Bethlehem, and His spiritual birth in the souls of men at Baptism and Holy Communion. Or again, the first Mass may be celebrated in union with the angels, Mary, and Joseph at the crib at night; the second Mass with the faithful shepherds at dawn; and the third Mass with all men who throughout the ages, past, present, and future, acknowledge the Christ-Child as their King and Redeemer.

The birth of the God-Man was the beginning and fountainhead of our redemption and sanctification. Without His coming, according to the present dispensation, there would have been no redemption, hence no sanctification. Already at Bethlehem men were divided into two camps. On the one side were

---

[7] The Greek word for Resurrection is *Anastasis.*

the persecutors of the Divine Infant, such as Herod and the majority of the Jews who neither believed in Christ nor accepted Him; to the other camp belonged the devout shepherds who came with true faith to adore Him, and who allowed themselves to be sanctified by Him.

Though the feasts immediately following Christmas may be to some extent more ancient than that feast itself, they were retained in their original position because of their appropriateness. By His birth at Bethlehem Christ sowed the first seeds of His kingdom which was to bear as its fruit all the members of the Church. It is proper, then, to place before us types of those who accepted Him as their King and became "living stones" in that kingdom, in the persons of Stephen, the first martyr, John, the virgin apostle, and the infant victims of Herod's wrath, the Holy Innocents. Each of these saints in his own way and in a supreme degree illustrates the loyalty and fidelity due to Christ. They demonstrate that the joys of Christmas are not an end in themselves, but they are to bear fruit in a life lived in close union with and according to the principles of the God-Man born on that day.

St. Stephen, Protomartyr — December 26

Stephen was the first Christian to bear witness to his faith in Christ with his blood. The vivid account of his martyrdom (Acts 6:8 ff.) testifies to his apostolic zeal and his Christlike love in pardoning his enemies. He was early honored among the saints, for his feast was already well established in the fourth

century and he is commemorated in the Canon of the
Mass immediately after John the Baptist.

The Mass of his feast is permeated with references
to his martyrdom bearing out the thought that the
kingdom of Christ is erected on the blood of martyrs.

ST. STEPHEN

The Introit introduces the thought, the Epistle illustrates it with its narration of Stephen's death, and the
Gospel reinforces it as we see Christ mournfully
gazing back at all the blood of the just that was shed
in the Old Testament from Abel to Zacharias, and
prophetically viewing the death of the "prophets and
wise men," who will make up His kingdom, while
He predicts the destruction of Jerusalem, the kingdom
of earth, "which shall be left to you desolate" (Matt.
23:34 ff.).[8]

In the Divine Office the Church links the death of
Stephen closely with the birth of Christ, inviting the
faithful to worship "the new born Christ who today

---

[8] In the illustration above, the *rays* express the words "Behold
I see the heavens opened, etc." (Acts 7:56); the *crown* is his
eternal reward; the *palm* is for victory; the *stones* derive from
the text, "And they cast him out of the city and stoned him."

crowned St. Stephen." St. Fulgentius (*circa* 533), in words used in the lessons of the second nocturn, beautifully contrasts Christ's birthday on earth with Stephen's birthday into heaven: "Today our King, coming forth from the virginal womb of His mother clothed in a robe of flesh, deigned to visit this world; today a soldier, going forth from the dwelling of his body, went victoriously to heaven. . . . Yesterday the Lord was born on earth that Stephen might be born in heaven; He entered into the world that Stephen might enter heaven."

Feast of St. John the Apostle and Evangelist —
 December 27

With the exception of His Blessed Mother, probably no human being was so close to Christ during His sojourn on earth as St. John the Apostle. Rightly, therefore, does the disciple to whom Mary was entrusted stand with her near the crib. He was the one "whom Jesus loved, the one who, at the supper, had leaned back upon his breast" (John 21:20). He himself reveals this close intimacy, "I write of what was from the beginning, what we have heard, what we have seen with our eyes, what we have looked upon and our hands have handled: of the Word of Life" (1 John 1:1). With Peter he shared some of the more hidden experiences of their Master, for they were both chosen, with James, to view Christ transfigured on the mount with Moses and Elias (Matt. 17:1-9); John went, too, with Peter to prepare the upper room for the Last Supper (Luke 22:8); and as Christ went up to the Garden of Olivet to enter upon His sufferings, John was in close attendance (Matt. 26:37; Mark 14:33). He alone of the apostles stood beneath His crucified Master on Calvary, and there received a most precious commission when our Lord charged him with the care of His Virgin Mother (John 19:27).

Of all the apostles, John alone did not suffer martyrdom, though actually he gave proof of his willingness to die a martyr when he was thrown into a cauldron of boiling oil in Rome (commemorated in the Feast of St. John before the Latin Gate, May 6).

The first chapter of his gospel which the Church daily prays at Mass gives the predominant message of Christmas: "But to as many as received him he gave the power of becoming sons of God; . . . And the Word was made flesh and dwelt among us" (John 1:12-14). His writings also include three Epistles and the great prophetic book of the New Testament, the Apocalypse. His symbol as an evangelist is the eagle[9] whose dauntless flight into the heights of heaven is comparable to the spirit of St.

---

[9] As the eagle soars into the lofty regions of the sky, so St. John's sublime gospel treats of the divinity of Christ.

John which soars immeasurably above the other evangelists in penetrating the mysteries of the Godhead.

In some churches wine is blessed in honor of St. John on this day, and distributed with the words, "Drink the love of St. John." Or the wine may be taken home to be kept for special family occasions such as reunions, engagements, marriages. The custom exists, too, in wine-growing countries of pouring some of this blessed wine into the casks. All of these practices have their origin in the fact that St. John was the apostle of love, and in the legend that at one time poisoned wine did not affect him.

Feast of the Holy Innocents — December 28

At the crib next to the martyr Stephen and the virgin Apostle St. John, the Church ranges a host of children, virgin martyrs, who were the first victims of man's hatred of Christ. In them He suffered as His Mother and Joseph hurried Him south to Egypt to safeguard His bodily life. For Herod, "perceiving that he was deluded by the wise men, was exceedingly angry; and sending killed all the boys that were in Bethlehem, and in all the borders thereof, from two years old and under" (Matt. 2:16).

The feast is very old, going back to the fifth century. Originally its attention was centered on the flight into Egypt, but as the veneration of the relics of the Holy Innocents grew, some of which are preserved in Rome in St. Paul's Without-the-Walls, it shifted to the infant martyrs who verified with their blood the words of the psalmist, "Out of the mouth of

HOLY INNOCENTS

infants and of sucklings, O God, thou hast perfected
praise, because of thine enemies" (Ps. 8:3).[10]

The death of Christ is prefigured in the death of
these children of Bethlehem. In this way the Church
reminds us how close to the crib is the shadow of
the cross, and how the joys of Christmas will yet lead
to the sorrows of Calvary.

With deep sympathy for the children and their
grief-stricken mothers, the Church clothes her ministers in the violet of mourning, or, if the feast falls
on Sunday, in the red of martyrs; the *Gloria,* used

---

[10] In this illustration, the *lily buds* recall that the earthly life
of these babes was taken by the *sword* before it could unfold.
The *curved line* above is for clouds and symbolizes heaven.

otherwise throughout the Octave of Christmas, is suppressed.

Feast of the Circumcision — January 1

The ceremony of circumcision was a kind of sacrament of the Old Law. As such it possessed a religious and sacred character, and was the outward sign which distinguished the chosen people from others. It made the individual a member of the nation and enabled him to participate in the promises and blessings of the chosen people. It was a divinely instituted means of expressing their faith in God and in the coming Redeemer, and was a type of Christian Baptism. At this ceremony, as at our Baptism, a name was given.

Christ, as the Redeemer who by His coming was to end the dispensation of the Old Law and establish the New, was not obliged to comply with this law, but in His humility He subjected Himself to it. He had come, as He said, "not to destroy but to fulfill" (Matt. 5:17). "And after eight days were accomplished, that the child should be circumcised, his name was called Jesus, which was called by the angel, before He was conceived in the womb" (Luke 2:21). The act involved the first shedding of Christ's blood, and thus keeps in the forefront the main motif of the Christmas season, that is, the thought of the redemption to be accomplished by the pouring out of His last drop of blood thirty-three years later.

The feast, however, has further significance, for it commemorates not only the Circumcision of our Lord, but also the Octave of Christmas. For this reason it borrows largely from the third Mass of Christmas. The feast also honors our Blessed Mother for her part in the redemption, particularly by the use of Oration and Postcommunion of her Mass and by frequent allusions to her in the Divine Office. For a time, three Masses were actually celebrated, one in honor of the Christmas Octave, the second in commemoration of the Circumcision of our Lord, and the third in honor of Mary, the Mother of God. As we have it, then, the feast in its Mass and its Office represents a condensation of these three feasts.

The Feast of the Holy Name[11] — January 2

The most sacred name of Jesus, meaning in itself *Saviour,* is so worthy of honor and so rich in meaning that it merits a special feast. God the Father Himself gave this name to His only-begotten Son and sent the angel Gabriel to announce it both to Mary (Luke 1:31) and to Joseph (Matt. 1:21). In the early centuries of the Church, the bestowal of the sacred name

---

[11] The symbol *IHS* is explained in a footnote on page 47.

upon the divine Child was commemorated in the Feast of the Circumcision. In the Middle Ages popular devotion began to clamor for something more; St. Bernard in the twelfth century and St. Bernardine of Siena in the fifteenth century were especially assiduous in promoting devotion to the Holy Name of Jesus. Later Pope Clement VII (died 1534) gave to the Franciscans the privilege of celebrating a feast in honor of the Holy Name. In 1721 this privilege was extended to the whole Church, and the feast was celebrated on the Sunday occurring between January 1 and January 6. Whenever no Sunday occurs between New Year's Day and Epiphany, this feast is celebrated on January 2.

It is appropriate to begin the New Year of the civil calendar with a Feast of the Holy Name at which "every knee should bow, of those that are in heaven, on earth, and under the earth" (Phil. 2:10).

Epiphany, or the Manifestation of the Lord — January 6

The Introit of the Mass indicates the underlying thought of the day: "Behold the Lord the Ruler is come: and the Kingdom is in His hand, and power, and dominion." It is the feast of the manifestation of the majesty and divinity of the new-born Saviour. As early as the third century, the eastern Church, in celebrating the birth of the Redeemer, viewed it primarily as the manifestation of God to man. Hence the name Epiphany, which means *manifestation*, was given to the feast. Toward the end of the fourth century, as the feast gradually came to be known and celebrated in the West, the adoration of the Christ-Child by the Magi or Wise Men was stressed. Soon these sages were looked upon as the Three Kings.

In the West Christ's birthday had already been celebrated for some time on December 25. But with this feast was associated all the poverty and helplessness of the cave of Bethlehem; Mary and Joseph watched beside the crib in poverty, and the shepherds that came to offer their humble worship were equally poor. This aspect was lost sight of in the Feast of the Epiphany. It is true that the Magi found a poor, weak child, attended by poor parents. But through their faith they recognized and acknowledged the helpless Infant as the Redeemer and King of the world, and as such they adored Him. In the Feast of Christmas Christ is shown as man to a few of His chosen souls; in the Feast of the Epiphany, on the other hand, He appears to the whole world as God.

In order to strengthen and reinforce this divine manifestation to the Magi, the Church commemorates on this feast two other incidents, both of which strongly testify to the divinity of Christ: His baptism in the Jordan and the first miracle at the marriage feast in Cana. In this way, the Redeemer, whose coming was known imperfectly at Christmas, is made known to the whole world.

While the Mass of the feast concentrates entirely on the coming of the Magi and their adoration of their new-found King, the Breviary abounds in references to the two other "manifestations." The antiphon for the *Magnificat* of second *Vespers* summarizes the threefold significance of the day in words that are unmistakable: "Three miracles glorify this sacred day: today the star led the Magi to the crib; today at the wedding feast water was changed into wine; today Christ willed that John baptize Him in the Jordan so that He might become our Redeemer, Alleluia." Thus we have three supernatural interventions: the star that guided the Magi from the East, the wine miraculously brought into being from water, and the voice of the Father ringing out from the heavens, "This is my beloved Son, in whom I am well pleased" (Matt. 3:17).

Various interpretations have been given for the gifts which the Magi offered the Christ-Child. In the responses at Matins the Church says that the gold represents kingly power, incense the great High Priest, and myrrh the burial of the Lord; and so she depicts the Wise Men offering their gifts to Christ is His threefold character of King, High Priest, and Man. In his homily for the third day within the octave, St. Gregory looks at the gifts from the viewpoint of the givers, and so sees in the gold, wisdom; in the incense, the power of prayer; and in the myrrh, the mortification of the flesh. Both interpretations are worthy of consideration, and some little reflection on them should prompt us to bring all the powers of our intellect to our King, the incense of our prayers to our great High Priest, and the myrrh of our sufferings and labors to our Man-God.

The Epiphany is the high point of Christmas and the fulfillment of Advent. It is the ancient Feast of Christ the King. Its dignity in the liturgy is superior

to that of Christmas. Because the feast commemorates
the baptism of Jesus, its vigil has long been a day
for solemn Baptism. In the present division of the
Church year, the baptism of our Lord in the Jordan
is commemorated on the octave day of the Epiphany.

The telling significance of this feast in the liturgy
of the Church is forcibly expressed in the custom,
still in use in some cathedrals and abbey churches,
of announcing on this day the movable feasts of the
current year that are determined by Easter. After the
Gospel, in their own peculiar chant, the dates of the
following feasts and the beginning of various seasons
are announced: Septuagesima (Pre-Lent), Ash
Wednesday (Lent), Easter, Ascension, Pentecost,
Corpus Christi, and the First Sunday in Advent. Thus
the position of Epiphany is made clear; as the climax
of the Christmas season, it announces the high points
of the Easter season, and reaffirms the four main
pillars of the Church year: Christmas (the birth of
the Redeemer), Epiphany (the manifestation of the
Redeemer to the whole world), Easter (the second
birth of Christ by His resurrection), and Pentecost
(the spiritual baptism of the apostles and the Church).

The Middle Ages, with its love for pageantry and
the picturesque, celebrated the Feast of the Three
Kings with much pomp and ceremony. Their lives
were dramatized, picturing them first as Magi,
members of a learned and respected priesthood, then
as counselors of a king, tutors of princes, skillful
astrologers, and interpreters of dreams, and finally
as kings with their offerings of gold, frankincense,
and myrrh. What little was known about them

offered fascinating material for dramatization: their call, their wanderings in the desert as they followed the star, their detention by Herod, their adoration of the Christ-Child, their return home to Babylon and Persia, and the subsequent conversion of their people to Christianity.

Another custom peculiar to this feast and prevalent in Germany and other European countries is "star caroling." Three young men, colorfully dressed, accompanied by a star-bearer, go singing from house to house. In return for their "star songs" they receive some little recompense. In many localities these young men are altar boys who are thus rewarded in some slight way for their serving at Mass.

Reminiscent of Christ's baptism in the Jordan and the administration of Baptism on the vigil of the Epiphany is the blessing of water as it is still done in many churches. This "Water of the Three Kings" is then taken home where the priest, or more generally the father of the family, sprinkles the various rooms with it as he prays:

> Bless, O Lord, almighty God, this place that there may be in it health, purity, victorious strength, humility, love, patience, obedience to God's laws, and thankfulness to God the Father, the Son, and the Holy Ghost; may this blessing remain in this house and upon all those dwelling herein. Through Christ our Lord. Amen.

In some places, too, blessed incense is burned with an appropriate prayer. Chalk is often blessed and used to write over the doors the initials of the three kings

(Caspar, Melchior, Balthasar) with the date of the year as, for example, $19 + C + M + B + 46$.

The relics of the Three Kings, formerly kept in Mailand, were preserved in the cathedral at Cologne, Germany. There the feast was celebrated with great festivity.

EPIPHANY

In the illustration above a threefold manifestation of the divinity of Christ is commemorated: The Heavenly Father and the Holy Spirit proclaim it at the baptism in the Jordan, the Magi recognize it by their tribute, and Christ Himself manifests it by showing His divine power over nature at the wedding at Cana. Shining over them all is the miraculous star.

If the Feast of Epiphany is to be fully understood as the Church sees it, it will have to be viewed from two aspects: that of God who manifested Himself to man, and that of man, typified in the Magi, who responded with wholehearted faith and love. It is, therefore, a day of faith and grace on which no other prayer ought to take precedence over that petition of the Our Father, "Thy Kingdom Come!"

Feast of the Holy Family — Sunday Within the Octave of Epiphany

Scripture tells practically nothing about the first years and the boyhood of the Child Jesus. All we know are the facts of the sojourn in Egypt, the return to Nazareth, and the incidents that occurred when the twelve-year-old boy accompanied his parents to Jerusalem. In her liturgy the Church hurries over this period of Christ's life with equal brevity.

The general breakdown of the family, however, at the end of the past century and at the beginning of our own, prompted the popes, especially the far-sighted Leo XIII, to promote the observance of this feast with the hope that it might instill into Christian families something of the faithful love and devoted attachment that characterize the family of Nazareth. Leo himself composed the texts of the Office for the new feast. In 1921 Benedict XV gave it further sanction when he extended the feast to the universal Church.

The primary purpose of the Church in instituting and promoting this feast is to present the Holy Family as the model and exemplar of all Christian families. The Mass is filled with beautiful texts, each of which is applicable to the individual members or to the family as a whole. The Introit is a hymn of praise to Mary and Joseph, the model parents: "The father of the just rejoiceth greatly, let Thy father and Thy mother be joyful, and let her rejoice that bore Thee." The Epistle summarizes in the stirring words of St. Paul the virtues of a Christian home. The Gospel contains that inimitable epitome of Christ's hidden life: "And he went down with them and came to Nazareth, and was subject to them . . . And Jesus advanced in wisdom and age, and grace with God and men" (Luke 2:52). The three prayers are so beautiful and so full of meaning that they might well be included in the daily prayer of every Christian family, as can readily be seen from the Collect:

> O Lord Jesus Christ, who when Thou wast subject to Mary and Joseph didst sanctify the home life with ineffable virtues: grant that by their assistance, we may be instructed by the example of Thy Holy Family and become partakers of their eternal happiness.

The Sundays After Epiphany

Six Sundays after Epiphany are listed in the missal. These picture the waning of this festal period, and at the same time develop more fully the primary motif of the Christmas season: the thought of God made manifest to man as man. The Church shows during these Sundays after Epiphany how Christ in His first public work labored to found and spread His kingdom in the souls of men, as the Gospels assigned to each Sunday clearly indicate. On the first

Sunday we see Him teaching the supremacy of His Father's will, on the second He illustrates His divine power by the miracle at the marriage feast at Cana, on the third He helps the poor and oppressed and heals the sick, on the fourth He demonstrates His power over the forces of nature, on the fifth He reveals Himself as a long-suffering but ultimately just and exacting judge, and on the last Sunday He is presented as the architect of the kingdom of God.

The first Sundays are closely associated in thought with Christmas and Epiphany, but as we near the end of the season, such thoughts recede into the background, and we are face to face with the Saviour and the Judge who is about to enter into combat with the powers of darkness in order to effect man's redemption. Thus the period is a gradual transition from the high point of the Christmas season, Epiphany, to the starting point of Lent, Septuagesima Sunday.

The fruits of our climb to the Christmas mount should be such that the coming ascent of the Easter mount can be undertaken courageously and confidently. For if we have lived the Christmas season intimately with the Church, we will have built up a firm, unwavering *faith* in Christ as our divine Redeemer and an ardent, trusting *love* for Him as our Brother. Both these virtues spring from the consciousness of being God's children; they will fill us with true Christian joy and prepare us to face undaunted the sufferings and delusions of this life. Christmas and Epiphany find their ultimate meaning in Good Friday and Easter Sunday. It is only the certainty that "A light has shone upon us" (Introit of the second Mass at Christmas) and that "the goodness and kindness of God our Saviour has appeared" (Tit. 3:4) which makes the ascent to the Easter mount possible.

The exact number of Sundays after Epiphany varies each year according to the date of Easter. If that feast occurs very early, there are only two Sundays; if it occurs very late, there are six. Sundays which fall out as a result of an early Lent are celebrated before the last Sunday after Pentecost. To ascertain the exact number of Sundays each year, a liturgical calendar should be consulted.

Feast of the Purification of the Blessed Virgin Mary — February 2

Two historical events form the foundation for this feast which goes back in origin to the fourth century. Both events stem from the ancient Mosaic Law.

The first event is the Purification. According to the Law of Moses (cf. Lev. 12:4–8), a mother was not permitted to enter the temple until forty days after the birth of a male child; then she was to present her new-born son with the twofold offering of a lamb and a pigeon; poor mothers, however, might substitute two turtle doves for the more expensive offering.

The second event is the presentation of Mary's first-born Son to God, for Mosaic Law required that "every male that opens the womb shall be called holy to the Lord" (Luke 2:23; cf. also, Exod. 13:2 and Num. 8:16).

These two incidents point to the double character

of the day. It is a feast of Christ, our Lord and Redeemer, who through Mary's hands offers Himself to His heavenly Father as He did previously at the fall of our first parents and at the moment of the Incarnation. It is, so to speak, the offertory of His morning sacrifice, which was begun at the crib and was to reach its climax on the cross of Calvary.

THE PURIFICATION

It is also a feast of the Blessed Virgin, and the Church indicates this particularly in the Divine Office where both the Vespers and Matins psalms are taken from the Common of her office; the antiphons of First Vespers, too, are those used on the Epiphany which praise her fruitful virginity. This is all the more fitting as it is our Lady's great offertory day; she repeats her *Fiat* as she gives herself and her Son to God. The price she is to pay before she completes her final oblation at the foot of the cross is unveiled in the words of Simeon, who, inspired by the Holy Spirit, warned her that "this child is destined for the fall and for the rise of many in Israel, and for a sign that shall be contradicted. And thy own soul a sword shall pierce . . ." (Luke 2:34-35).

In reality, Mary the Immaculate Virgin was not obliged by this Mosaic Law; she whom God had miraculously exempted from the stain of original sin had no need of purification. But as our Lord Himself had submitted to the rite of circumcision, so He wished His blessed Mother to obey the law in order to teach others the virtues of obedience and humility.

At the moment that Christ was presented by Mary and Joseph in the temple, His eternal priesthood was recognized by the gray-haired Simeon who was divinely inspired to see in this little child "the salvation" of the world, "a light to the revelation of the Gentiles, and the glory of thy people Israel" (Luke 2:30-32). Anna, too, the aged prophetess, saw her Redeemer in the newly offered Infant and "spoke of him to all that looked for the redemption of Israel" (Luke 2:38).

In a way, today's feast is a second Epiphany, another manifestation of the divinity of Christ. It is the final act in the drama of the Christmas scene which began in Advent and reached its climax in Epiphany. The Sundays after Epiphany showed us Christ's kingdom growing in the face of storms and opposition. The Feast of the Purification proudly announces to us the fact of redemption through the new-born Saviour; thus as we stand at the threshold of Lent, the feast, echoing for the last time in the liturgical year the message of Christmas, forms an easy transition to Lent and Easter.[12]

The Light of Candlemas

Simeon's greeting as he encountered the Child Jesus in the temple gives to this feast another aspect, for it is pre-eminently the feast of Christ, the Light of the world. The old prophet, who had looked forward for years with eager desire for the coming of His Redeemer, greets Him as "the light of nations" as he cries out, "Now thou dost dismiss thy servant, O Lord, according to thy word, in peace; because my eyes have seen thy salvation, which thou hast prepared before the face of all peoples: *A light to the revelation of the Gentiles,* and the glory of thy people Israel" (Luke 2:29–32). Simeon is but anticipating the words of John that His Master was "the true light, which enlighteneth every man that cometh into this world" (1:9), and Christ's own assertion "I am the light of the world" (John 8:12).

Of all material things, light is perhaps the most mysterious. Without it there is no life or growth. Unbelievably swift and vivifying in its action, it seems almost to be related to things spiritual. Most pagan peoples in their uncivilized ages associated it with a Supreme Being, and adored the sources from which it emanated, the sun, the moon, and the stars. But God, who once said, "Let there be light. And there

---

[12] "In the East the feast was celebrated as a feast of the Lord; in the West as a feast of Mary; although the Invitatorium (*Gaude et laetare, Jerusalem, occurrens Deo tuo*), antiphons, and responsories remind us of its original conception as a feast of the Lord" (*The Catholic Encyclopedia,* Vol. III, "Candlemas," p. 246).

was light" (Gen. 1:3), is infinitely greater than the material thing He created. Like all other creatures, it merely reflects some of the glory of its Creator.

The Church loves to use light in her liturgy as a symbol of God. Often she speaks of Him as "the Father of Light." At Christmas, references to Christ as the light of all "who received Him" are frequent: "A light shines upon us; . . . O God, who hast made this most holy night to shine forth with the brightness of true light; . . . upon us is poured the new light of thy Word made flesh . . . and the light shineth in the darkness . . ." At Epiphany, Isaias raises his voice urgently, "Arise, be enlightened, O Jerusalem: for thy light is come" (Isa. 60:1), and the *Magnificat* antiphon for the third day within the octave says, "As light from light, Thou hast appeared, O Christ."

Simeon's words "A light to the Gentiles" declare that the horizon of the light of Christ has been extended so that it will reach all men. The Church commemorates this vividly and dramatically by the blessing of candles and the Candlemas procession before Mass.[13] The candles, symbolizing the light of Christ, are put into the hands of the faithful and carried in procession to represent their carrying of

---

[13] Some authors believe that the procession on Candlemas Day was originally established by Pope Gelasius I (496) to counteract the pagan festivities of the *Lupercalia*. The Lupercalia was the principal feast of the old Italian deity Faunus, the god of fruitfulness and of rural life. This feast was celebrated in Rome by the heathens with a procession on February 15. Other authors question the relationship between the pagan and Christian feasts. (Cf. *The Catholic Encyclopedia*, ed. 1910, Vol. III, "Candlemas," p. 246b; Vol. VI, "Gelasius I," p. 406.)

Christ in their hearts as they go through life. The blessed candles are used, too, in the Church's liturgy wherever Christ is present in His sacramental power as at Mass or in the sacraments from Baptism to Extreme Unction. Because of the Church's blessing the candles become the bearer and intermediary of God's graces. As a sacramental, they are the outward symbol of the interior graces God gives to their users, and should, therefore, be lighted by the faithful in their homes on family feasts, during storms, in times of severe temptation, at the Communion of the sick, and during the administration of the Last Sacraments.

The lighted, blessed candle is in itself a stirring sermon. The pure wax, produced by the busy bees who sacrifice their short lives for others, represents human nature; the light represents Christ, the Redeemer and Light of the world. As the flame of the light melts and ultimately consumes the candle, so Christ's unending sacrifice of love consumed and destroyed the purely natural man on the altar of the cross and gave us a new life, akin to His own. It is for us to keep the flame of this new life glowing in our hearts so that we may be light-bearers, Christ-bearers in every sense of the word.

The light of Christ appears with new radiance during the Easter season, as the liturgy of that time will make clear. As "light eternal" the sanctuary lamp is a never failing symbol of the Eucharistic presence of Christ in our churches. Mother Church's final prayer for her children, happily, is that "eternal light may shine upon them," but perhaps there is no more beautiful epitome of what light means to her and her children than that which is found in the third prayer used in the blessing of the candles:

This illustration indicates the principal uses of light: At the Holy Sacrifice of the *Mass;* on Holy Saturday, the *Paschal Candle* and the *Triple Candle*; the *Baptismal Candle*, a symbol of sanctifying grace or the Christ-life; the *Sanctuary Lamp*, a symbol of Christ's love in the Holy Eucharist; the *Tenebrae Triangle*, used in Holy Week for Matins and Lauds; and the candles used on the feast of *St. Blaise* for the blessing of throats.

O Lord Jesus, the true light, who enlightenest every man coming into this world, pour forth Thy blessing upon these candles, and sanctify them with the light of Thy grace; and mercifully grant, that as these lights enkindled with visible fire dispel nocturnal darkness, so our hearts illumined by invisible fire, that is, the brightness of the Holy Spirit, may be free from the blindness of every vice; that our mental eye being purified, we may perceive those things which are pleasing to Thee and profitable to our salvation; so that after the dark perils of the world, we may deserve to arrive at never failing light.

The name Candlemas[14] comes from the custom of having all who are present at this Mass hold lighted candles during the Gospel and during the Canon of the Mass to acknowledge the presence of Christ at these times. During the remainder of the year, the altar boys with their lighted candles represent the faithful.

---

[14] The Feast of Candlemas or the Purification, on February 2, always falls between the third and fifth Sundays after Epiphany, though most frequently the date occurs between the fourth and fifth Sundays.

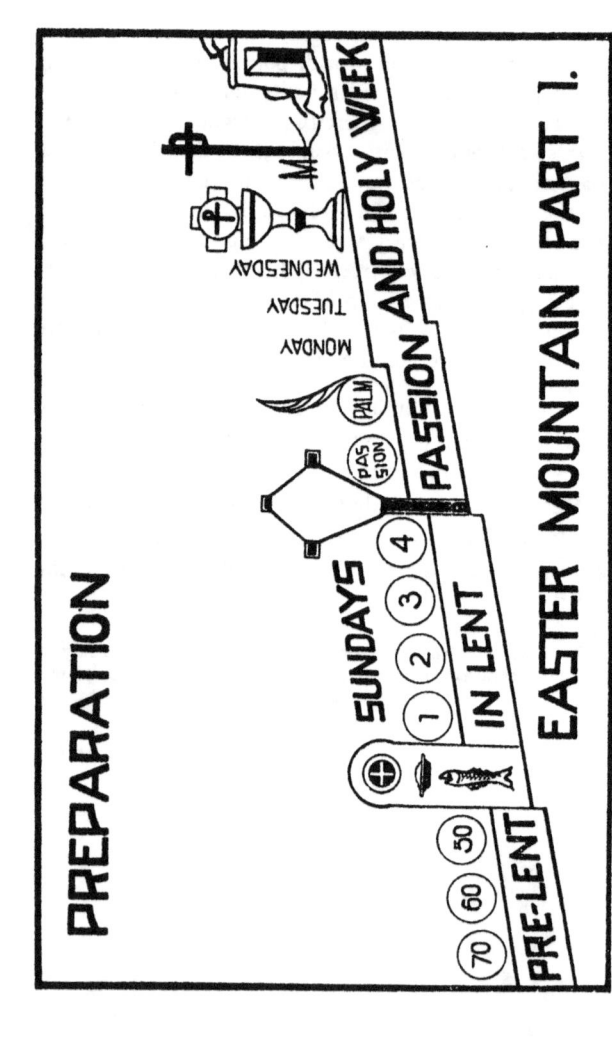

PREPARATION

SUNDAYS

1 2 3 4

IN LENT

PAS SION PALM

MONDAY
TUESDAY
WEDNESDAY

PASSION AND HOLY WEEK

70 60 50

PRE-LENT

EASTER MOUNTAIN PART I.

II. The Easter Cycle

The ascent of the Easter mount is by far the most serious and difficult climb the Christian will find in the liturgical year. This is in keeping with the fact that Easter is the high point of the entire year, the pivot on which our holy faith depends; for the resurrection of Christ was the greatest of His miracles and most strongly substantiated His claim that He was the Son of God. As St. Paul said, "if Christ be not risen again, then is our preaching vain, and your faith is also vain" (1 Cor. 15:14). More than anything else, the resurrection clearly and conclusively demonstrated that the dead Christ on the cross on Good Friday was God, and thus corroborated all His teachings as to the redemption of mankind and the institution of the one true Church.

As the greatest feast of the year, Easter is to be approached with the utmost care and most conscientious preparation. For Christ's coming at Christmas, the Church bids her children spend four weeks in

---

The *circles* in the illustration above represent the Sundays of pre-Lent and Lent; the *dish* with the *ashes*, the *cross* and *fish* represent Ash Wednesday, penance and abstinence, the blessing of the ashes and the words, "Remember, man, that thou art dust, and unto dust thou shalt return." The *veiled cross* signifies the beginning of Passiontide; the *chalice* and *host*, Holy Thursday; the *cross* and *Chi-Rho*, Good Friday; and the *tomb*, Holy Saturday.

preparation and anticipation. For the greater feast of Easter, with all due sense of proportion, she lengthens the preparatory period to nine weeks.

Preparatory Period

Easter and Pentecost are the two principal feasts of the Easter mount. The preparatory period begins on the ninth Sunday before Easter and continues for nine weeks; this period is usually divided into three parts, which are:

1. *The Pre-Lenten Sundays:* Septuagesima (the seventieth day before Easter; the number is a round one, for there are actually 9 weeks or 63 days before Easter), Sexagesima (the sixtieth day; again a round number for 8 weeks or 56 days); Quinquagesima (the fiftieth day; that is, 7 weeks or 49 days).

2. *Lent,* which begins on Ash Wednesday, and, together with Passiontide, lasts for forty days in imitation of Christ's fast of forty days in the desert. The four Sundays in Lent derive their names from the respective *Introits: Invocabit, Reminiscere, Oculi,* and *Laetare.*

3. *Passiontide,* which begins with Passion Sunday and includes Palm Sunday and Holy Week.

The Forty Days of Lent

We have spoken of nine Sundays, nine weeks of preparation for Easter, and then of Lent itself which, including Ash Wednesday, lasts for forty days. The question now arises as to where the forty days are, for there are actually forty-six in Lent proper. Counting the weekdays from Ash Wednesday to and including Holy Saturday, the number is forty exactly. Thus the early Christians kept forty days of Lent in imitation of Christ's fast of forty days in the desert.

ASH WEDNES-DAY	16	30
	3 SUNDAY	31
2		32
3	17	33
4	18	34
SUNDAY	19	PALM SUNDAY
	20	
5	21	35
6	22	36
7	4 SUNDAY	37
8		HOLY THURS-DAY
9	23	
10	24	GOOD FRIDAY
2 SUNDAY	25	
	26	HOLY SATUR-DAY
11	27	
12	28	EASTER EVE
13	PASSION SUNDAY	
14		EASTER SUNDAY
15	29	

The three pre-Lenten Sundays were added later before the year 1100. The Sundays do not count, for on them, as holydays of the Lord, we rejoice and do not fast.

Let us all keep Lent in the spirit of the Church, and thus prepare ourselves well and worthily for Easter;

LENTEN CROSS

This Lenten cross illustrates again the division and structure of Lent. The base of the cross is made up of the three pre-Lenten Sundays (*70, 60, 50*) ending with Ash Wednesday (*cross*). The second part of the base consists of the four Lenten Sundays. The third part is made up of Passion Sunday (*veiled cross*) and Palm Sunday (*palms*). The crosspiece comprises the sacred triduum of Holy Week, that is, Maundy Thursday (the *chalice* signifying the institution of the Holy Eucharist, Holy Mass, and Holy Orders), Good Friday (the *cross*), and Holy Saturday (the *grave* of the Redeemer). The top part represents Easter, with the *banner of victory* of the risen Christ, who by His suffering and death redeemed the world. Good Friday and Easter are related. They brought us redemption through Christ, the Son of God.

at the beginning of Lent let us make a firm resolution for this purpose. On Ash Wednesday the priest makes a cross on our heads with blessed ashes, saying, "Remember, man, that thou art dust and unto dust thou shalt return." In these words the Church says to each one of us: Remember, men, that all of you, sooner or later must die. In your lives strive earnestly to heap up treasures by good works and a holy life, for all good deeds, performed in the state of grace, will be rewarded in heaven. But all sloth and carelessness must be satisfied for in purgatory; sin itself entails the danger of hell.

This illustration shows the good works to which the Church calls all her children during Lent: prayer, fasting, and almsgiving.

During these weeks children should:

1. Pray well and gladly, and diligently attend Mass;

2. Be satisfied with their meals and not pilfer; refrain from sweets, making small sacrifices; save their pennies for the missions and pagan children (they are

bound only by the obligation of abstinence, not that of fasting);

3. Be obedient, industrious, assisting others to do good wherever possible.

' In this way they will prepare their hearts for Easter. And the loving Jesus, who suffered so much for all, will rejoice over their sacrifices, small and great, and will richly and infinitely reward them.

Lent as a Preparation for Solemn Baptism

The early Church was intent on fasting forty days in imitation of Christ's fast before He entered upon His public life. But there was another reason, a weightier one, for the long preparatory season for Easter. In the early days of the Church it was the training period, the final preparatory period, for catechumens who were to be baptized on Easter Sunday. Prior to Lent they had already undergone a period of instruction, perhaps a year or two in length. On Ash Wednesday they were admitted to instructions on Baptism; these continued until Whitsunday. Solemn Baptism was administered on Easter morning. As Christ rose from the dead, the children of men rise from the death of original sin in Baptism, become children of God, and heirs of heaven, brothers and sisters of the glorified Redeemer.

Baptismal Remembrance

Years ago we were baptized; we are all children of God. What good fortune for us! Consider the millions of pagans who have not been so blessed. We should often think of this special sign of God's predilection, especially during Lent and Eastertide. At the same time, we should thank God for it. Remember often your baptismal promises and repeat them: "Yes, dear God, I do renounce the devil and all his works and pomps. I do believe in God, the Father, and the Son and the Holy Ghost; I believe in the holy Catholic Church; in this belief I wish to live and die." Lent is for all of us a time to remember our Baptism.

The Administration of Baptismal Rites in the Early Church

In the early Church the administration of solemn Baptism extended over a long period of time. The individual ceremonies were performed, not in rapid succession as they are today, but one by one with intervals of time between. The whole period was a probation time for the catechumens.

On Ash Wednesday there was the imposition of hands upon those to be baptized; they were then signed with the sign of the cross. On the fourth Wednesday of Lent, prayers of exorcism against the devil were said over them. On the following Wednesday, the Profession of Faith and the Our Father were recited for them. Prior to this the priest (or bishop) moistened their ears with spittle, saying at the same time, "Ephpheta: be thou opened," the expression used by our Lord when He cured the deaf man (Mark 7:34). On the night between Holy Saturday and Easter Sunday, the catechumens made their baptismal promises and thus received the sacrament. They were anointed with chrism and, as a sign of their innocence, were given the white baptismal robes which were not laid aside until the end of Easter week, called White Sunday (*Dominica in Albis, sc. deponendis*). In their hands a lighted candle was placed to typify the light of grace now burning in their souls, which, through Baptism, became the dwelling place of the Trinity.

BAPTISM

This illustration shows the important ceremonies of Baptism and indicates how the grace of Baptism works.

1. The Exorcism: The priest says, "Depart from him, unclean spirit, and make place for the Holy Spirit." Through original sin, the devil lives in the soul of the unbaptized adult or child. Through Baptism, the devil is cast out and the soul becomes the habitation of the Blessed Trinity (depicted in the illustration by the *triangle*, and the *dove*, symbol of the Holy Spirit).

These ceremonies were carried out one by one in the early Church over the interval of time which extended from Ash Wednesday to the night before Easter. Today they are all performed at one time.

Readers might question themselves as to the number of times they have seen a priest administer this sacrament. These are beautiful prayers and ceremonies, all derived from ancient times and adopted to make the baptized person realize the great graces he receives in the sacrament wherein he is made a new man, a child of God.

The prayers and ceremonies of Baptism are among the most significant the Church uses, and each of them would repay closer study. Only then can we

---

2. The Profession of Faith: "I believe in God, the Father Almighty" and the *Our Father* which the adult catechumen himself prayed. Today the sponsors say these prayers for the child.

3. Baptismal Promises: "I do renounce Satan and all his works and all his pomps." These are renewed at solemn Holy Communion, at Confirmation, during retreats, and on other special occasions.

4. Anointing With the Oil of Catechumens: This is indicated by the *oil stock*, on the left of the baptismal font, which carries the inscription *O.C.*, that is, oil of catechumens.

5. The Outer Signs of Baptism: The pouring of the water on the head of the person to be baptized, and the saying of the words, "I baptize thee in the name of the Father and of the Son and of the Holy Spirit."

6. Anointing With Chrism: This is indicated by the *second oil stock*.

7. Presenting of the baptismal garment and of the lighted candle with the words, "Receive this white garment . . . this burning light." The *white garment* is indicative of innocence; the *lighted candle* typifies the state of grace and love and loyalty to God.

fully understand what God has done to our souls in this sacrament; only then can we fully appreciate His love and grace. A greater understanding of this sacrament would be a strong bulwark against sin, which is the greatest evil in the world because it destroys the divine life received in Baptism.

Renewal of Baptismal Promises

At solemn Communion and at Confirmation we renewed publicly the promises which were made in our name at Baptism by our godparents. Now that we are older, let us frequently renew them of our own accord. "I do renounce . . . I do believe." Above all, let us avoid sin, frequently recalling the admonition of the priest as he handed us the baptismal gown: "Receive this white garment, which thou mayest carry without stain before the judgment seat of our Lord Jesus Christ, that thou mayest have life everlasting."

The Ancient Church and Public Penances During Lent

In ancient times Catholics guilty of grave public sin were obliged to do public penance which was often very severe. On Ash Wednesday ashes were strewn on their heads. They were clothed in a penitent's garb, led out of the Church, and not permitted to re-enter until Maundy Thursday. During all this time they were deprived of Holy Mass and the sacraments. When the faithful assembled in church for divine services, the penitents stood before the church and begged for prayers. On Maundy Thursday they were taken into the church, and after having confessed their sins, were allowed to remove their penitential gown.

It can readily be seen how severe a penance the denial of attendance at Mass and Holy Communion must have been to them. How severe would it seem today when so many who could attend do not? Some are too lazy to rise on time; they are not sufficiently fervent and pious, nor do they love Christ in the Blessed Sacrament. They are careless or evil, and their hearts are filled with sin. Rather than belong to these, after the priest has strewn our heads with holy ashes on Ash Wednesday let us get busy and do voluntary penance that everything sinful may leave our souls. Then, on Easter day our hearts may be as pure as they were on the day of our baptism.

"During these days, therefore, let us add something to the usual amount of our service, special prayers, abstinence from food and drink, that each one offer to God 'With the joy of the Holy Ghost,' of his own accord, something above prescribed measure; namely, let him withdraw from his body somewhat of food, drink, sleep, speech, merriment, and with the gladness of spiritual desire await holy Easter" (*Rule of St. Benedict,* Chap. 49).

The Sunday of Joy During Lent: Laetare Sunday

Another name for this day is *Rose Sunday,* because vestments of that color may be worn. In accordance with the spirit of joy, the organ is played and the altar may be adorned with flowers. It corresponds to Gaudete Sunday (the third Sunday) in Advent when the Church rejoices at the nearness of the Feast of Christmas.

A good understanding of Laetare Sunday depends again upon some knowledge of the early Church and the first Christians. The catechumens, above all, were happy at the approach of Easter eve, for they were to be baptized, to become children of God, members of the Church, redeemed Christians, brothers and sisters of the divine Redeemer and heirs of heaven. With her children, Mother Church rejoiced. On this Sunday the early Christians brought fresh roses to church and gave them to the catechumens. Today, on Laetare Sunday, in memory of this practice, the Pope still blesses a *golden rose,* which he presents to some woman of royal rank.

PASSIONTIDE

The Church's joy will not continue much longer, for the earnest spirit of Lent becomes even more profound as we enter on the third step in our preparation for Easter, the steeper climb of Passiontide up to Passion Sunday and Palm Sunday.[15] In her lessons and prayers the Church turns more than ever to the approaching suffering and death of her Redeemer.[16]

Practices to enable us to think more frequently with the Church of the suffering Saviour are a careful reading of the scriptural account of Christ's passion; the Way of the Cross; recitation of the Sorrowful Mysteries of the Rosary; and prayers in honor of the Five Wounds. All of these remind us of what Jesus did for our immortal souls, how He redeemed us by His passion and death on the cross.

On our arrival in church on Passion Sunday, we will notice at once that the crucifix, statues, and holy pictures have been draped in violet. Two reasons are generally given for this practice:

1. It indicates the sad and serious spirit of the season. In the early centuries, Christians used to honor the cross on which the Son of God redeemed us by richly adorning it with gold and precious stones. But the glitter and splendor of jewels seemed inconsistent with the spirit of Passiontide. Hence, they were covered so that only the hard wood of the cross might be visible, the wood on which Christ suffered so intensely on Golgotha for the salvation of the world. Holy pic-

---

[15] See illustrations: Easter Mountain Part I and Lenten Cross, pp. 106 and 110.

[16] The *Tree of Knowledge* in the illustration, p. 118, with its *seven fruits* (seven capital sins) is the throne of the *serpent*, the devil, whence death came into the world. The *radiant cross* conquering the serpent is the sign of salvation, from which a new life springs and whereby the devil is overthrown. The *palm tree* is the symbol for the just One by whose passion the change was effected.

tures, too, had to give way to the sufferings and death of the Saviour, and were veiled accordingly.

2. The crosses are veiled, too, in memory of the fact that Christ, the Son of God, in His passion and death, hid and veiled His divinity. On the days of His suffering He let Himself be taken prisoner, mishandled, and crowned with thorns. He let His enemies crucify Him between two malefactors. The Gospel of Passion Sunday tells us that Christ "hid Himself" because the Jews wished to stone Him. But He hid His divinity only for a short time. On Easter morning He showed Himself in all His power and glory.

The Church expresses another serious thought in the liturgy of this season by placing the cross of the Redeemer adjacent to the tree of sin in paradise (cf. illustration, p. 118). From the cross came salvation and happiness, the new life of grace for men, their redemption; from the tree in paradise misfortune, sin (original sin), and death came upon mankind. On the tree in paradise the devil tempted and conquered; on the tree of the cross, Christ conquered Satan and overcame him, fully expiating the sin of our first parents. From now until Easter the priest very appropriately prays and sings in the Preface that "whence came death, thence also life might rise again, and that he who overcame by the tree (in paradise) might also be overcome on the tree (of the cross)."

Now we can appreciate the great difference between the high priest of the Old Testament and Jesus Christ, the High Priest of the New Testament. On days of propitiation the priest of the Old Testament took the blood of sacrificed animals and carried it into the

Holy of the temple. At his sacrifice he did not suffer personal harm. How different is the case of Christ, the High Priest of the New Testament. He sacrifices Himself to the last drop of His heart's blood, under unmentionable humiliations and injustices, interior and exterior sufferings and agony — on the Mount of Olives, at the scourging post, on the excruciating way of the cross. All this He suffers and bears and offers in order to redeem us sinful creatures, to make us happy, to give us peace of soul and life everlasting.

During these last two weeks of Lent, we shall thank our Redeemer from our hearts for His infinite love, and love Him with all our strength. We shall show our love by making sacrifices, praying more diligently, and being more obedient. We honor His cross particularly when we pray: "Holy cross, we praise thee! We adore Thee, O Christ, and we praise Thee, because by Thy holy cross Thou hast redeemed the world. Lord Jesus, crucified, have mercy on us. Dear Jesus, may Your cross and passion never be lost to my poor soul."

Friday in Passion Week: The Seven Sorrows of the Blessed Virgin Mary

Eight days before Good Friday the Church commemorates the unutterable grief that Mary, the Mother of Sorrows, publicly endured on the road to Calvary and under the cross of her divine Son. On the Feast of the Annunciation, when she replied to the angel: "Behold the handmaid of the Lord; be it done to me according to thy word," she took all things upon herself, joy and affliction, care and sorrow — everything which as Mother of the Redeemer she would be called upon to endure. It was indeed a heavy burden of suffering that Mary had to shoulder. The old man Simeon was indeed correct in his prophecy, "and thy own soul a sword shall pierce" (Luke 2:35). Mary, as co-redeemer, participated in all the bitter anguish which her Divine Son experienced.

In today's Mass the Church sings as the Sequence that impressive hymn, *Stabat Mater:* "At the Cross her Station keeping, stood the mournful mother weeping. . . ."

The seven events which the Feast of the Seven Sorrows depicts are the prophecy of Simeon, the flight to Egypt, the loss of the Child Jesus in the temple, His way of the cross, His death on Calvary, the piercing of His heart with a lance, and His burial.[17]

[17] Note to illustration above: The five-pointed *star* is always a symbol for the Blessed Virgin Mary who is greeted as the "Star of the Sea" and as "The Morning Star." It is often seen, too, on the coat of arms of members of the hierarchy.

Holy Week

The week from Palm Sunday to Easter is called Holy Week. It is the most important, the most serious, and, in its ceremonies, the richest week of all the year. Throughout its seven days, no feast of a saint may be celebrated.[19] On four days (Palm Sunday, Tuesday, Wednesday, and Good Friday) the Passion is read as it is recorded by the evangelists, Matthew, Mark, Luke, and John. The most important days of Holy Week are Palm Sunday, Maundy Thursday, Good Friday, and Holy Saturday.

To live these days well, one must first understand them. Probably nothing would serve better than to read aloud the Passion of our Lord according to the different evangelists. Such reading in common would make for a Christian celebration of Holy Week.

Palm Sunday

Palm Sunday puts before us Christ's solemn entry into Jerusalem (Matt. 21:1-11). Men, women, and children met the Saviour with palm branches in their hands; they strewed them in His path, spread their garments before Him, and joyously hailed Him as the great Miracle-worker, Benefactor, and Messias-King. "Hosanna to the Son of David! Blessed is he who comes in the name of the Lord! Hosanna in the highest" (Matt. 21:9). For this reason the church today blesses palms and has a solemn procession. We also carry palms in our hands and cry with joy to the

---

[19] For the transfer of feasts that may fall within this week, see page 255, note 24.

Saviour, "Glory and praise and honor unto Thee, Christ the King, Redeemer."

When the procession returns to the church, its doors are found closed. The subdeacon knocks three times with the foot of the cross on the closed door which then opens and the procession enters the church. The significance of this ceremony can readily be seen. The sin of our first parents closed the gates of heaven and no one could enter. Then Christ, by His passion and death on the cross, redeemed man and opened heaven. Now those who adhere to Christ, who serve Him faithfully, can enter by way of the cross into the new Jerusalem, represented here on earth by every parish church.

The procession with palms on this Sunday has a profound meaning for us. The blessed palms which we preserve in our homes should ever be a reminder that we will enter heaven only if, throughout our lives, we have served Christ faithfully and have kept our baptismal promises conscientiously. This is the promise we should make on Palm Sunday as we ask Him for the grace of perseverance.

When the Passion of our Lord is either read or chanted during Mass, at the words "and Jesus gave up His spirit" (that is, died), both priest and people kneel. The church is quiet. We adore the infinite love of our Redeemer who died for us on the cross.

Matins of Holy Week — Tenebrae

In the afternoon or early in the evening of Wednesday, Thursday, and Friday in Holy Week, in larger churches, a singular service is held such as is usually performed only in cathedral and monastic churches. This is *Tenebrae*.

Matins is that part of the Church's official prayer (the breviary, said daily by priests and religious in her name) which is prayed at night or very early in

During Tenebrae a triangular candelabrum with fifteen candles stands before the altar. Fourteen of these candles are yellow, and the middle one is white. As soon as a psalm is completed, one of the yellow candles is extinguished. The white candle, still lighted, is removed at the end of the service to a place behind the altar, and then, a few minutes later, is brought back. This act, too, has a meaning. The fourteen yellow candles represent the apostles and disciples, who one after the other, through fear or weakness, deserted Christ when He was taken captive. The white candle represents our Lord, who as the light of the world remained hidden in the grave for a short time only, and then at His resurrection shone brightly in His divinity. The withdrawal of the lighted candle reminds us of the darkness that came upon the earth at the death of Jesus. The noise made at the end of the service signifies the earthquake and all the dreadful manifestations of nature which accompanied the death and resurrection of Christ.

the morning. The Matins of the last three days of Holy Week are rich in content; they deal with the passion and death of the Redeemer and are among the most arresting and impressive of the Church's prayers. Particularly beautiful are the chanted lamentations, sung by the prophet Jeremias on the ruins of Jerusalem. He bemoans the destruction of the proud Jewish nation, its forgetfulness of God, and the subsequent captivity of his people. The words, "Jerusalem, Jerusalem, be converted unto the Lord, thy God," which are constantly repeated, are applicable not only to ancient Jerusalem but to all men. All of us should be sorry and do penance for our sins, since they were the cause of Christ's intense sufferings.

Maundy Thursday

The word *Maundy* derives from the Latin *mandatum:* order, command. It is the first word of the antiphon *"Mandatum* novum do vobis: a new commandment I give you" (John 13:34), and has reference to the occasion when our Lord washed the feet of His disciples (cf. John 13:1 ff.). For that reason the ancient ceremony of washing the feet is referred to as the *Mandatum,* and at the present time is still performed with great solemnity in cathedral, abbey, and other churches. In the liturgy this day is called *Coena Domini,* the day of the Last Supper, on which the Holy Eucharist was instituted.

To understand the celebration of this day, it is well to recall the experiences of Christ and His disciples on the first Maundy Thursday (cf. Matt. 26:1 ff.; Mark 14:1 ff.; Luke 22:1 ff.; John 13:1 ff.). They included: (1) The eating of the Easter lamb or the paschal meal; (2) The washing of the disciples' feet; (3) The institution of the Most Holy Eucharist (the first Mass at which Jesus Christ, the eternal high priest, is the celebrant; the first Communion of the apostles; the first conferring of Holy Orders); (4) The foretelling of Judas' betrayal and Peter's denials; (5) The farewell discourse and priestly prayer of Jesus; (6) The agony and capture of Jesus in the Garden of Olives.

In keeping with these happenings, the liturgy contains four divisions: (1) The holy sacrifice of the Mass; (2) The blessing of the holy oils in cathedral churches; (3) The stripping of the altars; (4) The washing of the feet in cathedral, abbey, and other churches.

1. *The Mass* is joyous in its theme, and yet beneath the joy there is an undertone of sorrow. It is joyful because it commemorates the institution of the great, grace-giving mystery of our faith, the Holy Eucharist as sacrifice and sacrament. In her joy the Church

adorns the altar with flowers and robes her priests and ministers in white garments. The Gloria is sung once more while the church bells ring exultantly; then they are silenced until Holy Saturday morning. In imitation of the Last Supper only one Mass is offered in each church even though more priests may be present; the highest ranking priest (bishop, abbot, dean, pastor) celebrates and the others receive Holy Communion from him as the apostles did from the hands of Christ.

The note of sorrow is evident in the preparations for Good Friday, which is already close at hand. On Holy Thursday two large hosts are consecrated; one the priest consumes at Holy Communion; the other, having been placed in the chalice, is solemnly carried at the end of the Mass to the altar of reposition where it is kept for the Mass of the Presanctified on Good Friday. No further consecration will take place until the morning of Holy Saturday.

2. In cathedrals, each bishop blesses the *holy oils* during the solemn Mass that he celebrates. These holy oils include: Oil of the Sick (used in the administering of Extreme Unction); Oil of the Catechumens (used in the blessing of baptismal water and in Baptism, in Holy Orders, and in the blessing of altars); and Chrism (used in Baptism, Confirmation, the consecration of a bishop, the consecration of churches and altars, chalices and patens, and in the blessing of bells). After Mass, each parish receives its holy oils for the year; oils remaining from the past year are burned in the Easter fire on Holy Saturday.

3. *The stripping of the altars:* After the Mass, the

altars are stripped of all coverings. Relics are removed, candlesticks are overturned so that nothing whatsoever remains on the altar. The altar represents Christ. For this reason the priest kisses it during every Mass and incenses it during a solemn Mass. Today's stripping is to remind us of the stripping of Jesus at the scourging and crucifixion, of His abandonment on the cross.

4. *The washing of feet:* In cathedral, abbey, and other churches twelve old men (priests or members of the order or of the parish) have their feet washed and kissed by the bishop, abbot, or priest, in imitation of the example Jesus gave when in all humility He washed the feet of His disciples, saying, "I have given you an example, that as I have done to you, so you also should do" (John 13:15). In some monasteries the superior serves his confreres at meals. In Rome the pope alone washes the feet.

Everyone should attend Holy Thursday services and make an afternoon's visit to the altar of repose.

Good Friday

This is the death and burial day of our Redeemer, the day of His mockery, His scourging, His crowning with thorns, His way of the cross, His crucifixion, the saddest of all the days of Christianity. The Church today is wrapt in sorrow and reveals it in all her ceremonies. No Mass is offered, for on this day the eternal High Priest offers Himself as a bloody sacrifice to God the Father for the redemption of mankind.

At the beginning of the services, no lights are burning, for Christ, the light of the world, has died. The

cross on the altar is draped in black. The priest and
his attendants, vested in black robes, prostrate themselves before the altar to reflect on the exceedingly
great love of Christ. Then follow:

1. *A prayer service.* First, two excerpts from Sacred
Scripture are read or chanted. These are followed by
the particularly beautiful account of our Lord's passion according to St. John. Then solemn prayers of
intercession are said for men in all conditions of life,
for Christ died for all men. Before every prayer a
solemn appeal is made to the faithful, telling them
for whom each prayer is to be offered. They are to
pray first for holy Church, then for the pope, the
bishops, priests, deacons, and all the different orders
of the hierarchy (for the emperor or the king), for
the catechumens, for heretics and schismatics, for Jews
and pagans, finally for all the unfortunate, the sick,
prisoners, travelers, sailors. The *"Flectamus genua:*
Let us kneel" is said and all kneel down to pray until
the *"Levate:* Arise" bids them rise. Then the priest
turns to God and formulates the prayer in the name

of all. Here we have an example of the oldest form
of the "Collect" or public prayer.

2. *The adoration of the cross.* The priest lays aside
his chasuble, receives the black-draped cross from the
altar, and gradually unveils it as he faces the people
and chants three times in an ever ascending pitch,
"Behold the wood of the cross on which hung the
Saviour of the world." The choir answers, "Come
let us adore," and all present fall on their knees in
silent adoration. The priest now puts the crucifix on
a pillow before the altar, takes off his shoes (other
priests present and altar boys do likewise), and after
kneeling three times in adoration at various distances
from the cross, approaches it and kisses the wounds
of the Crucified. This is the solemn ceremony of Good
Friday, honoring the Redeemer and the cross as the
sign of salvation. During this time, the choir sings
the soul-stirring *Improperia* (Reproaches), songs of
lamentation by our Lord to His unfaithful, unbeliev-
ing, and thankless people. These reproaches, inter-
spersed with invocations in Greek and chiefly taken
from the fourth book of Esdras, form one of the most
tragic episodes of the Good Friday service which is a
real drama and suggests the medieval Passion plays.

3. *The Mass of the Presanctified.* The name indicates that the offerings have already been sanctified
because the host had been consecrated on the previous
day; there is no consecration and, therefore, no real
Mass on Good Friday. In solemn procession, the sacred host is carried from the altar of repose to the
high altar, while the choir sings the hymn of the
cross, *Vexilla Regis,* composed in the sixth century by

the famous bishop, Venantius Fortunatus. After pouring wine and water into the chalice and reciting various prayers, among them, the Our Father, the priest with his right hand elevates the consecrated host for adoration. He then immediately breaks it into three parts, dropping one part into the chalice, into the unconsecrated wine which has been mixed with water. Then he receives Holy Communion, purifies the chalices, says a short thanksgiving prayer, and so concludes the Mass, which is in reality merely a long Communion service.

4. *Burial service.* In many dioceses this burial service takes place with a solemn procession to the grave or sepulcher.

On Good Friday we should pay frequent visits to our Saviour in His tomb, thanking Him from our heart for our redemption and for all our merited and granted graces. In Rome the Good Friday service is performed in the Church of the Holy Cross, where the most precious relics of our Lord's passion are preserved.

Holy Saturday

Holy Saturday is the Lord's day of rest, for on that day Christ rested in His tomb. In the liturgy this day is called the *Sabbatum Sanctum,* Holy Saturday. It should really be the quietest day of all the year. For this reason, for hundreds of years, no divine services were held. The early Christians gathered in church toward Easter morning to perform holy ceremonies, above all, for the solemn administration of the sacrament of Baptism to the catechumens who had been

preparing for its reception with special care since Ash Wednesday.

All that is now done on Holy Saturday morning was once done during the night (vigil) that preceded Easter. If we remember this throughout the services, we will understand better the many ceremonies of Holy Saturday morning. They, like all those of Holy Week, date from very early times and are full of that profound symbolism which characterizes the ancient liturgy. The resurrection of Christ is the central point of the entire celebration. Through His passion and death He has redeemed all men, He has merited grace for us all. From the grave He arose to a new life, magnificent and glorified. As He lay dead in His tomb, so our souls are spiritually dead when we come into this world, stained with original sin. Through Baptism our souls rise from the death of sin. Through this sacrament we are redeemed and freed from the devil and our souls receive a new life, the life of sanctifying grace. As long as we preserve this grace, as long as we are guilty of no grievous sin, so long do we remain children of God and heirs of heaven. When we appear before God with a pure soul, we, too, shall be gloriously transfigured in heaven, as Christ was transfigured at His resurrection.

In the early Christian centuries the ceremonies of Easter Eve began shortly before midnight. The new fire was lighted and blessed, the church was lighted, and the Easter candle was solemnly blessed. Then the catechumens received their final instructions on the sacrament of Baptism. The baptismal font was blessed and Baptism was administered. Immediately after Baptism, the candidates were confirmed since they were adults. These ceremonies would take place about the time that Christ arose, glorious and triumphant from His tomb. We know that He arose before dawn, because the tomb was empty when the holy women arrived there about that time. Appropriately, at that very time the newly baptized received the new life of grace — they arose from the death of original sin to the life of grace.

After Baptism and Confirmation, Mass followed in the early hours of Easter morning. Then the first solemn *Alleluia* was sung; the glad tidings of the resurrection were loudly proclaimed. This accounts for our interpretation of the glorious *Alleluia* sung by priest and choir in ever ascending tones. It is the church's cry of victory at the resurrection of its King; it is the happy *Alleluia* of the newly baptized at their good fortune of having received a new life in Christ and in His Church. At this solemn Easter night Mass, the new members of the Church receive their first Holy Communion.

Now we can understand how great a feast this Easter night was in the early Church. What a day of grace for the catechumens! They received three holy sacraments on this night: Baptism, Confirmation, and Holy Communion. Most of us have already received these sacraments — at least Baptism. During the ceremonies of Holy Saturday, we should thank our Redeemer for it.

The individual ceremonies of Holy Saturday are solemn and inspiring, and merit our closest consideration. They are:

1. *The Blessing of the New Fire.* Early in the morning the priest and the altar boys proceed to the entrance of the church where fire is ignited from sparks produced from flint.[18] This fire is solemnly blessed, sprinkled with holy water, and incensed. The new fire signifies Christ who arose victorious from His grave; the fire of His redeeming love allowed Him to die on the cross. Next the five grains of incense are blessed; they are to be put later into the Easter candle. These five grains represent the five wounds of our Lord, and are incensed to indicate that all His sufferings are at an end. A taper is lighted from the blessed fire with which the priest and his attendants enter the darkened church. For this entrance a white dalmatic is worn as the first outward sign of Easter joy; the white vestments are an Easter herald, the announcer of the happy tidings of the resurrection. As the priest makes his way to the high altar, he stops three times: at the entrance, in the cen-

---

[18] This is to symbolize the fact that Christ, the light of the world, came forth from a sepulcher of *stone*.

ter of the church, and at the Communion rail. Each
time he halts, one part of the three-branched candle[19]
is lighted from the newly blessed fire as the priest

    This illustration portrays the predominating thoughts and the
most important ceremonies of Holy Saturday.

    The *Lumen Christi*, the life-giving grace earned for us by the
Redeemer, is applied to our souls through the sacrifice of the
Mass. It is imparted in Baptism (*candle, font, garment*),
strengthened and brought to an adult stage by Confirmation
(*dove*), and nourished by Holy Communion (*host* and *chalice*).

---

    [19] The three-branched candle is a symbol of the Blessed Trinity,
made known to man by Christ, the second Person of the Trinity.

chants in an ascending tone the words, *Lumen Christi:* "The Light of Christ," while the congregation genuflects and answers *Deo gratias:* "Thanks be to God."

2. *The Blessing of the Easter Candle.* This is the largest and most beautiful candle burned in our churches. It typifies the risen Redeemer "who, shining in light, left the tomb." For this reason it is lighted each day during Mass throughout the Paschal season until Ascension Thursday. Having reached the high altar with the newly blessed lights, the priest sings the glorious Easter song, *Exsultet.* This magnificent hymn, which is remarkable for its lyric beauty and profound symbolism, announces the dignity and meaning of the mystery of Easter; it tells of man's sin, of God's mercy, and of the great love of the Redeemer for mankind, admonishing us in turn to thank the Trinity for all the graces that have been lavished upon us. During this solemn chant the five grains of blessed incense are inserted into the Easter candle; then from the tapers of the triple candle, it is lighted and after it, from the same tapers, the sanctuary light and all the candles on the altar, to indicate that through Christ, light and grace entered a sin-darkened world.

3. *The Twelve Prophecies.* Clad in violet vestments, the celebrant reads or chants the twelve prophecies of the Old Testament. They are often taken each by a different cleric, adding solemnity to the ceremony, and relieving the burden of their length on one reader. These prophecies represent the final instructions on the principal points of Christian doctrine received by the catechumens in the ancient Church. They were to be reminded again of the grace of the redemption

imparted to them in Baptism, thus recognizing the greatness of this hour of grace. For us, these prophecies are earnest admonitions to preserve our baptismal grace and to keep our baptismal promises throughout our lives.

4. *The Blessing of the Baptismal Font.* Accompanied by solemn chant, the celebrant and his attendants go to the baptistery to bless the baptismal font. The Easter candle is carried at the head of the procession. The ceremonies of the blessing with the accompanying prayers and chants have a profound significance. The priest touches the water, breathes upon it, blesses it, sprinkles it to the four directions; in like manner the graces of the redemption and of Baptism go out to the four corners of the world. The Easter candle is immersed in the water and the Spirit and the grace of God invoked upon the baptismal water. Finally the holy oils, blessed on Holy Thursday by the bishop, are mixed with water in order that the fullness of God's grace and the blessing of the Church may remain therein and pass to all who are baptized "in water and the Holy Ghost."

5. *Solemn High Mass.* Returning from the baptistery to the foot of the high altar, the priest and altar boys prostrate themselves to thank God and to beseech Him for the grace of perseverance. During this time the Litany of the Saints is sung up to the *Kyrie.* At its conclusion white vestments are donned, and the solemn Easter Mass begins, expressing in its prayers and chants the Easter joy of the Church and the happy gratitude of the newly baptized. After days of sorrow, the *Gloria* and the ringing of the bells an-

nounce the joyous Easter tidings. The thrice-repeated *Alleluia,* above all, sung in higher tones each time, tells of man's happiness now that his redemption has been effected.

In some monasteries at the Offertory of the Mass on Holy Saturday, a small boy, accompanied by a member of the community, leads a living lamb to the choir. The organ resounds, and the abbot with miter and crozier, approaches and blesses the lamb with these words:

> O God, who didst command Thy servant Moses to kill a lamb at the liberation of Thy people from the slavery of Egypt as a type of our Lord Jesus Christ, and who commandest the door posts to be sprinkled with the blood of a lamb, deign to bless and sanctify this living lamb which we, thy servants, shall eat in Thy name. Through the same Lord Jesus Christ, who liveth and reigneth with Thee forever. Amen.

The abbot then sprinkles the lamb with holy water. In the course of the afternoon it is slaughtered, and on Easter morning it is roasted whole and then carried, topped by a wooden cross, to the abbot's table. At the beginning of dinner, after the blessing has been given, the abbot puts on a white apron and carves the lamb, serving it to guests and monks in the order of their seniority. The symbolism of the whole ceremony is so apparent that it needs no further explanation.

Immediately after the Communion of the priest, Vespers is begun with the threefold singing of the *Alleluia.* It, too, is an expression of thanks and joy on the part of the Church to its risen Redeemer.

On Holy Saturday, let us unite heartily with a pure, loving, and thankful heart in singing and praying with the Church her glorious Easter hymn, *Exsultet*.

The Solemnity of Solemnities

"This is the day which the Lord hath made: let us rejoice and be glad therein. Alleluia." Thus the Church sings and rejoices today. The mountain has been scaled, the victory has been won. Christ, the light and redeemer of the world, has subjugated Satan, the prince of darkness, the tempter and corruptor of human souls. The sun of divine grace sends its enlightening and radiating beams over a world steeped in sin and death. Now is accomplished that for which we prayed during the Advent season, "Come, Lord, to save us!" Now is fulfilled the redemption which was begun at Christmas. The peace of Christmas now becomes the happiness of Easter and the jubilation of the resurrection. Easter, the "feast of feasts," the "solemnity of solemnities," as the liturgy calls it, is the pinnacle of the entire Church year. The great pope, St. Leo (461), wrote: "Among all the feasts which are celebrated in our faith, Easter is the greatest and most sublime, and all other feasts of the Church attain their worth only in their relationship to it." For this reason the Church never wearies of singing again and again, "Alleluia! Let us be glad and rejoice. Alleluia."

The fact of Easter, the resurrection of our Lord, gives us the greatest assurance that Jesus Christ is really the Son of God, that His teaching is pure truth, and that all of us will one day rise from the dead. Thus do we understand the oration of the Mass of this feast:

> O God, who on this day, through thine only-begotten Son, hast overcome death and reopened unto us the gate of eternity; even as by Thy grace Thou dost inspire our desires, so also follow them up with Thy continual help.

The risen Christ, the only-begotten Son of the Eternal Father, has conquered death and has reopened to us the gate of eternity which was closed because of original sin. Through His resurrection we have all become children of resurrection; through His victory all of us have become conquerors over sin, death, and the grave.

But it is not enough that we share in this joy and this jubilant *Alleluia*. We must form pious resolutions and carry them out with the aid of divine grace. For this Easter resolution is nothing else than the renewal of our baptismal vows: We believe in Jesus, in His resurrection from the dead, and in His Church; we renounce Satan and all his works, sin above all; with faithful love we adhere firmly to Christ and His Church; we will preserve unsullied in our hearts the blessings of Easter; we will remain forever redeemed and forever dead to sin and to all evil.

To this Easter resolution we may join the tender prayer:

> O dear Jesus, keep forever opened for us the heaven which you have unlocked for us through your sufferings, your death, and your resurrection! Do not permit that we again insult you with sin, that we return to our former condition as sinful, unredeemed people. Grant, O Saviour of the world, that we walk worthy of your glorious resurrection until we finally arrive at the participation of your glory, the eternal Easter in heaven!

This is the triumphant victory of Easter joy! This is the triumphant victory of Easter faith! This is the triumphant victory of Easter prayer!

The feast of Easter is the oldest feast in the Church.[20] In the Old Testament it was known as the Pasch, or Passover, and reminded the Jews of their sojourn in Egypt when the destroying angel passed by those houses which at God's command were sprinkled with the blood of a lamb. The Jewish Pasch served as a remembrance of their wonderful deliverance from Egyptian bondage. Each year they celebrated this feast for eight days, during which time they ate the paschal lamb. Christ ate the lamb with His apostles

---

[20] The English name *Easter*, from east or *oriens*, reminds us that Christ is the light of the world, and that as the sun rises in the east, so He left His tomb in the morning. (*The Roman Missal*, by Dom F. Cabrol, O.S.B.)

on Maundy Thursday for the last time, for the old covenant was ending and He was to become the paschal lamb of the new covenant, through the merits of whose blood we have all been saved.

That which the paschal lamb of the Old Testament prefigured was fulfilled and became reality on the first Good Friday and the first Easter Sunday two thousand years ago. For that reason the Church sings on these days, "Christ our Pasch is immolated." In the Divine Office and in the Mass prayers of the Easter season the liturgy again and again alludes to these prototypes of Easter: the eating of the paschal lamb, the departure from Egypt, and the destruction of Pharaoh and his people in the Red Sea.

Even to this day the Church celebrates the mystery of Easter for eight days. Each day of this *octave* has its own Mass text and its own lessons in the breviary which continue to keep before us the resurrection of Christ and our own resurrection in Baptism. The Gospels of these days relate the various appearances of the risen Saviour to His disciples.

The Feast of Easter ordinarily concurs with the coming of spring. Nature itself restrains its arising from the long sleep of winter as if it were waiting to join in the tremendous event which the resurrection of Christ brought about for the salvation of mankind. Resurrection, victory, light, life: spring in nature, spring in the Church and in the souls of men: this is Easter, "the day which the Lord hath made; let us be glad and rejoice therein. Alleluia!"

In many localities and in most monasteries the *blessing of foods* takes place during the divine services of Easter Sunday. Although eggs are commonly the object of this blessing, meat and bread are also included. This custom dates back to ancient times. It signifies that after the long season of fasting these foods are received again from the hand of Mother Church, sanctified through her blessings. For in some places, especially in monasteries, the Lenten fast is still observed in its original rigor, which means that during these forty days neither meat nor eggs are eaten. Furthermore, the blessed meat is to remind Christians of the Easter lamb. The egg is a symbol of the resurrection. The shell signifies the grave. As the chick breaks its way through the shell to come forth to light and life, so also did Jesus break open the sealed entrance to the grave, and so will all of us eventually come forth from the grave. Thus, the Easter eggs, used in so many homes, take on a deep, religious meaning — they are reminders of Christ's resurrection and they anticipate our own resurrection from the dead.

Easter and Easter Week

If Holy Week is the most sacred and most important week of the entire ecclesiastical year, it is because it draws its importance from Good Friday, the day on which Christ, the God-Man and Redeemer, died on the cross for us. Rightly therefore can this week be considered the most serious and awe-inspiring in the Church's calendar. But Easter Week is the very antithesis of Holy Week. Since the resurrection was the most significant event in the life of our Lord who by means of this wonderful and undeniable fact made His divinity known to the entire world, Easter is the highest Sunday and Easter Week the greatest week of the entire Church year. No other feast is ever celebrated during this week.

The Celebration of Easter, Until Pentecost

We have compared the festive cycle of Easter with mountain climbing. The season immediately preceding Lent and the Lenten season itself with the final steep stretch of Holy Week made a long arduous ascent.[21] Then during the night of Easter we arrived at the summit. Now we wander in the free and happy air of Easter faith, in the bright light of the joy surrounding the resurrection and of the grace of salvation. For a period of fifty days we shall wander on this mountain until we arrive at the highest point, the lookout point, the Feast of Pentecost, that grand birthday of the Church on which the first Christian community was formed under the visible workings of the Holy Spirit. After Pentecost we again begin the descent of the mount, which takes us from twenty-four to twenty-six weeks (Sundays).[22]

Easter and Pentecost are, therefore, the two high points of the Easter cycle. But they are surrounded by other feasts and Sundays which but increase the joys of Easter and prolong them in our souls. On the fortieth day after His resurrection, Christ ascended into heaven. Hence, on that day the Church celebrates the Feast of the Ascension. This feast is preceded by the three Rogation Days. On the fiftieth day after His

---

[21] See illustration: Easter Mountain Part I, page 106.
[22] The reason for this long period is given on page 176 ff.

resurrection, that is, ten days after His ascension, Christ sent the Paraclete, the Consoler, to His apostles. Hence, we solemnly celebrate the Feast of Pentecost on the fiftieth day after Easter. Between Easter and Pentecost there are six Sundays which are known in the missal as the *Sundays after Easter.*

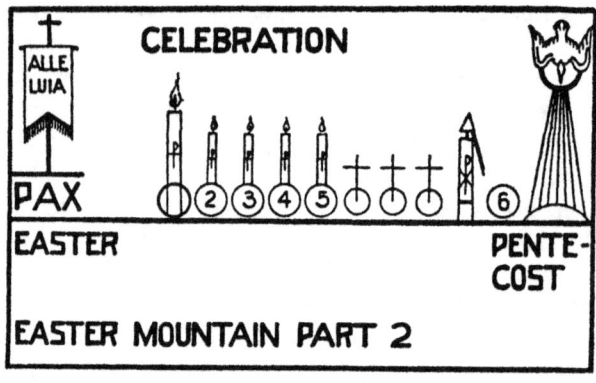

The *cross* and *banner* at the left of this illustration are symbols of the risen Saviour's victory over sin and death. With Easter the climax of the season is attained. The five Sundays after Easter are represented by *five paschal candles;* the first Sunday (Low Sunday) is of higher rank (greater double) than the four following ones. In many localities it is customary for children to receive their solemn Holy Communion on that day. The four Sundays that follow retain a definite reference to Easter in the fact that the Easter candle still burns during Mass. On Ascension Thursday, the day when the risen Saviour left this earth and returned to His Father, it is extinguished. The three Rogation Days preceding the Ascension are indicated on the picture by the *three crosses.* The last (the sixth) Sunday after Easter falls between Ascension and Pentecost. The *dove* and *seven rays* indicate the coming of the Holy Ghost on Pentecost.

Sundays After Easter

There are six Sundays after Easter. Five of these fall between Easter and Ascension. The first of these is Low Sunday or White Sunday (not to be confused with Whitsunday or Pentecost). The second is known as Good Shepherd Sunday, because on this day the Gospel tells the beautiful and consoling parable of the Good Shepherd. On the third Sunday the liturgy gives us Christ's prediction of His ascension. The Gospels of the fourth and sixth Sundays present Christ as speaking of the coming of the Holy Ghost. The fifth Sunday is sometimes known as Rogation Sunday because it precedes the three Rogation Days, and also because it reminds us of the duty, the necessity, the propriety, and the blessing of praying in the name of Jesus.

Low Sunday

The first Sunday after Easter, or Low Sunday, falls on the Octave of Easter. It is called *Low* in order to emphasize its difference from the greater Easter solemnity; it is also called *Quasimodo* from the first words of the Introit. Both the missal and the breviary refer to it as *Dominica in Albis* (*sc. deponendis*) or White Sunday. This name has its origin in the custom already mentioned (page 114) of "laying aside" (*deponendis*) the white baptismal robes (White Sunday). When the catechumens were solemnly baptized on Easter Saturday, they were given a white garment to symbolize the effects of Baptism on their souls. They continued to wear it during church services until the end of the week, "the Saturday on which the white garments were laid aside." The robes were preserved in the treasury of the church as a pledge of the catechumens' fidelity, and as a constant reminder that their baptismal vows were to be faithfully kept. There they would also be a reproach to those who might become unfaithful to these sacred promises.

The visible white garment is put aside by the neophytes. Yet, the invisible white garment of the soul, that is, sanctifying grace, must be spotlessly preserved by them and by all of us if we are to become worthy of the glorified garment in heaven.

In many localities Low Sunday has an additional significance, for on this day children make their solemn Holy Communion.[23] It is the day of the renewal of their baptismal vows. In the presence of the entire congregation, in the presence of Christ in the Blessed Sacrament, the Communicants solemnly promise, "We do renounce . . . we do believe." Truly it is a serious hour, the like of which they may never again experience.

We rejoice today with these innocent children, and renew with them our own baptismal vows with a faithful and loving heart. Let us also receive Holy Communion with them. And may every Communion Sunday be a blessed White Sunday for our souls. Then we shall remain truly happy children of our heavenly Father. Let us unite our prayer with that of

---

[23] In the early centuries the faithful assembled on this day in the Church of *St. Pancratius*. This brave fourteen-year-old lad, with God's grace received in Holy Communion, was enabled not only to preserve his baptismal vows through cruel sufferings but to seal them with his death; he is a magnificent example to First Communicants and to all. May we, too, as did this youthful patron, remain faithful to our baptismal promises.

the priest and the communicants at the Oration of the Mass:

> Grant, we beeseech thee, O almighty God, that we who have now come to the end of the Easter festivities, may through Thy goodness, always keep its spirit (that is, the grace of Baptism, the blessings of our First Communion) in our life and conduct.

Easter — Eastertide — Easter Cycle

A clear distinction must be made between these three terms. The word *Easter* is used in the narrowest sense to refer to Easter Sunday, the festival of the resurrection of our Lord from the dead. In a broader sense the word means Easter Week or the Octave of Easter which ends with Low Sunday. *Eastertide* refers to the fifty days from Easter Sunday up to and including the Saturday before Pentecost Sunday. The *Easter cycle,* however, includes all the days from Septuagesima Sunday to the first Sunday in Advent.[24]

Because the Feast of Easter is the greatest feast of the whole liturgical year, it is celebrated not only with an octave like other great feasts, but for seven weeks, exactly fifty days, ending with the Feast of Pentecost. The number fifty has its historical foundation in the fact that the risen Christ remained on earth forty days after His resurrection; ten days later the Holy Spirit descended upon the apostles on the first Pentecost. Furthermore, the number fifty was symbolical of joy in ancient times.

---

[24] In general usage in America *Easter time* covers the period from the first Sunday in Lent to and including Trinity Sunday, the time during which all Catholics must perform their "Easter duty" by receiving the sacraments of Penance and Holy Communion.

These fifty days from Easter to Pentecost reflect a glad and jubilant character, because they commemorate the resurrection of our Lord, the most glorious event of His life, the most conclusive proof of His divinity, the accomplishment of our redemption, hence the foundation of our faith. The entire liturgy of the Church sings and speaks of Easter victory and Easter joy at this time. Taken as a whole, these fifty days are the one comprehensive celebration of Easter in the Church. Only as Sundays after Pentecost succeed one another does the echo of the Easter bells gradually grow more faint.

That new life in Christ, which we received in Baptism and have nourished and strengthened through the renewal of our baptismal vows and the worthy reception of the sacraments of Penance and the Holy Eucharist, will be brought to fruition by the frequent reception of these sacraments. And what we cannot attain to this year, we must strive anew to attain in the years that follow so that ultimately we will be permitted to participate in that eternal Easter celebration in heaven.

Rejoice during this holy season with holy Mother Church that Christ is risen from the dead and that through Baptism, Penance, and the Holy Eucharist we are His redeemed brothers and sisters, members of His holy Church. Strive earnestly and steadfastly ever to remain children of God, true friends of the loving Christ, and worth-while members of the Catholic Church. Keep your baptismal robe and baptismal and Communion candles as witnesses of your fidelity to your baptismal vows.

Characteristics of the Liturgy of the Easter Season

1. During this season there is very frequent repetition of the exultant *Alleluia*, the Hebrew cry of joy, meaning *Praise the Lord!* In all changeable chants — Introit, Offertory, and Communion verse in the missal and the Versicles and Responses of the breviary — the Church is constantly singing *Alleluia*.[25]

2. After the Epistle, instead of the Gradual, the *Alleluia* is repeated together with a verse of some psalm. The Gradual was always considered a song of penance.

3. During the sprinkling of the faithful with holy water on Sundays, instead of the usual *Asperges* with the accompanying verses of the *Miserere* (a petition to God to cleanse our souls of sin), we hear the *Vidi aquam* and the first verse of Psalm 117: "I saw water well forth from the right side of the temple, Alleluia. And all toward whom this water flowed were saved, and they shall sing Alleluia, Alleluia. Praise the Lord for He is holy and His mercy eternal." This happy and joyful song of thanks is a reminder of the solemn administration of Baptism in the early Church on the vigil of Easter. To us it should be a reminder of our resurrection through Baptism from the death of original sin, and of the new life we are bound to live in Christ.

4. The *Regina Coeli*, Easter hymn to the Blessed Virgin, is an invitation to all of us to unite ourselves with Mary, the mother of the risen Lord; an invitation to rejoice and ask her intercession that we may

---

[25] For a fuller discussion of the *Alleluia*, see page 43 ff.

attain to eternal life. The *Regina Coeli* is sung or recited *standing* until Trinity Sunday; it also takes the place of the *Angelus*. Every Christian who lives the liturgy of the Church should know by heart and gladly pray this beautiful and joyful hymn to Mary.

5. Two interesting precepts for paschal time were already enacted in the early Church: *Not to fast* during Easter time, and *not to kneel* during solemn services. From the earliest days, Christians were not expected to fast on Sunday, the day which reminds us of Christ's resurrection and our redemption. When the Church extended her prohibition of fasting to the paschal season, she was clearly indicating that she wished this whole period of time to be regarded as an uninterrupted Sunday. As St. Ambrose wrote, "During these fifty days the Church omits fasting as she does on Sundays . . . all these fifty days are one and the same Sunday." The eastern Church still has this feature of not kneeling during solemn services. In the western Church it is customary for the laity to kneel, but if one attends a solemn High Mass in a Benedictine monastery, he will notice that the monks remain standing and kneel only during the elevation (except during Advent, Lent, and a Requiem High Mass).

The liturgical color of paschal time is white or gold to express joy, though violet is worn on Rogation Days. The *Gloria,* omitted during Lent, is recited or sung daily, except on Rogation Days and during Requiem Masses.

Let us deeply realize this spirit of joy at our redemption, this spirit that permeates the whole of

Easter time, and thank Christ, our risen Redeemer and Saviour, and love Him with our whole heart. We will manifest our love in every deed if we show, through the keeping of all His precepts, that our conversion has been a real one.

The Easter Sun

Easter Sunday is the greatest and holiest of all Sundays of the Church year. It is appropriately called the Feast of Feasts. The Easter Sun simultaneously completes the redemption and eclipses the darkness and malice of sin. The Light, the King of light, the God of light has conquered the spirit of darkness. Brighter than the Christmas light, the Easter sun sends forth its rays upon the earth and warms and brings to life and maturity. Louder and more joyfully than the angelic *Gloria* at the crib does the Easter *Alleluia* of angels and men resound through heaven and earth. The jubilation and happiness of the Church because of Christ's Easter victory is especially evident in the Mass prayers of the Sundays after Easter: "*Jubilate Deo* . . . Shout with joy to God, all the earth, alleluia! *Cantate Domino* . . . Sing ye to the Lord and bless His name. *Benedicite, gentes, Dominum* . . . O bless the Lord our God, ye peoples."[26]

Again and again the liturgy tells us why we should rejoice and be glad and praise and glorify God, for "the Lord hath sent redemption to His people. Alleluia." For us Christians the Easter bells ring more than once a year. They ring every day, but especially

---

[26] See the Introits, Alleluia verses after the Epistles, Offertories, etc., of these Sundays.

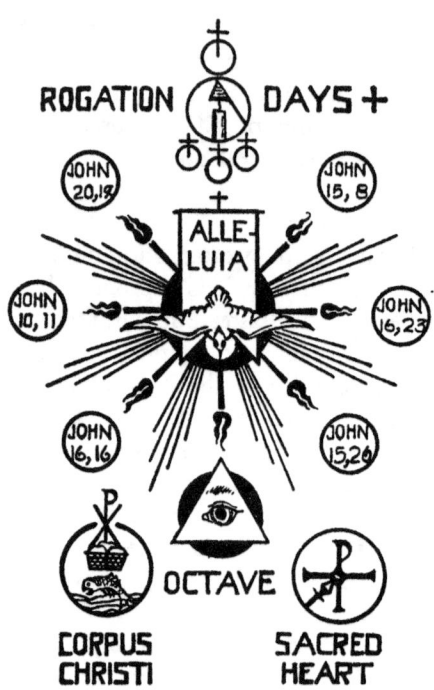

This illustration, called "The Easter Sun," is the counterpart of the "Lenten Cross," showing the relation between the Feast of Easter and Easter time. In the center is the Easter *sun*, emitting *rays* of light and fiery *tongues*, that is, the great Feasts of Easter and Pentecost. Directly above is the Feast of the Ascension with its accompanying Rogation Days. Underneath are the Feasts of the Blessed Trinity, Corpus Christi (with an octave), and the Feast of the Sacred Heart (with an octave). The six small *circles* surrounding the Easter Sun as planets are the Sundays between Easter and Pentecost. The *numbers* in the small circles give the context of the Gospel for those Sundays. On the fourth and sixth Sundays the Lord speaks of the Holy Ghost. He promises the Holy Spirit as comforter and teacher, as light, and strength, as a help in every need. Before His ascen-

on each Sunday, on each Communion day. "Declare it with the voice of joy, and make it known, alleluia; declare it even to the ends of the earth: The Lord hath delivered His people,.alleluia, alleluia!" (Introit, Fifth Sunday after Easter.)

The liturgy is meant to imprint deeply on our hearts the proud and happy knowledge that we are the redeemed children of God, brothers and sisters, heirs of heaven. It is our duty as redeemed brothers and sisters of Christ to live a truly Christian life, and to thank our Redeemer by word and deed. This is the purpose of all liturgical worship: to praise and thank God, to beseech Him for His grace, and to atone for the sins of mankind. It is just these ideas that the Mass prayers of the Sundays after Easter manifest so well.

St. Augustine once remarked: "He who loves, sings." Christians have always sung to God in the Church's public service, prompted by gratitude, joy, love, and inspiration. The priest sang at the altar; the deacon and subdeacon, in their appointed places. Following the dictates of their hearts, the faithful also sang their allotted parts and answered the priest's chant. The choral chant we have today is of such early

---

sion Christ commanded the apostles to remain in Jerusalem, there to await the coming of the Holy Spirit. The apostles and the Blessed Virgin, therefore, awaited the coming of the Paraclete in the room of the Last Supper. We, too, should ask His graces, especially during the public novena to the Holy Ghost before Pentecost. Those to be confirmed should attend this novena with special fervor, and those already confirmed should renew the sacramental grace of confirmation, and strive to live as soldiers of Christ and the Holy Ghost. This would be a genuine preparation for the feast in the spirit of the liturgy.

origin. As redeemed children we should sing our praise and thanks to God, for then it will be "truly meet and just: *dignum et justum est*" (Preface).

Rogation Days

Our blessed Lord said, "Ask, and it shall be given you; seek, and you shall find; knock, and it shall be opened to you" (Luke 11:9). This was His conclusion to the story of a man who, having nothing at home to feed a hungry friend, knocked persistently and boisterously at the door of another friend until he let him in for a loaf of bread. Then Christ told the story of a child asking its father for food — "for bread, will he give him a stone? or a fish, will he for a fish give him a serpent? or if he shall ask an egg, will he reach him a scorpion?" (Luke 11:11.)

This Gospel is read on Rogation Days to show how Christ wants us to persevere in prayer.

Obedient to this teaching and exhortation, the early Christians prayed much and, above all, prayed in common. They gathered in one of the many churches in Rome, the "meeting church" for the day,[27] whence with the bishop and priests they proceeded to another church, called "the station church" because the procession halted there to celebrate Mass.[28]

We still have four such processions, on the four Rogation Days. April 25 is called the Major Rogation Day; the three days before the Feast of the Ascension are the Minor Rogation Days. On all these days the Litany of the Saints is said, continuing a tradition of the early Christians, for during the processions priests and faithful sang and prayed, alternately, short petitions to God and the saints. The Litany of the Saints is our most ancient and liturgical litany; it was in use as early as the third century. It gives a long list of apostles, martyrs, bishops, monks, and virgins, primarily saints who were specially venerated in Rome. This list is followed by an enumeration of the mysteries of the redemption: Christ's birth, sufferings, death, and resurrection. Other petitions follow, and the litany concludes with a psalm, versicles, and several orations. When the route of the procession was

---

[27] Called *ecclesia collecta*. The name *Collect* for the Oration of the daily Mass comes from the fact that a prayer was said before they left this church.

[28] In the missal, especially during Lent and Easter Week, there are notations like "Station at St. Peter's," "Station at St. Mary Major," etc. The minor procession (*statio*) that now takes place in monasteries on Sundays and holydays is a reminder of the processions in the early Church.

very long, other psalms and hymns were chanted in addition to the litany.

Even the ancient pagans had a kind of intercessory procession. The helplessness of the people, when faced with the forces of nature, storm and tempest, hail and drought, sickness and epidemics, taught them to turn hopefully to a divine power in order to obtain help and protection or a blessing on the harvest. For this purpose the ancient Romans celebrated a well-known "flower procession" on April 25, in honor of the god Robigo to whose "evil glance" the wheat rust was attributed.

In accordance with her practice of adopting a pagan custom and christianizing it, the Church took over this observance of April 25, already in the fifth century, and changed it into the Christian rogation procession. Its meaning and purpose were made clear: that through communal prayer and sacrifice God's anger, aroused by our sins, might be appeased and He might deign to bless and increase the crops. Instead of ending in a temple dedicated to the gods, as they did in the days of pagan Rome, these spring processions terminated in St. Peter's, the church which Gregory the Great appointed as the station for the Major Rogation Day, April 25. There is no relation between the Feast of St. Mark, celebrated on this day, and the Rogation Day prayers; but another reason, frequently alleged, for additional solemnities on April 25 is the belief that this is the day on which St. Peter first came to Rome.

The Minor Rogation Days, the three days preceding the Feast of the Ascension, were instituted by Bishop

Mamertus of Vienns in modern France. This city and the surrounding country were visited about the year 450 with a series of dire misfortunes: plagues, crop failure, war, pestilence, and earthquakes. To avert these, and to implore God's grace and mercy, St. Mamertus called upon his people to spend three days in penance and prayer. It became a custom in Vienns and was soon imitated everywhere. Pope Leo III (795–816) introduced the practice into the entire Church. The intention behind these days is that all our prayers, whether for ourselves, our families, or the parish, for a good harvest, or for the entire Church and everything related to it, may be put in the hands of our Lord that He may take them with Him to heaven on Ascension Day.

We offer these prayers in the spring of the year, when all things sprout and blossom, when the expected harvest is often threatened with bad weather and frost. Let us pray earnestly together, beseeching our Lord to bless our fields and gardens and their fruits. Let us ask God for our daily bread, as Christ Himself taught us in the Our Father.

Christ taught us how to pray. In the Gospel of the fifth Sunday after Easter, Rogation Sunday, we hear these words. "Amen, amen I say to you: if you ask the Father anything in my name, he will give it you" (John 16:23). The prayers of the liturgy end repeatedly with the words, "Through our Lord Jesus Christ," for the Church prays always, as He taught her, through His mediatorship. Whether we pray for ourselves or for others, for the living or for the dead, whether we ask God's grace for our souls or upon the fields and forests, we constantly beg our heavenly Father to hear our prayers "through Jesus Christ our Lord."

The rogation procession leaves the parish church and proceeds each day, if possible, in a different direction through the fields. Then it returns to the church where the rogation Mass is celebrated. The Mass is the climax of the day and for this reason may never be omitted; in it Christ prays in a most perfect manner for the necessities of mankind. Our prayers and petitions during these days might be vitalized and take on a new meaning if we directed them to more specific intentions each day; for instance, we might pray for our own needs and cares the first day, for our family and parish the second day, and for the world-wide family of the Holy Father on the third day. Let us unite our voices fervently and devoutly to the recitation of the Litany of the Saints and the other prescribed prayers: One for all and all for one! This is the spirit of the prayers of the Church.

The Ascension of Our Lord

After His glorious resurrection our Lord remained on earth forty days longer. The two great events of this period were the institution of the sacrament of Penance and the conferring upon St. Peter of the dignity of the papacy. On the fortieth day the Lord appeared to His assembled apostles for the last time and took them with Him, as he did on Maundy Thursday, into the Garden of Olives. There He gave them His last commands, especially the commission to go out into the whole world to preach the Gospel and to baptize the nations, "in the name of the Father and of the Son and of the Holy Ghost." For the last time their beloved and glorified Master raised His hands in blessing and, in heavenly majesty, ascended into heaven "to the right hand of the Father."

"Father, I come to Thee, Alleluia." In these words the Church rejoices with Christ who Himself had said, "I ascend to my Father and to your Father, to my God and your God" (John 20:17), and "I go to prepare (in heaven) a place for you" (John 14:2).

Ascension Day is thus a doubly happy feast, first for Christ and then for us and all His followers. He, as conqueror and king, triumphantly enters heaven. In the words of St. Bernard, "The ascension of our Lord is the completion and fulfillment of all other feasts, and a blessed conclusion to the earthly life of the Son of God. It is the feast of Christ's ascension to His throne and His crowning as king of heaven and earth" (Pius Parsch).

It is a day of happiness for all of us, for "Christ's glorification in His ascension is also the glorification of human nature; it is also our glorification" (Pius Parsch). In heaven Christ is our mediator who constantly intercedes for us. "We have an advocate with the Father, Jesus Christ the just; and he is the propitiation for our sins; and not for ours only, but also for those of the whole world" (1 John 2:2). He ascended (into heaven) to make us partakers of His godhead (Preface of the feast). He has returned to His Father to prepare a home for us there. Should we not attain this place in heaven we ourselves would be to blame.

For this reason Mother Church, in the Preface of the Mass, asks us all to raise our hearts to heaven: *Sursum corda!* You must not only look toward heaven as did the apostles on this day, until reminded of their duty by angels; but you must strive heavenward, you must exert yourselves by a good, Christian

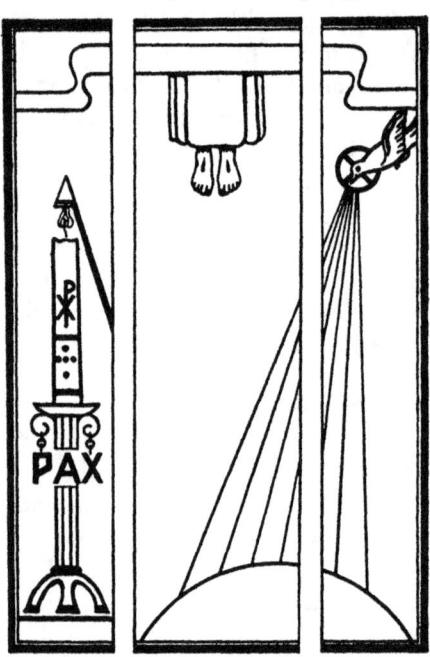

A simple but expressive ceremony signifying Christ's departure from this earth is the extinguishing of the Easter candle after the Gospel; this is depicted in the *left* part of the illustration above. The *right* side pictures the novena of prayers which the apostles and the Blessed Virgin offered for the coming of the Holy Ghost, the Spirit promised by Christ. Let us also pray on these nine days before Pentecost, "Come, Holy Ghost."

life so that you will really attain heaven. St. Paul concisely and clearly sums up the part Christ's resurrection and ascension should play in our lives when he says, "Therefore, if you be risen with Christ, seek the things that are above, where Christ is sitting at the right hand of God. Mind the things that are above, not the things that are upon the earth. For you are dead, and your life is hidden with Christ in God. When Christ shall appear, who is your life, then you also shall appear with Him in glory" (Col. 3:1-4).

Vigil of Pentecost

Two thoughts readily suggest themselves in the liturgy of Pentecost:

1. It reminds us of Baptism and the renewal of our baptismal promises, as did Holy Saturday. In the early Church the vigil of Pentecost was also a day for solemn Baptism. For this reason holy water is solemnly blessed in all parish churches. The six prophecies preceding the blessing are taken from the twelve sung on Holy Saturday. The Easter candle is not blessed again, but it is lighted and immersed three times in the baptismal water. After the blessing of the font, the Litany of the Saints is sung. During the *Gloria* of the Mass, which concludes the ceremony, the bells are rung again, for on this day as on Holy Saturday the newly baptized Christians marched solemnly into the church.

The vigil of Pentecost is a fitting time for administering Baptism. The Holy Ghost who "renews the face of the earth" grants in this sacrament a new supernatural life, the life of sanctifying grace, makes

new creatures, children of God, temples of the Holy
Trinity, and strengthens those who are born anew in
Baptism. On this day, remember again the graces you
received at Baptism, thank God for them, and renew
your baptismal vows.

2. Pentecost also prepares those who are about to
receive Confirmation, and reminds all who have been
previously confirmed of the promises of fidelity they
have made. It is a day on which to pray for the graces
and gifts of the Holy Ghost. Baptism makes you a
child of God, an heir of heaven; Confirmation makes
you a soldier of God, a defender of all that is good,
a perfect Christian.

Powerful enemies — the devil, wicked men, and our
own evil inclinations — conspire to draw us from the
kingdom of all that is good and pure and holy, to
separate us from God and rob us of our heritage of
heaven. The saints fought this battle. If we are to
follow them, we need the graces of the Holy Ghost;
we need His gifts of wisdom, understanding, counsel,
fortitude, knowledge, piety, and fear of the Lord. Let
us pray much and earnestly for these gifts during
these days. Let us think, too, of the end of this warfare and of heaven, where dwells the Blessed Trinity.

Pentecost

The Feast of Pentecost, from the Greek word
pentecostes, meaning fiftieth, occurs fifty days after
Easter and is the jubilee-octave of Easter. At the same
time it is the culmination of the Easter cycle, the fulfillment and conclusion of the Feast of Easter. The
sending of the Holy Ghost — teacher, leader, and

comforter — seals Christ's work of redemption, firmly establishes its fruits, and makes them operative in the Church. Christ, the heavenly Sun, rose on Easter Day; on Pentecost this Sun reaches its zenith where it warms and begets life.

THE SPIRIT OF THE LORD HATH FILLED THE WHOLE WORLD

The Jews in the Old Testament also celebrated a feast of pentecost. But for them it was a commemoration of their receiving the Ten Commandments on Mount Sinai, an event that took place fifty days after their departure from Egypt. Besides, they made it a day of thanksgiving for the God-given harvest of the year by offering to Him their first fruits.

For Christians, however, Pentecost is the Feast of the Holy Ghost, commemorating the day when the third Person of the Blessed Trinity, in the midst of a mighty wind, descended upon the apostles assembled in the room of the Last Supper, and in the form of fiery tongues, endowed them with wondrous power to speak in diverse tongues, made them zealous and enthusiastic preachers of the truth of Jesus Christ the crucified and risen Redeemer of the world, and prepared them to suffer persecution and martyrdom for this truth, "rejoicing that they were accounted worthy to suffer reproach for the name of Jesus" (Acts 5:41).

Pentecost is the birthday of the Catholic Church. So powerfully did the Holy Ghost begin to work on souls on that day that in Jerusalem itself three thousand souls were baptized. Now begins the speedy victory march of the Church, which neither cunning nor force nor persecution nor martyrdom can thwart, for "the gates of hell shall not prevail against it" (Matt. 16:18).

The Church and her liturgy enter even deeper into this Pentecostal time; they concern themselves with all things that the Triune God has, from the beginning of the world, produced through the Holy Spirit. "The Spirit of the Lord fills the earth," says the Introit of the Mass. In the opening lines of Genesis we read ". . . and the spirit of God moved over the waters" (1:2). Hence, we are grateful to the Holy

Ghost for the grandeur of creation, for the miracles of God in nature.

It was the Holy Ghost also who made Mary the Mother of God. It was this same Spirit that guided Christ in His earthly life, as our Lord Himself indicated in the words, "The Spirit of the Lord is upon me" (Luke 4:18). The redemption, too, is the work of the Holy Spirit, and is continued in the Church under His guidance, pre-eminently in the Mass and the sacraments, until the end of time.

This same Holy Spirit entered into us in Baptism and Confirmation. We, too, are imbued with the Holy Spirit. By means of the sacraments and blessings of the Church, the third Person of the Blessed Trinity works unceasingly, sanctifying us. We can never pray too often with the Church, "Come, Holy Ghost, fill the hearts of Thy faithful, and enkindle in them the fire of Thy divine love." We shall never be able to honor the Holy Ghost sufficiently nor bring to sufficient fruition His gifts of love and peace, but we shall live on this earth as true "temples of the Holy Ghost," fight as brave "knights of the Holy Ghost," and let ourselves be led by the Spirit of truth and love.

Let us celebrate Pentecost with great happiness, with firm faith, and with holy longing. The Spirit of God within us will be our Sanctifier, our Comforter, our Strength!

Like Easter Week, Pentecost Week is a week of joy. Each day has its proper Mass to tell of the workings of the Holy Ghost in the world, in the Church, and in the souls of men. The color of the Mass is red, which is the color of fire and love.

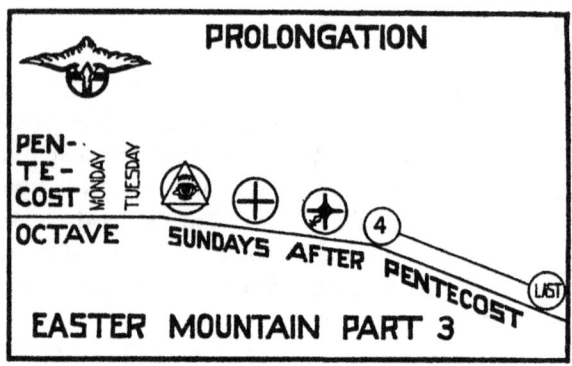

The entire story of the redemption is reviewed during the Church year. Advent reflects the long expectation for the Messias. The period from Christmas to the Ascension gives us the life of Christ and His redemptive work. Pentecost depicts the sending of the Holy Ghost, the divine consoler and sanctifier.

Now follows the long succession of Sundays after Pentecost, twenty-four or twenty-eight, depending upon the date of Easter. This period represents the working of the Holy Ghost in the Church until the end of time.[29] The feasts occurring at this time sum up the redemptive love of God. We may call them feasts of faith, because each commemorates a mystery of our holy faith. They are:

1. The mystery of the unity of three Persons in one God: *Feast of the Holy Trinity,* first Sunday after Pentecost.[30]

[29] For further reference to this time, see page 181 ff.
[30] In the illustration above, Trinity Sunday is represented by the *triangle,* the feast of Corpus Christi by a *host,* and the feast of the Sacred Heart by the *cross* and *spear.*

2. The mystery of the Holy Eucharist, the sacrament of the altar: *Corpus Christi,* the following Thursday.

3. The mystery of the "fullness of grace": *Feast of the Sacred Heart,* on the third Friday after Pentecost. Through Christ's death on the cross out of love for mankind, grace has flown into the treasury of the Church. It is communicated to the individual soul through the channels of the sacraments. The culmination of Christ's surrender to love was manifested in the piercing of His Sacred Heart, the source of this great redeeming love.

The Feast of the Holy Trinity (First Sunday After Pentecost)

After Mother Church has invited us in the course of the year to view and meditate on the great deeds of the individual persons of the Trinity, she asks us to praise and bless and thank the Trinity: "Praised be the Blessed Trinity and the undivided Unity. Let us praise Him because He has shown His mercy to us" (Introit).

The mystery of the Trinity will never be fully understood by man, for it is the greatest, the most profound, the most incomprehensible and most exalted mystery of our faith. The catechism tells us there is but one God in whom there are three persons, the Father, the Son, and the Holy Ghost. Each of these three persons is true God; there are not three gods but only one eternal, almighty, all-knowing, and incomprehensible God.

How do we know this? Jesus Christ, the only-begotten Son of God has told us so, and He is eternal truth which cannot err or deceive. How frequently did Christ speak of His Father in heaven and make clear that He came only to do the will of His Father, and that upon its completion, He would return again to Him. Christ speaks of Himself as the Son of God; He tells us that He is begotten of the Father,

that He is coeternal with Him, that He came obedient (to the Father) unto death in order to redeem man, in accordance with the will of the Father. Our Lord also reveals to us the existence of the Holy Spirit who proceeds from both Father and Son, who will sanctify and enlighten the Church until the end of time. One who believes in Christ and His teachings must also believe in His Father and the Holy Spirit. If we knew nothing more of the Blessed Trinity than the fact that Christ commissioned the apostles to go into the whole world and to "teach all nations, baptizing them in the name of the Father, and of the Son, and of the Holy Ghost" (Matt. 28:19), this mandate would give us positive certitude that there are three persons in one God.

We were baptized in the name of these three blessed persons, we whom God created and called to the true faith, whom the Son of God redeemed, whom the Holy Spirit sanctified and ordained as temples of the Blessed Trinity. The work of the Trinity continues in us as often as we are absolved from our sins in the sacrament of Penance, as often as we are blessed in the name of the Father and of the Son and of the Holy Ghost.

On the Feast of the Trinity, on every Sunday, on every day, we acknowledge our faith in the Trinity, and praise and thank God as often as we devoutly make the sign of the cross, or say that beautiful prayer from the Divine Office, "Glory be to the Father, and to the Son, and to the Holy Ghost." The *Gloria* and *Credo* of the Mass and the *Te Deum* are songs in praise of the Trinity. Holy Mass itself is the most beautiful prayer of all and the most efficacious offering. It is a prayer of praise, thanksgiving, petition, and propitiation offered to the Father through the Son in union with the Holy Ghost. Each Sunday is especially dedicated to the Blessed Trinity. For this reason the Preface of the Trinity is generally used.

Corpus Christi (Second Thursday After Pentecost)

The Latin name, *Festum Sanctissimi Corporis Christi* (Feast of the Most Holy Body of Christ), indicates the meaning of the feast. It is the mystery of the Holy Eucharist, the most Blessed Sacrament of the altar, the real and true presence of Jesus in the consecrated species of bread and wine. On the eve of His passion and death, Christ instituted the sacrament of the altar. It was the first *Corpus Christi* day and the celebration of the first Mass. At this time, too, He gave the apostles His great power of transubstantiation.

In the liturgy of Maundy Thursday out of sympathy for Christ's approaching passion and death, the Church gives little attention to the great Eucharistic gift in which the Redeemer gave Himself to be the food and nourishment of mankind until the end of time. To commemorate more fully and with greater solemnity the institution of the Blessed Sacrament, the Feast of Corpus Christi was finally established in 1264 for the entire Church, though it already had been celebrated for some time in Belgium as a result of a vision granted to St. Juliana of Liege († April 5, 1258). The most learned theologian of the Middle Ages, the angelic doctor of the Church, St. Thomas Aquinas († 1274), composed the beautiful liturgical texts for the feast. His hymn, the *Lauda Sion,* has always been considered a masterpiece from every point of view.

Now Mother Church is enabled to express her joy over this great gift. Appropriately she voices her thanks and her praise in the most beautiful time of the year, when green buds are appearing on shrubs and trees, when the first blossoms of spring unfold their petals to greet and praise the Saviour of the world. For further solemnity, this feast is usually celebrated with a procession, on the feast itself or on the following Sunday. This procession signifies the triumph and progress of Christ's blessing in our cities, villages, and countrysides.

The most Blessed Sacrament of the altar which we

call the "holy of holies" is our Lord's greatest miracle of love. It is time during this joyous feast and its octave (*a*) to acknowledge openly our faith in God's presence in the Blessed Sacrament, (*b*) to manifest our thanks for the innumerable graces granted to us here, (*c*) and to propitiate and make amends to our Saviour for the many blasphemies and dishonors heaped upon Him in this sacrament.

The Feast of the Most Sacred Heart of Jesus (Third Friday After Pentecost)

The deep meaning and significance of this feast is indicated in the body of the Preface which reads:

> It is truly right . . . to give thanks to Thee . . . Eternal God who didst will that Thine only-begotten Son should be pierced by the soldier's lance as He hung upon the cross: that from His opened heart, as from a sanctuary of divine bounty, might be poured out upon us streams of mercy and grace; and that in His heart always burning with love for us, the devout may find a haven of rest and the penitent a refuge of salvation.[31]

The limitless love of the Redeemer is continued in the most Blessed Sacrament. Through it, voluntarily given to mankind, graces and blessings stream forth from an inexhaustible treasury. It is these unending streams of love, emanating from the Sacred Heart, that we celebrate today. It is this love which has been scorned, spurned, and mocked by many who have been redeemed by Christ. Our part as His

---

[31] *St. Andrew's Missal*, Bruges, 1937.

This illustration expresses clearly the mysteries of the feast. The redeeming death of Jesus, symbolically expressed by the pierced *Chi-Rho,* has merited for us heaven and all graces. These flow to us primarily through the life-giving sacrament of Baptism (*Baptismal font*) and the life-sustaining sacrament of the Holy Eucharist (*altar* and *chalice*). All graces and merits are entrusted to the Church (*Ecclesia*); here lies the inexhaustible reserve, the treasury of all graces. And from the "fountain of life and holiness" (Litany of the Sacred Heart) all graces flow to us through the seven sacraments.

faithful followers is to give Him a return of ardent love, to be sincere and fervent in our gratitude for this sacrament, and as Christ-loving souls to strive earnestly to atone and make satisfaction to His Sacred Heart for the faithlessness of others. This is the meaning and purpose of the Feast of the Sacred Heart and all devotions to the Sacred Heart, the First Fridays in particular. Pope Pius XI emphasized its importance by introducing beautiful new Mass-prayers, and, in 1929, by raising the rank of the feast, giving it a privileged octave of the third order.

Sundays After Pentecost

The Easter season, including the Octave of Pentecost, really ends on the Saturday after Pentecost. The time after Pentecost, with twenty-four to twenty-eight Sundays, constitutes a new period, the aftermath of the Easter season, the descent from the Easter mount.[32]

Why such a long period of time? It comprises half a year, but for all the great feasts, which conclude with Pentecost, only half a year is used, that is, the time from Christmas to Pentecost. Then, why so many Sundays after Pentecost?

The answer to these questions is helpful in making us realize the depth of meaning that is to be found in the Church year. During each year the Church relives for us the complete history of the redemption from the beginning to its completion at the end of the world. In comparison to the thousands of years which the earth has existed, the earthly life of Christ

---

[32] See illustration: Easter Mountain, Part 3, page 168.

was very short — a mere thirty-three years. Since Christ's death, for a period of almost two thousand years, the Holy Ghost has been working in and for the souls of men and He will continue His work until the day of the last judgment. Fittingly, then, the time after Pentecost which commemorates this long period is also the longest part of the Church year.

During this time each individual Christian, in union with the entire Church, should guard and strengthen the new divine life received in Baptism. We should nourish this life by the frequent reception of the sacraments and intimate participation in the holy sacrifice of the Mass. We have time to strengthen it and make it impregnable, to bring it to fruition and perfect it. Thus we will fulfill our high purpose in life, that of becoming more like our Redeemer, perfect Christians, other Christs. Thus prepared we will await with holy longing the final coming of the Redeemer as the Judge and Rewarder of the world.

The liturgy puts the following thoughts and admonitions before us on these Sundays after Pentecost as it asks us to think of the past, the present, and the future:

1. The prayers of the first few Masses of the Sundays after Pentecost constantly revert to the past. We must never forget what the Blessed Trinity, especially the Second Person, has done for us and our salvation. Above all we should celebrate on these Sundays His resurrection and our resurrection into a new supernatural life. Each Sunday reminds us of our baptismal day, hence the *Asperges me;* it is a day of thanksgiving for the grace of Baptism. Each Sunday causes

joy to well up in our souls. In every holy Mass the priest cries to us *Sursum corda:* "Lift up your hearts!" Lift up your hearts to heaven, to a better and ever-lasting life beyond — to the life for which we were created, which, through faithfulness and the grace of God, we can and must attain.

2. Later, in the Sunday Masses, the Church looks to the present and uses prayers of petition in the liturgy. We have all received the grace of becoming children of God, but the devil, God's great adversary and the enemy of our soul, permits us no peace. He wishes to prevent us from entering heaven and to bring about our eternal ruin. For this reason our whole life is a constant battle with this evil enemy and his aides. At Mass, in confession, Communion, and the other sacraments and blessings of the Church, her power and strength are available to us. We can find new courage and spirit to wage this battle. We should meditate on this and petition for this courage.

3. Toward the end of the Church year, there are many prayers which express our longing for heaven. These prayers look to the future. We have received the grace to be happy eternally, but we must co-operate with it; this co-operation requires effort and care on our part. We must wage war against the enemy and his allies who wish to seize and lay waste the land of our soul. The mere thought of heaven and eternal reward makes this battle easier, for victory and its reward are certain. The Church exposes the enemy; she gives us powerful weapons, and with her heavenly Founder for a guide, who conquered death

and hell, she leads us to certain victory. Christ Himself does battle and is victorious in His faithful.

The Gospels of the Sundays after Pentecost show us:

1. The divine Redeemer as a merciful Friend, Shepherd of the poor and sinners, the great Miracle-Worker, the Physician and Aide in every need, the Lord of life and death. Let us have confidence and courage. Our great Helper and Friend can and will cure the ills of soul and body and fill our needs.

2. Various pictures and concepts in which the kingdom of God and kingdom of the world are contrasted, as are good and bad Christians, temporal and eternal happiness. It is for us as baptized Christians to put ourselves unconditionally on the side of God's kingdom, to be soldiers of God and of His kingdom, brave and courageous as were the saints.

3. The Christian hope and longing for the reappearance of the Redeemer as Judge of the world, eternal Rewarder of good and Punisher of evil. There are joyful thanks for the grace of Baptism, for the fact that we have been chosen to be children of God and heirs of heaven; there is firm "will to battle and victory" over "the flesh, the world, and the devil"; there is holy longing after heaven, and a firm hope of being united with the Triune God above.

These items are an outline of our conduct after Pentecost.

Characteristics of the Liturgy During the Time After Pentecost

The statement already made, that the time after

Pentecost is the waning of the glory of the Easter cycle, is brought out in the liturgy of this season:

1. By the less frequent use of *Alleluia* which since Easter concluded every variable chant, such as Introit, Communion verse, and Antiphons.

2. By the insertion of a versicle after the Epistle: the Gradual which has a penitential character, and which, therefore, was replaced by the joyful *Alleluia,* twice-repeated, during the paschal season. By the return to the Gradual the Church tells us that we are back again to the commonplace, ferial day with its "earnestness and joy, its penance and praise."

3. By the singing of the *Asperges me* and the *Miserere* at the customary Sunday sprinkling with holy water: "Thou shalt sprinkle me with hyssop, O Lord, and I shall be cleansed; Thou shalt wash me and I shall be made whiter than snow. Have mercy on me, O Lord, according to Thy great mercy. Glory be to the Father. . . ." The holy water reminds us of the waters of Baptism which cleansed us from original sin. So may this blessed water (together with contrition and confession for serious sins) purify us from the sins of the past week. The garment of our soul should be as clean and white as it was on our baptismal day. Each Sunday the *Asperges* signifies our baptismal renewal which is to be realized in devout participation in the holy sacrifice of the Mass and in partaking of the sacred banquet of Holy Communion.

4. By replacing Easter's joyful salutation to Mary, the *Regina Coeli,* with a cry for help to Mary, Mother of mercy, in the *Salve Regina.* Three times a day at

the sound of the *Angelus,* we recite "The angel of the Lord," etc., meditating on the Incarnation of the Son of God with which our redemption began.

Green is the liturgical color for most of the Sundays after Pentecost, as well as for weekdays on which the Sunday Mass is celebrated. It is the color of the verdant life of nature. The time after Pentecost is the time for the growth and maturing of the kingdom of God on earth, both in the Church at large and in the individual soul. Green is also the color of hope, for the postpentecostal season is the time of joyous hope in the blessed fulfillment of all things in heaven.

The Working of the Holy Ghost

In the Acts of the Apostles (2:14 ff.), we read with what courage and success St. Peter delivered his first sermon at Jerusalem on the first Pentecost after the coming of the Holy Spirit. It was the same Peter who a few weeks before had denied his Master out of fear of a mere maidservant. This courageous frankness and the fact that "about three thousand were baptized" was the work of the Holy Ghost.

A little later the apostles went out to all parts of the world at the express, apostolic command of our Lord. All the apostles, except St. John who was miraculously preserved from death, shed their blood as martyrs for Christ and His Church. It was the work of the Holy Ghost, and everything great and noble that was realized in any of the saints is the work of the Third Person of the Trinity. That is why, in the time after Pentecost, the Church now celebrates so many feasts of the Mother of God and of the saints. They are put before us as models. We can become saints like them by faithful co-operation with the grace of the Holy Spirit and by a persevering battle against evil.

The Church follows a strict order in the honor she shows the saints. This is best exemplified in the Litany of the Saints, the only litany used in the liturgy (on Rogation Days, Holy Saturday, etc.). Following the invocation of the three divine Persons and before all the angels and saints, comes Mary the Mother of God, who is Queen of all the angels and saints. After her come the angels, first the Archangels, Michael, Gabriel, and Raphael. Then come two great saints, John the Baptist and St. Joseph. The other saints follow in groups: apostles, martyrs, confessors, holy women, and virgins. Each state of life, every age, and both sexes have their types and ideals among the blessed in heaven. To imitate them is our first and holiest task.[33]

Remembrance of Christ in the Summer and Fall

The liturgical celebration of the mysteries of salvation, as they are presented mystically in the Church year, ends with the Feast of Pentecost. During the long period after Pentecost, there is time, especially on Sundays, to ponder upon the principal mysteries of our faith. We should devotedly look back upon the birth of our Saviour, upon His sufferings and death and glorious resurrection. We should be reminded of our holy Baptism which incorporated us

[33] For lengthier details about the saints and groups of saints, see the sanctoral cycle, pages 196 ff.

into Christ and into His Church. Through an intelligent and devout participation in the holy sacrifice of the Mass, through frequent reception of the sacraments, especially Holy Communion, we can receive nourishment and gather strength in the battle of life for the eternal warfare of our souls. Then we may look forward hopefully to the glory and bliss of heaven, which awaits us as the divinely gracious reward for love and loyalty to Christ.

That we, who are so forgetful and so fickle in our attachments, may more easily keep Christ and His love for us before our minds, the Church, in her wisdom, celebrates five feasts in His honor during the summer and autumn months. These are: (1) The Feast of the Most Precious Blood of Our Lord Jesus Christ, July 1; (2) The Transfiguration of Our Lord Jesus Christ, August 6; (3) The Finding of the Holy Cross, May 3;[34] (4) The Exaltation of the Holy Cross, September 14; (5) The Feast of Christ the King, on the last Sunday in October.[35]

The Church's Autumn

Signs of autumn now appear all over the land. In nature it is the season of harvest and death, the falling and dying of summer fruit. Nature spreads joy by its rebirth in springtime and by its budding and growth in the summer months; now it is gradually dying. The leaves turn yellow and fall from the trees. The sun loses its strength and warmth. Thick clouds of

---

[34] Although strictly speaking the month of May is not a part of summer, it is here loosely embodied in the summer season.

[35] An explanation of these feasts is to be found in the sanctoral cycle.

fog and cold showers sweep over the land. The days become shorter and the nights longer. What is still to be gathered from the fields, the farmer now brings home, rejoicing in the harvest which he recognizes as God's gift and God's reward for work done faithfully.

This illustration expresses the predominant thought of the Church's autumn which begins with the eighteenth Sunday after Pentecost. It is a hopeful anticipation of the second coming of Christ at the end of time. The just, having attained perfection through grace, are garnered by the divine Reaper (often the fifth Sunday after Epiphany is transferred to autumn). With expectant joy they look to Christ as the divine Rewarder rather than the fear-inspiring Judge. The *grape harvest* (*grapes* and *vine*) and the grain harvest (*sickle* and falling *shafts of grain*) symbolize the thoughts of the autumn ember days.

The Church does not pass by without notice these manifestations in nature and life. She, too, celebrates autumn. In the third week of September after the Feast of the Exaltation of the Holy Cross (September 14) Mother Church has her autumn ember days, in imitation of the ancient week of thanksgiving for the blessings of the harvest. One Sunday of this season is celebrated as a feast of thanksgiving for the harvest. Fruit, grain, and grapes are brought to the altars, and all the people join in a thankful *Te Deum* (Holy God We Praise Thy Name).[36]

On the last Sundays of the Church year which now follow, the Church repeatedly thinks of and warns about the autumn of human life. She reminds us of the four last things: death, judgment, heaven, and hell.

Before everything else, one thought was prevalent in the consciousness of the early Christians. It was the second coming, the *Parousia,* of Jesus Christ as judge of the world. For this reason the liturgy reminds us in these last weeks to think of death and judgment, not, however, in fear and anxiety, but with a strong and noble Christian hope, with a holy confidence in the eternal reward that the Lord God will give to all those who have faithfully served Him. God as the solicitous Father of the household will gather into the barns of heaven all who stand before Him as good fruit. Only the weeds, souls spotted by mortal sin, will be rejected; they will be damned. All of this is impressed upon us during the last weeks of the Church year. Death and decomposition are not the final things in a man's life. What is final is the continued and eternal life of the soul — eternal blessedness for the soul which has been loyal to God. Let us become a part of the good harvest of the Lord of heaven and earth.

---

[36] This thanksgiving feast is sometimes celebrated on the Assumption (August 15) with the blessing of flowers and herbs. See page 285.

Hope in the eternal reward gave the first Christians courage to suffer patiently in the face of persecution and horrible mistreatment. This hope has made saints of all times joyful in every suffering and affliction, and helped them renounce this world and its transitory goods and pleasures in order to gain the eternal and imperishable gift of heaven.

Hence, it is the intention of the Church in her liturgy of the autumn season to warn us to appraise this earthly existence rightly. With all its blessings and good fortune, as well as its sufferings and cares, it is often very short. Life on this earth is primarily an instrument for use in the service of God, so that we may receive good fortune eternally, so that we may reach our heavenly goal. "Only one thing is necessary: save thy soul!" "For what does it profit a man, if he gain the whole world, but suffer the loss of his own soul?" (Mark 8:36.)

The Church's autumn suggests very serious thoughts; for men of good will, however, they are comforting, even happy thoughts. Not only the last Sundays of the year, but the feasts occurring at this time speak impressively, too, of the harvest and of man's goal, of judgment, and of eternal happiness.

The harvest-thanksgiving feast warns us to live as good grain so that the harvest time of our lives will find us ripe and worthy for the heavenly granaries.

The Feast of St. Michael the Archangel (September 29), mighty confederate in our battle for heaven against sin and the powers of darkness, calls on us to step into the ranks of the loyal soldiers of Jesus Christ.

The Feast of the Holy Guardian Angels (October, 2) reminds us of our heavenly guardian, the friendly messenger from God and the protector of our soul, who is untiring in his admonitions and never betrays us in his warnings against all that is evil. Let us listen to him.

The Feast of All Saints and *the Feast of the Commemoration of the Poor Souls* suggest that our transition from the militant church to the triumphant church must occur at the closing point of our life even though the way be by the hard and difficult route of the suffering church in purgatory.

The Feast of Christ the King, on the Sunday before the Feast of All Saints, finally places before our eyes the glorious and triumphant Christ, the just and all-powerful Judge of the world, the omniscient and eternal Rewarder of souls who have been true to Him. We who, according to our strength, have loyally served this Christ, our Saviour, who have preserved the faith, and have loved Him and our neighbor in word and deed, need never fear the judgment. Such souls have Jesus for a brother and a friend, God Himself for a father, and Mary, Queen of Angels and Help of Christians, for a mother.

Above all, the Church wishes to give us courage, to strengthen our confidence, to breathe new fervor into our love and good will, to make us strong in faith, hope, and charity, and to direct our thoughts heavenward, to the never ending happiness "that God has prepared for those who love Him."

The readings and prayers of the last Sundays after Pentecost beautifully corroborate these thoughts. A

good example is found in the eighteenth Sunday after
Pentecost:

> I give thanks to my God always for you, for the
> grace of God that is given you in Christ Jesus, that in
> all things you are made rich in Him, in all utterance,
> and in all knowledge; as the testimony of Christ was
> confirmed in you, so that nothing is wanting to you
> in any grace, waiting for the manifestation of our
> Lord Jesus Christ. Who also will confirm you unto
> the end without crime, in the day of the coming of
> our Lord Jesus Christ (1 Cor. 1:4–8).

This is an appropriate autumn reading. Holy
Church tells us in the words of the apostle that we
have been enriched through the grace of God, that we
should grow ripe with it and through it, and that
Jesus Christ rejoices over the good harvest. For many,
however, there is still a long way, a prolonged,
danger-filled journey upon the sea of life before the
Lord of the harvest will appear. For this reason we
pray God at the Introit of this Mass (eighteenth Sunday after Pentecost), "Give peace, O Lord, to them
that patiently wait for Thee." And in the Oration,
we pray, "In Thy tender mercy, direct our hearts, we
beseech Thee, O Lord, for without Thee we are not
able to please Thee." In the Gradual we tell God how
even now we rejoice over the great day of the harvest,
over the time when we shall be allowed to enter
heaven: "I rejoiced at the things that were said to me:
We shall go into the house of the Lord."

To arrive at this goal, we need the help of God's
grace. Hence, even now, we should very frequently
and willingly come into the house of God "with joy"

to receive this grace at Holy Mass, in the sacraments, and in devout prayer. Like Moses, we should wish to make our offering together with the priest "for an odor of sweetness to the Lord God," as today's Offertory verse so beautifully puts it. At Holy Mass, at Holy Communion, and in the sacrament of Penance Jesus often speaks to our weak and sickened souls the healing and peace-giving words which He says to the paralytic in today's Gospel: "Be of good heart, son . . . Arise . . . go into thy house" (Matt. 9:2–6). We shall be securely at home for the first time only in heaven. There is our true and eternally blessed dwelling. Our view now in autumn should be directed heavenward. We should foster in our hearts a great desire and love for heaven, and always live so true and devout a life that we may one day arrive there in eternal happiness.

At Home: All Saints . . . All Souls

The time after Pentecost reveals the working of the Holy Ghost in the Church of God and in the souls of men: building, strengthening, perfecting, and sanctifying. The sun makes the fruits of the earth large and ripe and beautiful for the day of harvesting. Similarly, the Holy Spirit sends the sunshine of His grace into the souls of men that they may grow, ripen, become beautiful and holy for heaven. The day of death will come for each of us, when the heavenly Lord of the harvest, God Himself, will test us to find out whether we are pure and ripe and holy enough for heaven.

Every man realizes that he is not entirely at home

upon this earth. Here, "we have no lasting city"; we are wayfarers on the way to an eternal home in our Father's house. Holy Mother Church celebrates many feasts in the course of the liturgical year to remind us of our true homeland. For this reason she constrains us to come to church, at least every Sunday and on some feast days, to make a good confession and Communion at least once a year. For this same reason she celebrates two feasts at the end of the Church year in which she gathers together all these earnest thoughts of our destination and of the care-laden journey through the strange country of this world to our everlasting home. At the same time they are feasts of consolation and encouragement: *the Feast of All Saints* and *the Feast of the Commemoration of All Souls.*

The Close of the Church Year

At the end of the Church year, with advice and a warning, holy Mother Church solemnly reminds all her children of the end of the world. The sign of the Son of Man, the holy cross, will appear shining gloriously in the heavens. Sun, moon, and stars will darken and fall from heaven. Flames of lightning and a storm will rage over the earth. The Lord will send His angels amid the loud blasts of trumpets to summon all men for the final judgment. Souls will be united to their bodies which will arise from the grave. It will be a day of terrible woe for the wicked, of supreme happiness for the good. All who have lived on the face of the earth will show themselves in their true character before the all-knowing, heavenly Judge to see whether they are genuine good grain or chaff to be discarded, to see how they have conducted themselves during life in their relation to the truth, to God, to Christ and His Church. On this day, as at the moment of their death, all men will see and know what happiness, what blessedness the Lord God has prepared for them, what glory Christ, the Redeemer, has earned for them through His suffering and death. All will discover and know what the Son of God, by His incarnation, by His death on the cross, by His resurrection and ascension, by His sending of the Holy Spirit, by His holy Catholic Church with her doctrines and her sacraments, wished them to be and what they could have been. They will recognize all this and agree that, if they have missed the true and eternal goal of their life, they alone are culpable. For no one enters heaven against his will. And no one enters hell unless he has brought about his own damnation.

The great question is: How have I used the past liturgical year? How have I celebrated the feasts? Christmas, Easter, Pentecost? And all the others? How have I lived the Sundays? How have I used the abundant graces God showered upon me? Many I did not accept; many I lost through my own fault. These will never be given to me again. The saints of the Church year with Mary at their head stand before us and ask: Was our example in vain? And what about the prayers and protection of our guardian angels and our patron saints?

Holy Mother Church has taken us along into the Holy of Holies so often in order to teach us to be

"The sun shall be darkened and the moon shall not give her light, and the stars shall fall from heaven   and then shall appear the sign of the Son of man in heaven (*cross* and *Chi-Rho*)   and they shall see Him coming in the clouds (*curved lines*) with much power and majesty (*lightning* and the *alpha* and *omega*), and He shall send His angels with a trumpet Heaven and earth shall pass away" (the *hourglass* represents the end of time) On "that day he will separate them one from another" (the *scale,* a symbol of judgment), that is, judge them according to the commandments (*tablets*)

concerned about the one thing necessary, the salvation of our immortal souls. How many instructions have we listened to in the readings and Gospels of the Mass, in sermons, and in catechetical instructions? How frequently has the Church, the Communion of Saints, the Mystical Body of Christ, whose members we are, offered the holy sacrifice of the Mass and prayed for us! How often has she called upon us to be loyal to our baptismal promises and exhorted the wicked to renounce their sins and to do good, to come frequently to the holy sacraments and to serve Christ, our King!

First, we must be sorry for all our negligences and unfaithfulness. Then, we want to thank God at the end of the Church year for all the graces, all the helps, for every success and progress in our spiritual life. We want to thank our divine Saviour and Redeemer, for making us royal children of the King, and sons of God and heirs of heaven through His love and death. If suffering has been our lot, we should be nearer now to God and Christ.

This is the time to make a firm resolution for the new Church year. We shall try to understand more fully the liturgy of the Church. We shall live more and more zealously and intensely according to the mind of the Church. We will follow her counsel as it is given in the Epistle for the last Sunday after Pentecost, "that you may be filled with the knowledge of His will, in all wisdom and spiritual understanding; that you may walk worthy of God, in all things pleasing; being fruitful in every good work, and increasing in the knowledge of God" (Col. 1:9-10).

The new Church year with its feasts and graces will bring us nearer to our eternal home. And Christ will speak the comforting and cheering words which the last Sunday of the Church year puts before us, "I think thoughts of peace, and not of affliction; you shall call upon Me and I shall hear you, and I will bring back your captivity from all places" (Introit of the Mass), that "where I am, there you also may be" (John 14:3), at home in God — at home next to the heart of the Father, at home in the heart of the Holy Trinity, at home in the heart of Mary, the Queen of All the Saints. At home — with all the saints of heaven, our brothers and sisters in Christ, with all the clean of heart, the strong, the noble. At home — in the possession of all we wished for: truth and wisdom, virtue and holiness, beauty and happiness, honor and favor with God. At home — in the possession of the love of God, in the love of Christ and of His blessed Mother, in the love of all the saints of heaven. At home in the eternal fatherland of our souls. That is the goal which the liturgy of the Church makes known to us. It is the goal which she helps us reach by means of her holy prayers and sacrifices, her holy seasons and sacraments. It is the same goal which St. Benedict had in mind when he wrote his great maxim for all his followers: "That in all things God may be glorified" (*Ut in omnibus glorificetur Deus*).

THAT
IN
ALL THINGS

GOD

MAY BE GLORIFIED

SANCTORAL CYCLE: THE PROPER OF THE SAINTS

Feasts of the Blessed Virgin Mary

The greatest of all the saints, the queen of all the saints is Mary, the mother of God. Mary is the mother of Jesus, our Saviour, distinguished from all eternity in a special way, the favored daughter of the Father. Free from original sin as well as from all personal sin, she is the immaculate bride of the Holy Spirit. Next to her divine Son, Mary played the most significant role in the whole work of our redemption. Through her perfect co-operation with the will of God at the Annunciation and at the foot of the cross, she became our co-redeemer and mother, and as such she is honored and venerated by the Church. Full of grace and close to the Trinity in heaven, she is invoked (though never worshiped) for her protection and for her intercessory power.

One who knows Mary's unique position as Queen of Heaven and Mother of Mercy will not be surprised that in the course of a year so many feasts are celebrated in her honor. The greatest feasts of our redemption — Christmas, Epiphany, even Easter and Pentecost — are in a certain respect also feasts of Mary. Who can think of the crib at Christmas or the worshiping Magi at Epiphany without including

Mary in the picture? Throughout Christmastide the Holy Family is before our eyes. Easter and Pentecost are no less inseparably bound up with our Lady. On Good Friday she stands at the foot of the cross, and the dying Christ proclaims her the mother of the re-

The *Mystical Rose*, with its five *petals* and the five-pointed *star* as background, signifies the five major feasts which pertain to the divine motherhood, to Mary as the Christ-bearer.

deemed, there represented by St. John. On Easter morning Mary was undoubtedly the first person to whom the Risen Saviour appeared. On Pentecost Mary was in the midst of the apostles when the Holy Ghost descended on them in the form of fiery tongues. She plays a prominent part during Advent in preparing the Church for the coming of her divine Son at Christmas. In Lent she recedes into the back-

IMMACULATE CONCEPTION

"Thou art all fair, O Mary, and there is not a spot in thee" (Mass: Song of Sol. 4:7). "I will put enmities between thee (*serpent*) and the woman, and thy seed and her seed: she shall crush thy head" (Lesson 4: Gen. 3:15). "This day a rod came forth from the root of Jesse (Isa. 11:1), this day Mary was conceived without any stain of sin: this day the head of the old serpent was crushed by her, Alleluia" (Second Vespers).

ground to permit her Son to engage in combat with the powers of darkness, but she stands undaunted at the foot of the cross in Passiontide. In the postpentecostal season, she is honored as the Refuge of Sinners and Mediatrix of Grace, as Queen of the Rosary, Comforter of the Afflicted, and most powerful Help of Christians. Popular devotion has established special services in her honor during the month of May.

Besides recognizing the part our Blessed Mother plays in the temporal cycle, the Church celebrates a series of special feasts in her honor. The most solemn of these commemorate the beginning and end of her life: the *Immaculate Conception* on December 8 which reminds us that Mary at the moment of her conception was miraculously preserved from all stain of original sin, and the *Assumption* on August 15 when her children rejoice at her triumphal entry into heaven and her coronation as Queen of heaven and earth. Both feasts have a vigil and an octave.

Other feasts of our Lady may be divided into three groups according to their rank in the Church year.

Her major feasts are: the Nativity of Mary, September 8; the Annunciation, March 25; the Visitation, July 2; the Purification, February 2; the Maternity, October 11; and the new Feast of the Immaculate Heart of Mary, August 22.

Lesser feasts of Mary make up a second group; these are: the Most Holy Name of Mary, September 12; the Seven Sorrows, September 15 (and on Friday of Passion Week); the Holy Rosary, October 7; and the Presentation, November 21.

Feasts of still lesser rank are: the Apparition of our

ASSUMPTION

"Mary is taken up into heaven (*empty tomb*); the angels rejoice and bless God (*circle*) with songs of praise" (First Vespers). "I was exalted as a rose plant in Jericho" (Epistle: Ecclus. 14:18). "Rejoice for she reigns (*crown*) with Christ for evermore" (Second Vespers).

Blessed Lady at Lourdes, February 11; the Commemoration of our Lady of Mount Carmel, July 16; the Dedication of the Church of our Lady of the

Snow in Rome, August 5; and Our Lady of Ransom, September 24.

In all, there are approximately seventeen feasts of the Blessed Virgin Mary celebrated in the Church's liturgy. To these may be added a few which are celebrated locally or by certain religious orders, such as the Feast of our Lady of Guadalupe in Central America, the Feast of our Lady of Perpetual Help by Redemptorists, and the Feast of the Blessed Heart of Mary by Benedictines. The proper for such local feasts is found in the different *Supplements* to the missal, compiled for the various countries, dioceses, or religious orders.

The more important feasts of our Blessed Mother will be considered separately as they occur in the calendar of the year. But it is to be remembered that *Saturday* is also dedicated to Mary in a very special way. Unless an important feast falls on this day, the Church says the Office and Mass of the Blessed Virgin for Saturday; the proper, of course, varies with each season.

The Holy Angels in the Liturgy

The angels[1] hold a place of honor in the liturgy as the foremost creatures and friends of God. As pure spirits they are messengers and servants in the court of heaven. We are reminded of their power in every holy Mass, for in the Gloria and Sanctus we sing their

---

[1] The word *angel*, taken from the Latin *angelus*, means *messenger*. They are generally represented with wings in order to indicate the speed with which they fulfill the commands of God. As pure spirits, they have no bodies, but from Holy Scripture we know that occasionally angels have appeared in visible form.

The nine choirs of angels: Angels, Archangels, Thrones, Dominations, Principalities, Powers, Virtues, Cherubim, Seraphim. *The
Archangel Michael*, the warrior, the defender in battle *(sword and
shield with symbol of the Trinity)*, "Who is like to God?" *The
Archangel Gabriel*, "power of God," who proclaimed the mystery
of the Incarnation *(Fleur-de-lis)*. *The Archangel Raphael*, "God
heals," the healer and faithful companions, Tobias 12:7-15 *(Staff,
pouch, and fish)*.

songs of praise; in the Preface we ask them to thank
God with us; in the Confiteor, we invoke the help
of their great leader, Michael; after the Consecration
our sacrifice is carried to the altar on high "in the
sight of Thy divine majesty" by the hands of an
angel; and finally, in the prayers after every low
Mass, the protection of Michael, the archangel, is invoked against the malice and snares of Satan. In her
official night prayer (Compline) the Church also im-

plores the help of angels that "they may dwell in our house and keep and protect us in peace."

The Votive Mass of the Holy Angels may be celebrated on Tuesdays if no other feast falls on that day. This Mass contains beautiful prayers which not only enlighten us as to the work of the angels but also urgently appeal to us to render to God a comparable service of honor and praise. The Communion verse presents the nine choirs in all their glory, "Angels, Archangels, Thrones, and Dominations, Principalities, and Powers, the Virtues of the heavens, Cherubim and Seraphim, bless ye the Lord forever."

There are several special feasts of the angels in the course of the Church year:

1. Feasts of the Archangel Michael

Already in early times Michael, the archangel, whose name means "Who is like to God?" was honored as the patron of the Church. Assisted by the host of good angels who rallied to his side with his name as their battle cry, Michael defeated Lucifer and his malicious followers (Apoc. 12:7 ff.). Ever since this victory he has been considered the Church's most valiant defender against the powers of Satan, and for this reason we pray to him daily after low Mass:

> Holy Michael the archangel, defend us in battle; be our safeguard against the wickedness and snares of the devil. May God restrain him, we humbly pray. And do thou, O Prince of the heavenly host, by the power of God cast into hell Satan and all the evil spirits who wander through the world seeking the ruin of souls.

In the Offertory verse of the Mass for the dead, the Church prays that Michael may lead the souls of the departed "into the holy light":

> O Lord Jesus Christ, King of glory, deliver the souls of all the faithful departed . . . from the lion's mouth that hell engulf them not . . . but let Michael, the holy standard-bearer, bring them into the holy light.

a) *The Dedication of the Church of St. Michael, the Archangel, September* 29

This church is in Rome. The oldest church of St. Michael was built by the emperor, Constantine, who in 313 established freedom of worship and so ended the persecution of the Christians. The Feast of the Dedication of the Church of St. Michael in Rome later became the chief feast of the archangel. The Mass prayers of this feast, however, are not directed to St. Michael alone, for the Church sees Michael above all as the leader of the heavenly host and therefore turns to him and all the angels in prayer; she asks them all to protect the Church and its members, and to join the Church Militant in honoring, praising, and thanking God.

b) *The Apparition of St. Michael the Archangel, May* 8

This feast was already celebrated in the sixth century because of the marvelous appearance of St. Michael on the summit of Monte Gargano in southern Italy about the year 500. At that time he expressed the wish that a church be built there in honor of himself and the holy angels. The church which was built was dedicated on May 8, and was subsequently the site of many miracles. The feast was later extended to the universal Church, and thus offered all Christians an opportunity to honor and invoke this mighty patron and his angelic hosts. The Mass used on this occasion is that of September 29.

Pictures or representations of St. Michael are frequent in Catholic churches. He is usually depicted as a warrior knight, armed with shield and sword and battling with Satan who is represented as a dragon or serpent. Sometimes artists portray him at the altar with the censer in the role of a mediator or intercessor, a picture which undoubtedly has its origin in the Offertory verse of his Mass for September 29:

> An angel stood near the altar of the temple, having a golden censer in his hand, and there was given to him much incense: and the smoke of the perfumes ascended before God, alleluia (Apoc. 8:3-4).[2]

2. The Feast of the Archangel Gabriel, March 24

The archangel Gabriel, whose name signifies "Power of God," was also highly honored in the early Church. He was chosen by God especially to proclaim the mystery of the Incarnation of His Divine Son in both the Old and New Testament. Already to the prophet Daniel, Gabriel clearly disclosed the coming of the Messias; to Zachary he announced the birth

---

[2] The following beautiful prayer is used for the blessing of incense at the Offertory of a solemn High Mass: "Through the intercession of blessed Michael the Archangel standing at the right of the altar of incense, and of all his elect, may the Lord vouchsafe to bless this incense, and to receive it for a sweet savor. Through Christ our Lord. Amen."

of John the Baptist, the great precursor (cf. Luke 1:5 ff.); at Nazareth he greeted Mary with the angelic salutation and announced to her that she was to become the mother of God (Luke 1:26 ff.). For this reason Gabriel is often called the "angel of the Incarnation." In 1921 Pope Benedict XV ordered his feast to be kept by the universal Church on March 24, the day before the Annunciation.

The closing prayer of the Mass of this feast is one that might well be repeated frequently: ". . . that we to whom Thine Incarnation was made known by the message of Gabriel, may likewise obtain through his help the benefits of that same Incarnation" (Postcommunion).

The archangel Gabriel is frequently pictured with a lily in his hand, especially in the Annunciation scene.

3. The Feast of St. Raphael, the Archangel, October 24

St. Raphael, whose name means "God heals," appears in the Old Testament where he guides the young Tobias safely on a journey, arranges for his marriage, and ultimately brings him back to his aged parents where, following Raphael's instructions, the young man restores sight to his father. In the New Testament the health-giving power of the water of the pool of Bethsaida in Jerusalem is attributed to Raphael (cf. the Gospel for his feast, John 5:1 ff.). The Church honors him, then, as protector of the sick, as "messenger of divine help," and "patron of travelers." In her official prayer for those who go on a journey she prays, ". . . may the holy archangel Raphael accompany us on the way that we may return home in joy, peace, and safety." The proper of the Mass for his feast pictures him offering our prayers to God:

> Vouchsafe, O Lord our God, to send down Thy holy archangel Raphael for our helper; and may he, whom we faithfully believe ever to stand before Thy majesty, present our humble prayers to Thee for Thy blessing (Postcommunion).

In 1921 the Feast of St. Raphael was extended to the universal Church by Pope Benedict XV. St. Raphael is usually pictured with a pilgrim's staff as companion of the young Tobias. "May the angel Raphael, physician of our salvation, help us from the heights of heaven, heal all diseases, and guide our faltering steps toward the true life" (Hymn at Lauds).

4. The Feast of the Holy Guardian Angels, Ocobter 2

The Feast of the Holy Guardian Angels was celebrated by the Spaniards in the sixteenth century, and extended to the whole Church by Pope Paul V in 1608. Today we honor the heavenly guide and friend whom God in His fatherly kindness and love has given to each of us. It is a day on which we should remember the numberless benefits to body and soul which we have secured through the intercession of our guardian angel, and give him due thanks for them. We should also remind ourselves of our duties to our guardian angels, particularly those of obedience and veneration, so clearly expressed in the Epistle of the feast:

Thus saith the Lord God: Behold, I will send My
angel, who shall go before thee, and keep thee in thy
journey, and bring thee unto the place that I have
prepared. Take notice of him, and hear his voice, and
do not think him one to be contemned, for he will
not forgive when thou hast sinned . . . (Exod. 23:20–
21).

We ought also to have reverence and respect for the
guardian angels of our fellow men. This will prompt
us never to tempt another to sin, never to scandalize
another. Our own guardian angel is to be obeyed
when he warns us of dangers, when he exhorts us to
good, when he speaks to us lovingly, when he leads
us on the way of virtue. Let us keep an intimate, true
friendship with him. He will one day be our powerful
intercessor or our stern accuser at the Last Judgment.

At least once a year, on the Feast of the Holy
Guardian Angels, the liturgy of the Church brings
our heavenly companions vividly before us. In the
lessons of the breviary, St. Bernard urges us to put
our trust in them:

They are faithful, wise, and powerful; why then
should we fear? Let us only follow, let us be faithful
to them, and we shall dwell under the protection of
God. As often as you perceive that you are being
threatened by severe temptations, call upon your protector, your guide, your helper in every situation and
need . . .

Let us not forget to greet and pray to our guardian
angel daily:

O my good angel, whom God by His divine mercy
hath appointed to be my guardian, enlighten and
protect me, direct and govern me this day and always.

Angel of God, my guardian dear,
To whom God's love entrusts me here,
Ever this day be at my side
To light and guard, to rule and guide.

Feasts of the Apostles and Evangelists

In the Litany of the Saints, the invocations to Mary, to the angels, to John the Baptist, and to St. Joseph precede those of the twelve apostles. In the *Te Deum,* which is thought to be as old as the fourth century, after the angels who praise the Triune God are enumerated, these words follow: "The glorious choir of the apostles, the admirable company of prophets, the white-robed army of martyrs praise Thee."

That only these few groups of saints are mentioned in the *Te Deum,* and not others like confessors and virgins, shows that this part of the *Te Deum* is very old, and can be traced to a time when feasts of confessors, doctors, and virgins were not yet celebrated. It also implies that the liturgical veneration of saints began with the celebration of the feasts of apostles and martyrs. On the anniversary day of their martyrdom, the divine service was celebrated at their graves. Only several centuries later did the Church begin to honor nonmartyrs as saints. They were called *confessors,* a term which in the first centuries of Christianity was used to designate those good Christians who by word and deed, in the face of persecution, confessed Christ and their faith in Him, but did not suffer martyrdom.[3]

The apostles were already highly honored in the

---

[3] For further explanation of the word *confessor,* see page 226.

GO AND TEACH ALL NATIONS BAPTIZING THEM

THE SYMBOLS OF THE EVANGELISTS

Matthew is symbolized by a *man* because his gospel begins with the humanity of Christ, that is, with the human genealogy of the Child Jesus. St. Matthew stresses "the human and kingly character" of Christ.

Mark is symbolized by the *lion* because he begins his gospel with the penitential sermons of John the Baptist, whom he likens to the "Voice of one crying in the desert," that is, the voice of a lion. St. Mark emphasizes the miracles of the Saviour.

Luke is symbolized by the head of an *ox*, since he starts his gospel with the sacrifice of Zachary, the father of John the Baptist. The Jews offered all kinds of animals for burnt sacrifice in the temple. St. Luke emphasizes the universal priesthood of Christ.

earliest Christian centuries as the friends and co-workers of Jesus Christ, for they were the first priests and bishops of the Catholic Church, the first missionaries, the founders and pastors of the first Christian communities. After the descent of the Holy Spirit, they were the courageous men who went about "rejoicing that they had been counted worthy to suffer disgrace for the name of Jesus" (Acts 5:41). They were the first to seal with their own blood their belief in Christ and His Church. They were the groundwork and pillars of the Church, which, according to St. Paul, is "built upon the foundation of the apostles" (Eph. 2:20). After spending the whole night in prayer on a mountaintop, Christ chose from among His disciples twelve apostles to help Him in the foundation of His kingdom and His Church (Luke 6:12 ff.; Mark 3:13 ff.; Matt. 10:1 ff.). They were to be His special friends, the witnesses of His

---

John is symbolized by the *eagle*, because he, like a high-soaring eagle, begins his gospel with the highest theme of all, the divine origin and nature of Christ.

In the visions of the prophet Ezechiel (1:1–10), these four symbols are described as combined into one face, and it is this picture that the Church has applied to the four evangelists who wrote the one Gospel of Jesus Christ. This illustration is easy to understand. Jesus Christ (His *Chi-Rho* symbol is in the center) called the apostles to be His representatives. His life, sufferings, death, and glory in heaven make up the content of the four Gospels, which are set forth in their symbols. "Going therefore, teach all nations, baptizing them in the name of the Father, and of the Son, and of the Holy Ghost" (Matt. 28:19). With a great command He sent the apostles out as His bishops and priests; their episcopal dignity is indicated by the *staff* and *miter*. The *palm* signifies that all of them except St. John suffered a martyr's death.

life, His teaching, and His miracles. They were to be His special family, His messengers,[4] and His representatives among men. They were to share likewise in His own fullness of power. They were to continue among men His teaching, His priestly and pastoral work. The government of His Church was to be upon their shoulders. They were to transmit their own fullness of grace to other men until the end of time.

One of the twelve (Judas), despairing of the goodness and mercy of his Divine Master, became a traitor and took his own life. His place was taken after the first Pentecost by Matthias. Later Paul and Barnabas were received into the group, giving us fourteen in all. Since the Church considers the evangelists, Mark and Luke, to be of equal rank with the apostles, we arrive at the number of sixteen whom we invoke in the Litany of the Saints.

The oldest and highest ranking feast of the apostles is that of the two princes of the Church, Peter and Paul. Similarly Philip and James are honored together, and Simon and Jude Thaddeus. In the course of the Church year the following feasts of apostles and evangelists are celebrated: St. Andrew, November 30; St. Thomas, December 21; St. John, December 28; St. Matthias, February 24; St. Mark, April 25; SS. Philip and James the Less, May 1; St. Barnabas, June 11; SS. Peter and Paul, June 29; St. James the Greater, July 25; St. Bartholomew, August 24; St. Matthew, September 21; St. Luke, October 18; and SS. Simon and Jude, October 28. Most of these feasts are very

---

[4] The word *apostle*, from the Greek, means "one sent forth," a messenger.

(1) St. Peter — (2) St. James — (3) St. John — (4) St. Andrew
— (5) St. Philip — (6) St. Matthew — (7) St. Bartholomew —
(8) St. Thomas — (9) St. James the Less — (10) St. Jude —
(11) St. Simon — (12) St. Matthias.

old and have a vigil; that of SS. Peter and Paul also
has an octave.

There are also *six lesser feasts of apostles.* Three
of these are in honor of St. Peter: (1) *St. Peter's
Chains, August 1,* which commemorates the miraculous escape of St. Peter from prison; (2) *St. Peter's*

Chair at Rome, January 18; (3) *The Chair of St. Peter at Antioch, February 22.* The latter two honor St. Peter as first bishop and pope in Rome and as first bishop of Antioch. They are a liturgical testimony to the primacy of honor and jurisdiction which he had.

Two feasts are celebrated in honor of St. Paul: (1) *The Conversion of St. Paul, January 25,* to commemorate the miraculous conversion of the saint before the Damascus Gate; (2) *The Commemoration of St. Paul, June 30,* to honor the saint as the great, indefatigable Apostle of the Gentiles.

The last *lesser feast of an apostle* is that of *St. John before the Latin Gate, May 6,* which recalls the ancient tradition that he was thrown into a cauldron of burning oil outside this gate. Having miraculously survived the ordeal, he was banished to the island of Patmos where he wrote the Apocalypse.[5]

The feasts of apostles and evangelists, so remarkably distributed throughout the Church year, are a constant exhortation to renew and strengthen our faith in Christ and His Church, and to awaken in us an interest in Sacred Scripture, especially the New Testament. What a salutary practice it would be for Catholic family life if the custom could be revived of reading aloud in the family circle from Holy Scripture or the Lives of the Saints.

Feasts of One or Several (Holy) Popes

On January 9, 1942, mindful of the needs and

---

[5] See also the account of St. John given on his feast day, December 27, page 83.

The *tiara* in the illustration above is the papal crown worn only at nonliturgical functions. The second cardinal deacon places it on the pope's head at his coronation saying: "Receive the tiara adorned with *three crowns* and know that thou art Father of princes and kings, Ruler of the world, Vicar of our Saviour Jesus Christ." The *keys* are a symbol of the power and office of the pope, as the successor of St. Peter to whom our Lord said: "And I will give to thee the keys of the kingdom of heaven" (Matt. 16:19). They denote the power to bind and to loose.

The crowns of the tiara have also been explained thus: The *first crown* symbolizes the pope's universal episcopate, the *second* his supremacy of jurisdiction, and the *third* his temporal influence.

desires of the entire Church, Pope Pius XII took the very unusual step of introducing a special Mass into the Common of Saints to be said on the feasts of Sainted Popes.

"Holy Mother Church," it is pointed out in the decree publishing the new Common, "has always held in particular honor those Roman Pontiffs who by their holiness of life and precious death have become an example to the faithful of the flock committed to them." The decree goes on to explain why the time chosen for paying them this new and added honor was so fitting: "In these days the enemies of the Church, not satisfied with their long, cruel, and often bloody attacks in the past on the firmness of the Apostolic Rock, are seeking in their impious hate to assail the Supreme Pastors themselves and to insult them with the vilest accusations." By singling out Holy Popes from among other Holy Bishops for special honor, this new Mass serves to reassure and strengthen the faith of the whole Church in the supreme dignity and spiritual power bestowed by Christ Himself on St. Peter, the first bishop of Rome, and on the popes, his lawful successors.

As the Mass opens we see our Lord, already risen from the dead, addressing the first pope with the words, "If thou lovest me, Simon Peter, feed my lambs, feed my sheep" (Introit). The sheep and the lambs all belong to Christ and He calls them "mine." Yet Peter is over every one of them, the great and the small, the most exalted bishops and the humblest of the laity, the sheep and the lambs. He is to be their shepherd, ruling them in the Saviour's name. He is to feed them the word of Christ, teaching them with the infallible authority of the divine Master. And all this, because Christ's solemn word has made him His vicar on earth, His spokesman and representative, the visible head of His Church.

Precious as this scene is to the faith of the Church, the Gospel is perhaps more remarkable and important for the way it indicates that the Church will continue to have a visible head even after Peter's death. Before going up to Jerusalem to be crucified, Christ declares, "Thou art Peter, and upon this rock I will build my Church." Against this rock foundation the gates of hell — the devil's malice and the impious hate of men — shall not, cannot, prevail. Clearly, Peter is to be with the Church as her support and strength as long as Christ Himself remains her invisible head, and *He* has promised to remain with her "until the consummation of the world," that is, until the end of time. In fact, it is of the very nature of a rock foundation to endure, never to be removed, never to decay. Only such a lasting rock (the name Peter means the rock) could keep the Church secure and immune to the forces of evil and decay. In this promise to build His Church upon the rock against which even hell itself would be powerless, our Lord was making it unmistakably clear that Peter's power, Peter's authority, Peter's infallible teaching voice would live on in his lawful successors, the bishops of Rome, until the end of time.

It is this sure teaching voice that we hear in the Epistle, a selection from the first papal encyclical (1 Pet. 5). The Prince of the Apostles describes there how a worthy minister of Christ should live and act. The unselfish service in behalf of others that he urges upon his bishops and priests, he himself practiced, even to the point of death by martyrdom. The particular saint whose feast is being celebrated followed in Peter's footsteps and at the moment of death, "when the Prince of Pastors (Christ)

In this illustration the *rock* symbolizes Peter, the first pope to whom Christ said: "Thou art Peter, and upon this rock I will build my Church" (Matt. 16:18). The shepherd's *staff* and *pouch* signify the pastoral obligation which Christ, the divine Shepherd, imposed upon Peter and his successors: "Feed my lambs, feed my sheep." When Christ commissioned His apostles to teach all nations He promised to be with His Church to the end of the world (Matt. 28:20). He does this in a twofold manner: through the Holy Ghost and the Eucharist. The *rays* proceeding from the *dove* indicate the guidance of the Holy Ghost, the Advocate, the Spirit of truth, who will dwell with the Church forever. (Cf. John 14:15–17, 26; 16:13.) The *chalice and host* signifies the Holy Eucharist by which Christ's Sacrifice on Calvary is re-presented and its merits applied to the faithful throughout the centuries. The divine Shepherd offers Himself as "the bread of life" to His flock (John 6). He does so through the ministry of His sacerdotal representatives.

appeared, received a never fading crown of glory."

It is to this same saint of the day that the "Thou art Peter — *Tu es Petrus,*" repeated this time as the Communion verse, is principally addressed. But it too, like the Gospel, is meant to reassure the children of God that as truly as they have one divine Father in heaven, they have a Holy Father on earth who is His agent, His mouthpiece, the channel for His loving goodness and mercy.

However, the petitions and longings of the Catholic people, as well as their needs, are satisfied by this new Mass. The more the Holy See has been deprived of earthly power and spendor — the present Vatican City is but a tiny fraction of the former Papal States and hardly more than a token of temporal sovereignty — the greater has its spiritual prestige and influence grown. Even those outside the Church listen when the pope speaks. But especially among Catholics all over the world have his words been received with steadily increasing attention, reverence, and active support. The Common of Popes gives the faithful fresh opportunity to show their devotion to the Apostolic See. At the same time it will strengthen their loyalty, awaken prayerful remembrance of the Holy Father, and deepen their appreciation for the providence of God, who has given the faith and charity of His children so mighty a safeguard and so unfailing a guide.

The new Mass, *Si diligis me,* is used on the following feasts of popes, except for those parts which may be proper to them (like the Collect of St. Marcellus, January 16; of St. Gregory VII, May 25, etc.):

January 5, *St. Telesphorus*
January 11, *St. Hyginus*
January 16, *St. Marcellus*
March 4, *St. Lucius*
March 12, *St. Gregory the Great*
April 11, *St. Leo I*
April 17, *St. Anicetus*
April 22, *SS. Soter and Cajus*
April 26, *SS. Cletus and Marcellinus*
May 5, *St. Pius V*
May 19, *St. Peter Celestine*
May 25, *St. Gregory VII*
　　　　　St. Urban
May 26, *St. Eleutherius*
May 27, *St. John I*
June 20, *St. Silverius*
July 3, *St. Leo II*
July 11, *St. Pius I*
July 13, *St. Anacletus*
August 2, *St. Stephen*
August 26, *St. Zephirinus*
September 23, *St. Linus*
October 7, *St. Mark*
October 14, *St. Callistus*
October 26, *St. Evaristus*
November 12, *St. Martin*
November 19, *St. Pontianus*
November 23, *St. Clement*
December 10, *St. Melchiades*
December 11, *St. Damasus*
December 31, *St. Sylvester*

IF YOU SUFFER WITH CHRIST YOU WILL REIGN WITH CHRIST

The palm signifies victory over trials and triumphant martyrdom. According to the vision of St. John, the saints in glory wear *crowns* upon their heads (Apoc. 2:10; 4:4; 7:9) and carry *palms* obtained by victory through Christ.

Feasts of Martyrs

Veneration of the saints began with the Martyrs, victorious champions and heroes of the Church. Every year on the anniversary of the death of a martyr, Holy Mass was celebrated over his grave. The custom soon arose of having a eulogy or sermon delivered at this Mass which recounted the main facts of the life and death of the respective martyr. This usually followed the Gospel. Through these eulogies (a large number are still extant) runs the theme that every Christian should strive always to become more like the Redeemer, to become an "other Christ" as did those faithful men, women, and children who suffered persecution and martyrdom for love of Christ and His Church. In laying down their lives, they were but imitating their Divine Master who gave up His life on the cross out of love for mankind.[6]

Three facts, above all, indicate how highly the early Christians esteemed the martyrs:

1. In the unchanging parts of the Mass, particularly in the Canon, both before and after the Consecration, the names of several martyr saints are mentioned.

2. In that part of the missal which contains the "Common of the Saints," there are nine Masses of martyrs, divided into three groups: (*a*) four separate Masses in honor of *one* martyr; (*b*) three in honor of *several* martyrs; and (*c*) two in honor of one or several martyrs during Paschal-time. In the first group of Masses mentioned (*a*), there is distinction made between martyrs who were bishops and those who were not; the proper of these Masses is of very early origin.

3. In the *Te Deum* and in the *Litany of the Saints,* the holy martyrs are named immediately after the apostles.

---

[6] The word *martyr* is from the Greek meaning "witness" which in the language of the Church means "blood witness." By shedding their blood the martyrs "gave witness" to their faith in Christ and His Church.

Red, the color of blood and fire, is used for the feast of martyrs whose ardent love for Christ gave them strength to sacrifice their blood for Him.

Two of the Church's favorite martyrs are St. Stephen and St. Lawrence. The Feast of St. Stephen is celebrated on December 26 (see page 81), though on August 3 there is a second feast which commemorates the finding of his relics in 415. The Feast of St. Lawrence, August 10, is privileged to have both a vigil and an octave day. Both of these saints are mentioned in the Canon of the Mass, after the consecration, and enjoy first place among the martyrs in the Litany of the Saints.

Other martyrs whose names are enrolled in the Litany of the Saints are:[7]

St. Vincent, a holy deacon in Spain, January 22. St. Anastasius, a Persian martyr, is honored on this same day.

SS. Fabian and Sebastian, January 20. The first of these two saints was a pope (236–250) who died a martyr. St. Sebastian, an officer of the Roman imperial household, was caught consoling and encouraging his soldier companions who were being subjected to torments for their faith. Diocletian ordered him to be shot to death with arrows. Left in a dying condition, he was secretly nursed back to health by fellow Christians. Then he went before the emperor and courageously reproached him for his crimes, with the result that he was condemned to be flogged to death. St. Sebastian is a much-

---

[7] Of this group SS. John and Paul and SS. Cosmas and Damian are also mentioned in the Canon of the Mass.

honored saint. He is a favorite of men and often invoked for help against pestilence and contagious diseases. Many confraternities have been established in his honor.

SS. John and Paul, June 26, two wealthy brothers, who gave all their property to the poor. They were beheaded in Rome in the year 362.

SS. Cosmas and Damian, September 27. These two brothers were physicians, who healed not only bodies but also countless souls. Due to their unwillingness to sacrifice to the heathen gods, they were beheaded about the year 303.

SS. Gervase and Protase, June 19, were also brothers, sons of SS. Vitalis and Valeria. They were the first martyrs in Milan, about 170.

The prayers of the *Canon* of the Mass also mention *before the consecration,* Linus, Cletus, Clement, Sixtus, Cornelius, Cyprian, and Chrysogonus. The first five were popes. Cyprian was a bishop in Carthage, Africa, and Chrysogonus belonged to the nobility. *After the consecration* come Ignatius, Alexander, Marcellinus, and Peter. St. Ignatius was a disciple of St. John the Evangelist and bishop of Antioch in Asia Minor; about the year 107 he was thrown to the wild beasts in the Roman amphitheater. St. Alexander was a pope, St. Marcellinus a priest, and St. Peter his Mass server. All of these martyrs, together with the women who are mentioned in the Canon of the Mass,[8] were highly venerated in Rome from earliest Christian times.

Among other martyrs whose feasts the Church celebrates, the following are especially noteworthy:

---

[8] For further reference to them, see page 232.

St. Timothy, January 24, a disciple of St. Paul, to whom that great apostle wrote two letters.

St. Polycarp, January 26, the disciple of St. John the Evangelist, and bishop of Smyrna.

St. Irenaeus, June 28, whose writings are a valuable link between the apostolic age and the early Church Fathers.

St. George, April 23, the soldier martyr.

St. Blaise, February 3, the sainted bishop who worked many miracles during his lifetime. By one of the most outstanding of these miracles, a child who had swallowed a fishbone was saved from choking to death. For this reason, St. Blaise is recognized as a protector against diseases of the throat, and a special blessing of the throat is usually given on his feast.

SS. Celsus and Pancratius. The saintly youths Celsus, July 28, and Pancratius, May 12, were sons of prominent families. Rather than deny their God and break their baptismal vows, they courageously refused to offer sacrifice to the heathen gods.

St. Tarcisius, August 15, as a young boy, let himself be stoned to death in order to protect the Blessed Sacrament from desecration by his pagan companions.

The glorious example of the martyrs should inspire and encourage us to be faithful to our baptismal promises which we solemnly renewed at our first Holy Communion and on other important occasions of our life. Faithfulness to these promises will secure for us the heavenly crown, promised by Christ, who is eternal truth itself, "He who loses his life for My sake, will find it" (Matt. 10:39; 16:25).

> Blessed is the man that endureth temptation; for when he hath been proved, he shall receive the crown of life which God hath promised to them that love Him (James 1:12).

Feasts of Confessors

While the liturgical veneration of apostles and martyrs reaches back to the first centuries, that of confessors began later. The first feasts of confessors were celebrated in honor of such saints as had suffered for Christ and their faith during the early persecutions without actually meeting death by martyrdom. Later the title "Confessor" was given to all who faithfully followed Christ in word and deed, with an extraordinary degree of perfection. They were those wise and faithful servants who with "girt loins and lamps burning in their hands" (Luke 12:35) awaited the return of their Lord.

The liturgy of the Church groups the confessors under four different headings:

1. *Doctors.* This is the title given to those saints who accomplished much for the Church by their writings. Many of these men have left us volumes of profound treatises on our faith; with the exception of Sacred Scripture, there is nothing more instructive and edifying in ecclesiastical literature than the works of the Doctors of the Church. The Church honors twenty-seven of these learned and saintly men. Among these, the most eminent are the two great popes, *St. Gregory I,* March 12, and *St. Leo I,* April

11. Other great doctors are: *St. Ambrose,* December 7; *St. Augustine,* August 28; *St. Jerome,* September 30; *St. Basil,* June 14; *St. Bernard of Clairvaux,* August 20; *St. Anselm,* April 21; *St. Bede,* May 27; *St. Thomas Aquinas,* March 7; and *St. Alphonse Liguori,* August 2, and (most recently) *St. Anthony of Padua,* June 13.

THE JUST SHALL FLOURISH LIKE THE PALM

The quotation in the illustration above is from Psalm 91, verse 13. It is used in the Masses of Confessors as Offertory verse, Introit, and Gradual.

2. *Confessor-Bishops.* To this group belong the saints who were popes, cardinals, archbishops, and patriarchs. Three of these are invoked in the Litany of the Saints: Pope *St. Sylvester,* December 31; and the bishops *St. Martin,* November 11, and *St. Nicholas,* December 6. Other great bishops are: *St. Patrick,*

March 17; *St. Boniface,* June 5; *St. Norbert,* June 6; *St. Bruno,* September 6; *St. Ulric,* July 4; *St. Augustine of Canterbury,* May 28; *St. Willibrord,* November 7; *St. Lambert,* September 17; *St. Hubert,* November 3; and *St. Virgilius,* November 27.

3. *Abbots.* "Abbot," meaning *father,* is the title given to the head of a monastery of one of the older religious orders, such as the Benedictines or Cistercians. When he enters upon his office, which he normally holds for life, the abbot receives a special blessing as the father of the monastic family. The most renowned of abbots is *St. Benedict,* March 21, the founder of the order which bears his name. It is the oldest of the monastic orders in the West which, in the course of its fourteen hundred years of existence, did much to keep alive both faith and culture. *St. Bernard of Clairvaux,* whom we have already mentioned among the doctors of the Church, was also a distinguished abbot.

In the Litany of the Saints, *St. Anthony* of Egypt, January 17, the father of eastern cenobites and the wonder-worker of his day, takes precedence over all other abbots. Other saints honored in this group include *St. Maurus,* January 15, and *St. Placid,* October 5, who were among the first disciples of St. Benedict; and *St. Columba,* June 9, *St. Brendan,* May 16, and *St. Leonard,* November 7.

4. *Confessors Who Were Not Bishops.* This group includes all the saintly men, nonmartyrs, who were neither bishops nor doctors nor abbots. Of the multitude of confessors — emperors and kings, priests and monks, married and unmarried men — only a few can

be listed here, such as: *St. Joachim,* August 16, the
father of the Blessed Virgin, and the grandfather of
Christ; *St. Henry,* July 15, the saintly emperor; *St.
Louis,* August 25, king of France; the founders of
great religious orders, *St. Dominic,* August 4, *St.
Francis of Assisi,* October 4, and *St. Ignatius of Loyola,*
July 31; *St. Anthony of Padua,* June 13; *St. Aloysius,*
June 21; *St. Stanislaus Kostka,* November 13; *St. Con-
rad of Parzham,* April 21; *St. Don Bosco,* January 31;
St. John Vianney, the Curé of Ars, August 9; and
St. Cloud, September 7.

For the Mass of feasts of confessors *white,* the color
of innocence, joy, and glory, is used.

The many feasts of saintly confessors in the ecclesiastical year should always be an earnest exhortation
for us to confess our faith zealously under all circumstances, to do penance for our sins, and like these
"good and faithful servants" to live continually in
the fear of the Lord, ready to sacrifice self for God
and neighbor so that we can calmly look forward to
death and judgment. Then will be fulfilled in us what
the Church sings in the Introit (Second Mass of a
Confessor not a Bishop) on the feasts of confessors,
"The just shall flourish like the palm tree: he shall
grow up like the cedar of Libanus: planted in the
house of the Lord, in the courts of the house of our
God" (Ps. 91:13–14).

It will be easier to understand and enter into the
meaning of the six different Mass formulas for the
feasts of confessors if you know the life of the saint
whose feast is being celebrated and are able to apply
the Mass texts to him. A more intimate knowledge of

the lives of the saints will greatly simplify your efforts to live according to the mind of the Church.

Feasts of Holy Women

In the Litany of the Saints, after the confessors comes the group of women saints. The same order is preserved in "the Common of the Saints" in the missal where there are eight different Masses in their honor. Here again the Church distinguishes between martyrs and nonmartyrs so that there are four divisions and, correspondingly, eight Mass formulas. If the saint is a martyr, red vestments are worn, otherwise white ones are used. Many individual dioceses have their own feasts of saints in this group.

1. Virgin Martyrs

To this division belong first of all the four great saints of the early Church who have been especially honored:

St. Cecilia, November 22, the patroness of Church music. About the year 230 she died a courageous death for her faith.

St. Lucy, December 13, was born in Sicily of noble parents. She gave away all her riches to the poor and, having sacrificed all material things, gave her life also to her divine Spouse in 303 rather than lose the treasure of virginity.

St. Agnes, January 21, the first and earliest patroness of youthful purity. Though still a child, she guarded her purity so bravely that she died a martyr's death after terrible torture about the year 300. In Rome on her feast day the Holy Father blesses two lambs from whose wool the *pallia,*[9] the special insignia of arch-bishops, are woven.

This sketch illustrates the Gospel of the Wise and Foolish Virgins. The burning *lamps* represent the wise virgins who were ready to meet the bridegroom. The *light* signifies sanctifying grace which is fed by the oil of charity.

---

[9] The *pallium* consists of a narrow band of white woolen tissues which is worn over the chasuble. After the *pallia* are blessed by the Holy Father on June 28, they are placed in a receptacle on the tomb of St. Peter.

St. Agatha, February 5, was cruelly martyred in 251 because she refused to sacrifice her innocence and faith at the order of the pagan judge.

These four virgin martyrs, who were already venerated in Rome in ancient times, are commemorated after the Consecration in daily Mass.

St. Catherine of Alexandria, November 25, is another well-known virgin martyr, honored by the Church since her death at the beginning of the fourth century. She is included in the Litany of the Saints and is invoked as one of the fourteen "auxiliary saints."[10]

Other virgin-martyrs of prominence are *St. Christine,* July 24, *St. Ursula* and her companions, October 21, who were martyred by the Huns in the third century; *St. Ottilia,* December 12, and *St. Victoria,* December 23.

2. Other Women-Martyrs

The Canon of the Mass after the Consecration mentions *St. Anastasia,* December 25, the noble Roman woman who, though born of a pagan family, secretly became a Christian while in the school of St. Chrysogonus (see page 224). She was forced, however, to marry a pagan of high position. After the sudden death of her husband, she gave all her goods to the poor and died a martyr's death on December 25 in the fourth century. She is commemorated in the second Mass on Christmas Day and her name is invoked in the Litany of the Saints.

---

[10] Two other virgin martyrs belong to this group of "auxiliary saints": *St. Barbara,* December 4, and *St. Margaret,* July 20.

Both the Canon of the Mass and the Litany of the Saints include the names of *St. Perpetua* and *St. Felicitas,* March 6 (the first, a noble, wealthy woman of Carthage in Africa, and the other, her young slave), who about the year 202 were scourged and then left to be mangled by wild beasts in the arena. The Acts[11] of these two women martyrs are among the most beautiful and impressive writings of this period.

3. Virgins — Not Martyrs

The first to be considered here are the two women who were friends of our Blessed Saviour, *St. Mary Magdalen,* July 22, the penitent and faithful disciple, whose intercession is also asked in the Litany of the Saints, and *St. Martha,* July 29, the oversolicitous hostess at Bethany, at the house of their brother Lazarus.

This section includes many holy women who belonged to the religious state, and who in the cloister, through prayer, self-denial, and self-sacrificing love of God and neighbor, sanctified themselves and others. Space permits mention of but a few:

St. Scholastica, February 10, the sister of St. Benedict, patriarch of western monks;

St. Hildegard, September 17, and *St. Gertrude,* November 16, two illustrious and learned Benedictines

---

[11] "In a strict sense the *Acts of the Martyrs* are the official records of the trials of early Christian martyrs made by the notaries of the court. In a wider sense, however, the title is applied to all the narratives of the martyrs' trial and death" (the *Catholic Encyclopedia,* Ed. 1910, Vol. IX, p. 742, by James Bridge).

of the Middle Ages whose writings still rank high in mystical literature;

St. Clare, August 12, the courageous disciple of St. Francis of Assisi, who went out against the licentious pagan soldiers with the Blessed Eucharist, and thus miraculously routed them;

St. Teresa of Ávila, October 15, one of the most gifted saints of all times;

St. Teresa of the Child Jesus, October 3, the "Little Flower," the beloved saint of Lisieux, who believed that her mission in life was "to make others love the good God as I love Him . . . to teach my little way to souls";

St. Catherine of Siena, April 30;

St. Rita, May 22;

St. Brigid of Ireland, February 1;

St. Margaret Mary Alacoque, October 17, the great advocate of devotion to the Sacred Heart of Jesus; and

St. Rose of Lima, August 30, the first flower of sanctity to bloom in South America; she died in Peru, August 29, 1617.

4. Other Women Saints — Not Martyrs

St. Anne, July 26, the mother of the Blessed Virgin and the grandmother of the Child Jesus, merits the first position among this group of nonmartyr saints;

St. Monica, May 4, was the mother of the great St. Augustine, who by continual prayers and sacrifices obtained from God the conversion of her wayward son;

St. Helena, August 18, was the holy empress to whom we are indebted for the finding of the true cross of Christ. Like her son, Constantine, who granted religious freedom to the Church after three centuries of persecution, she built splendid churches, among others the wonderful Church of the Holy Sepulcher in Jerusalem;

St. Frances of Rome, March 9, the model of all married women, an angel of mercy, who during her own life had the grace of seeing and speaking intimately with her own guardian angel;

St. Elizabeth of Hungary, November 19, whose great love for the poor and afflicted prompted her to supply them generously with food; later she was basely persecuted by the very people she had helped;

St. Hedwig, October 16, patroness of Poland, who was renowned for her love of her husband, but far more illustrious for her resignation to God's will;

St. Cunigunda, March 3, saintly empress, daughter of Count Siegfried of Luxemburg, who in the midst of most dreadful calumny retained a remarkably stanch faith in God. Her love of neighbor extended even to her calumniators whom she was ever ready to forgive. She was the wife of the emperor, St. Henry II, after whose death she lived fifteen years in a convent as a simple nun.

The Gospel which is read most frequently in the Masses in honor of Virgins relates the story of the wise and foolish virgins (Matt. 25:1–13), one of the most beautiful and instructive of all the parables of our Lord. Here, especially, is shown how the Church, by her celebration of the feasts of the saints, keeps our eternal goal before us. We should always live, free from mortal sin and so prepared that we will be

ready to come into the presence of our eternal Judge
at any moment of any day. For we do not know
when and how we shall die. "At midnight there was
a cry made: 'Behold the bridegroom cometh, go ye
forth to meet him!' . . . and they that were ready,
went in with him to the marriage, and the door was
shut. . . . Watch ye, therefore, because you know not
the day nor the hour" (Matt. 25:6–13).

Women of all ages, children, young girls, young
women, married women, and widows, have models
in heaven, whose example they ought to follow faithfully so that they, too, may be permitted to enter into
the eternal marriage feast in heaven.

Special Feasts

The major feasts of the Church year, such as
Christmas, Easter, Pentecost, Corpus Christi, are celebrated in the *entire* Catholic world. This is also true
of most of the feasts of the Blessed Virgin, of the
apostles, and of other outstanding saints, who, included in the Church's calendar of saints, are venerated for the most part in the liturgy of the universal
Church.

But every country, diocese, and religious order has
its own special feasts, that is, feasts of certain saints
which are celebrated only in that particular country,
diocese, or order.[12] The saints so honored may have
lived and worked in that country or diocese, or were
members of the certain order which gives them special

---

[12] Supplements for the missal are available which contain the
proper feasts for the various countries, dioceses, and religious
orders.

veneration. The place is often the site of the saint's grave or the church in which his relics are preserved.

The highest special feast of every country is that of its own patron. For the diocese, it is the feast of the patron of the diocese. In a religious order, it is the feast of the founder of the order. The feast of the patron of a country is celebrated in every parish of the country, whereas the feast of the patron of the diocese is observed only in the parishes of that particular diocese. There it is a first-class feast with an octave.

Interesting examples of *local patrons* may be cited. For instance, on February 5, the Roman calendar has listed the Feast of St. Agatha. In the Archdiocese of Baltimore and the Archdiocese of Los Angeles, the feast of the patron of the City of Mexico, St. Philip of Jesus, martyr, is observed. On February 1 the Roman missal gives the Feast of St. Ignatius, bishop, martyr. The country of Ireland celebrates the feast of the great first abbess of Kildare, St. Brigid, styled the "Mary of Ireland," on that day.

The Feast of St. Benedict, March 21, is observed in the whole Church as a feast of third rank, *a double major;* in the Benedictine Order, however, it is regarded as a first-class feast. Besides, since this feast regularly falls in Lent at a time when it is not fitting to solemnize it, there is a special feast, the Solemnity of St. Benedict on July 11, which is celebrated with an octave. Similarly, St. Augustine is honored among Augustinians by a first-class feast with an octave, though the liturgy of the Church accords him, as a doctor of the Church, only a Mass of the fourth rank on his feast, August 28. In like manner, St. Francis is honored by the Franciscans, St. Ignatius by the Jesuits, St. Alphonsus Liguori by the Redemptorists, as are other founders of religious houses or institutes by their respective followers.

Patrons[13]

The name of a saint was given each of us at Baptism when we first became members of the "Communion of Saints." Since we received them at Baptism, they are called *baptismal names.* Many of us have several saints' names. The saints whose names we bear are our patrons. One purpose for choosing them is to obtain their special protection; thus they are called our protectors. By the example of their saintly lives and by their intercession for us at the throne of God they can help us to reach our eternal goal. On our part, then, we should know the life of our special patron and imitate his virtues, his love of God and neighbor, his great courage and faith in fearlessly keeping God's commandments and doing His will always and everywhere. We should also pray diligently to our patron. Many pray to all possible saints except their patron whom, sad to say, they seem to ignore entirely. Such neglect is blameworthy. Our patron should be invoked every morning for protection in the following or some similar manner:

> O guardian patrons given me,
> My guide-protectors ever be![14]

[13] *Patron* comes from the Latin word, *patronus,* meaning father, guardian, protector.

[14] It was once the custom in Christian homes to read the lives of the saints aloud in the evening. This custom should be revived, so that we will learn again to know more about the saints, especially our patrons.

Patrons of States of Life: Just as every Christian has a patron, so also have the various states and vocations of life a special protecting saint. Some of these patrons are: St. Joseph for workingmen, St. Anne and St. Monica for mothers, St. Aloysius for boys and young men, St. Agnes for girls, the holy Curé of Ars, St. John Baptist Vianney, for pastors, St. Francis Xavier and St. Teresa of the Child Jesus for missionaries.

Patrons for Churches: Every Catholic Church has its patron, a fact which is especially significant for parish churches, for there the saint is not only the protector of the church, but of the entire parish family. Every child in a parish should know something about this patron and be urged to pray to him. His feast is celebrated with solemnity every year.[15] The name of a patron of a church is mentioned in the Church's prayer "To implore the Intercession of the Saints" (the *A cunctis*), as often as that Oration is said at Mass or in the Divine Office. In this way the liturgy does special honor to the patrons of its churches, and begs them to intercede with God for the protection of the entire parish family.

Other Patrons: Besides the patrons of parish churches, there are also many *patrons of places,* such as villages, towns, and cities. They are chosen to protect the inhabitants of these districts from all misfortune, both of body and soul. For example, St. Louis is the patron of the city of St. Louis, and St. Paul of the city of St. Paul. Moreover, there may be a patron

---

[15] Note what is said about the feast of a patron of a church under the section on "the dedication of a church," page 315 ff.

for each diocese or bishopric.[16] This patron may have been the first missionary to preach the glad tidings of the Gospel in that region, or he may have been a great saint living in that very place. Perhaps he was the one who was held in highest esteem by the people through some accidental connection. The patron of the diocese of St. Cloud, for example, is the French St. Cloud, after whom the city of St. Cloud, Minnesota, has been named.

Most *Christian countries* also have their patrons. *The United States* honors Mary under the title of her

---

[16] For a definition of a bishopric or diocese, see page 12.

Immaculate Conception, December 8; *Canada,* St. John the Baptist, June 24; *Mexico,* Our Lady of Guadalupe, December 12; *France,* both the Blessed Virgin and Joan of Arc, the holy Maid of Orleans, May 30; *Belgium,* St. Joseph, March 19; *Germany,* St. Michael the Archangel, September 29; *Scotland,* the Apostle St. Andrew, November 30; and *Ireland,* the great missionary bishop, St. Patrick, March 17.

Above these protector-saints stand the *patrons of the universal Church.* The holy apostles, St. Peter and St. Paul, have been so honored since the first Christian centuries. St. Michael the archangel has been thus venerated, too, since the Middle Ages. And in 1870, by the proclamation of Pius IX, St. Joseph was declared "protector of the universal Church," with a special feast called the Solemnity of St. Joseph on the third Wednesday after Easter.

Special Feasts of Our Lord and the Saints

St. Andrew, Apostle, November 30: St. Andrew, whose name means "the brave," was the brother of Simon Peter.[17] Andrew and the beloved disciple, St. John, were the first of the apostles invited to follow their Master, according to the beautiful account John gives in his gospel (1:35 ff.). Andrew immediately told his brother about this blessed meeting with the Messias and led Simon to Jesus who gave him the name of Peter. Even though Sacred Scripture reports little more about the Apostle Andrew, we know from tradition that he was very zealous in preaching the

---

[17] With many other zealous and devout young men, he belonged to the disciples of St. John the Baptist.

Gospel in Asia Minor and in the Balkans; he so loved the cross that he died a martyr's death by crucifixion at Patras in Greece. It is handed down in tradition that after he had seen the cross on which he was to die for Christ, he cried out:

> Hail, O holy cross that was made holy by the Body of Christ! O precious cross which I have greatly desired, intimately loved, sought unceasingly, and found at last! Take me out of this world and lead me to my Master, and may He who through thee redeemed me, through thee also receive me![18]

The body of the apostle was taken to Constantinople in 357; centuries later, in 1210, it was transferred to the Cathedral of Amalfi near Naples. In 1462 the head was placed in the basilica of St. Peter in Rome.

Because of his great love for the cross, St. Andrew has been called "the Apostle of the Cross," and he is always pictured with a cross shaped like the letter X, the so-called St. Andrew's cross. Each time the holy sacrifice of the Mass is offered, his name is mentioned twice, at the *Communicantes* before the Consecration, and at the *Libera nos* after the *Pater noster*.

From the "Apostle of the Cross" let us learn to love Christ and His cross; it is the sign of our redemption, of Christ's victory and a presage of our own victory, for when it will appear glorified in the heavens on the day of judgment, it will mean for us, not fear and trembling, but everlasting happiness.

THE IMMACULATE CONCEPTION OF THE BLESSED VIRGIN MARY, December 8: On December 8, 1854,

---

[18] The antiphons for I and II Vespers of this feast are particularly beautiful, and will repay special study.

in the presence of an immense and enthusiastic crowd in St. Peter's basilica, Pope Pius IX solemnly announced the dogma of this great feast in the following words:

> "To the greater glory of God and to the exaltation of the most Blessed Virgin, I, as Vicar of Christ and the successor of St. Peter, declare the doctrine that the Blessed Virgin Mary in the first instant of her conception, by a singular privilege and grace granted by God, in view of the merits of Jesus Christ, the Saviour of the human race, was preserved exempt from all stain of original sin. This doctrine is to be taken as one revealed by God, and must, therefore, be firmly and steadfastly believed by all the faithful."

Mary is, therefore, the first among the redeemed, the first and holiest fruit of the redemption. The fruits of the redemption, which her divine Son later won on the cross, were applied to her, the mother of the Redeemer, at the moment of her conception. She, the Mother of God, was from the beginning entirely pure, holy, pleasing to God, "full of grace." Although all other men have to be cleansed from the curse of original sin in Baptism, Mary's soul was never in the least touched by it.

This unique distinction has made Mary the inspiration of all Christians who are her children and has rendered her ineffably worthy of their respect and love. In the eastern Church, this feast was celebrated as early as the sixth and seventh centuries. By the ninth century, we find it being observed in the West, especially in Italy and in Ireland. Pope Clement XI (1708) ordered it to be celebrated in the whole

ELECT AS THE SUN

By accommodation the Church applies the words of the Apocalypse (12:1) and of the Canticle of Canticles (6:9) to the Immaculate Conception. In reality the prophecy pertains to the Church herself under the Old and New Covenants.

Church, and in 1854 it became a holyday of obligation. Pope Leo XIII raised it to the rank of a first-class feast with vigil and octave, in 1879.

With the Archangel Gabriel, let us greet Mary Immaculate often and devoutly as the Virgin "full of grace." And with the liturgy of the Church, in the Mass and the Divine Office, let us praise "the lily among the thorns," the "spotless mirror of justice." "Thou art all fair, O Mary, and the stain of original sin is not in thee."[19]

ST. THOMAS, THE APOSTLE, December 21: There is not much in Sacred Scripture about the apostle, St. Thomas. What there is, however, is important for our faith. Thomas had doubted the truth of our Lord's resurrection. The Saviour thoroughly convinced him (cf. John 20:24 ff., used as the Gospel of the feast), and Thomas, the doubter, became a stanch and faithful believer in the divinity of Christ. He went as a missionary to Armenia, Persia, and India, and died in the last-named place, pierced with a lance, a martyr to his faith. He is honored, appropriately, therefore, as the patron of India. St. Thomas' name appears in the Canon of the Mass before the Consecration.

The words which our Lord spoke to St. Thomas are also applicable to us: "Be not faithless, but believing. . . . Blessed are they that have not seen, and have believed" (John 20:27-29). In the Child in the crib and in the consecrated host on our altars, we see in faith the Son of God become man, our Saviour and Redeemer, the Lord and Judge of the world. During the elevation at Mass, let us contemplate with deep faith and reverence the elevated host, saying with St.

---

[19] For the place of this feast in Advent, see the section on Advent, page 69.

Thomas, "My Lord and my God," a practice highly indulgenced by Pope Pius X.[20]

ST. PETER'S CHAIR AT ROME, January 18, and ST. PETER'S CHAIR AT ANTIOCH, February 22: The Feast of St. Peter's Chair at Rome recalls St. Peter's occupation, in the year 42, of the episcopal chair in the eternal city as vicar of Christ, bishop of Rome, and first pope. It may have been celebrated as early as the year 300, but there is positive evidence that it was celebrated on February 22 before 450. On January 18 it was customary in some places to commemorate the binding and loosing power bestowed on St. Peter by our Lord. Later in the sixth century the custom arose of having two feasts of St. Peter's Chair; in addition to the one at Rome, the Church commemorated the fact that he had first been bishop of Antioch. In 1558 Pope Paul IV confirmed both feasts by decreeing that on January 18 the possession of the episcopal chair at Rome should be celebrated, and on February 22 the Feast of St. Peter's Chair at Antioch. The purpose of these feasts is to renew and strengthen our love and fidelity to our holy mother, the Church, to the pope, and to all our bishops and priests.

ST. SEBASTIAN, January 20: According to legend the martyr, St. Sebastian, who is especially honored among Catholic men, was an officer of the imperial household and commander of a cohort in Rome. Because he became a Christian and protected and

---

[20] The important feasts occurring between Christmas and Epiphany are to be found in their respective places in the temporal cycle. See page 81 ff.

encouraged his fellow-Christians against their persecutors, he was to be shot with arrows at the command of the emperor Diocletian, who had tried in vain to turn the brave officer from his faith. The soldiers left him lying seriously wounded, but a good Christian woman by the name of Irene nursed him back to health. With undaunted courage he came again before the emperor and reproached him for his godlessness and cruelty. The emperor was furious and ordered Sebastian to be flogged to death. Thus he died a martyr about the year 285. Many miracles, especially cures of the sick, were wrought through his intercession. He is often invoked as a patron against plagues. Let us beg St. Sebastian to intercede for us that we may have a faith as ardent as his, and courage to confess it at all times.

St. Agnes, January 21 and January 28: The Litany of the Saints names five virgin martyrs who were among the first to be honored in the Church. By what seems a coincidence, the feasts of all these saints fall during the winter months. The Church celebrates the Feast of *St. Cecilia* on November 22, of *St. Catherine* of Alexandria on November 25, of *St. Lucy* on December 12, the two feasts of *St. Agnes* in January, and *St. Agatha's* on February 5.

The most lovable of these virgin-martyrs is undoubtedly St. Agnes. St. Ambrose, bishop and doctor of the Church († 397) had already placed her before his contemporaries as an example and model of virtue. The name Agnes derives from the Greek meaning "pure," but in Latin the word *agnus* means lamb. It is a word nobly dignified by the fact that John applied

it to our Lord in a salutation that the Church has
always revered and loved: "Behold the Lamb of God,
behold Him who taketh away the sin of the world!"
(John 1:29.)

St. Agnes, herself a pure and patient lamb, is
usually pictured holding one in her arms. Born of a
noble family, she was only thirteen years old when
with childlike innocence but with a mature love for
her divine Bridegroom, she became a sacrificial lamb
by martyrdom. The rich pagan son of the Roman
prefect wanted her for his bride and loaded her with
presents. But she did not wish to marry. To his pro-
posal she replied, "The one to whom I am betrothed
is Christ whom the angels serve." He overwhelmed
her then with threats and reported her to the authori-
ties as a Christian. His wickedness and cruelty were
so great that he even went so far as to attempt to dis-
honor her by violence, to force her to sin. The courageous child, however, said, "I have an angel of God
as my protector." And truly, as soon as anyone tried
to harm her, she was enveloped in so brilliant a light
that those about were blinded. Next she was thrown
on a funeral pile, but "the flames did her no harm."
The judge finally commanded her to be beheaded,
at which sentence Agnes joyfully exclaimed, "Now I
shall be united in heaven to Him whom on earth
I have loved so much." Her death occurred about
the year 304. The emperor Constantine built a magnificent basilica over her tomb in Rome to honor this
heroic maiden.

The Divine Office of the feast is rich with beautiful
passages depicting her courage and love, her purity

and faithfulness. It summons us also to a life of purity and sacrifice. Let us ask St. Agnes to obtain these graces for us so that with her we may be happily united forever to our Lord and Saviour, Jesus Christ.

The missal has a second Feast of St. Agnes on January 28. Legend tells us that eight days after her death (the octave-day), when her parents came to pray at her tomb, she appeared to them surrounded by a "bevy of virgins" (Introit).

"On her right hand was a lamb whiter than snow; it was Christ consecrating His union with the one who by her virginity and martyrdom became His bride" (Magnificat Antiphon).

A more appropriate reason for the second feast, however, is the fact, mentioned in several Sacramentaries,[21]

---

[21] In the Roman Rite, the first complete liturgical books we know are the Sacramentaries (*Sacramentaria*). A Sacramentary is not a missal. It is the book for the celebrant, containing all and only the prayers that he says. When these books were written it was not yet the custom for the celebrant to repeat at the altar whatever is sung by the ministers or choir. Thus Sacramentaries contain no Lessons, Introits, Graduals, Offertories, etc., but only Collects, Prefaces, the Canon — all that is strictly the celebrant's part. On the other hand, they are used at other occasions besides Mass. As the celebrant is normally supposed to be a bishop, the Sacramentary supplies him with the prayers for ordinations, for the consecration of a church and altar, and many exorcisms, blessings, and consecrations now inserted in the Pontifical and Ritual. This is the order of a complete Sacramentary. Many of those now extant are more or less fragmentary.

The so-called *Sacramentarium Leonianum* is the oldest. Only one manuscript of it is known, written in the seventh century. It was published by Joseph Bianchini in 1735 and attributed arbitrarily to the saintly Pope Leo I (440–461) (*The Catholic Encyclopedia*, 1910, Vol. IX, p. 297).

that January 28 was St. Agnes' birthday, celebrated already in the early Christian centuries because of the great honor in which the young saint was held.

THE CONVERSION OF ST. PAUL, January 25: The marvelous conversion near Damascus of Saul, the zealous young Pharisee, who was on fire with eagerness to persecute the Christians, is graphically related in three different passages of the Acts of the Apostles (Chapters 9, 22, and 26). In his epistles, too, St. Paul refers to the vision that was granted him (1 Cor. 15:8; 2 Cor. 12:2). The conversion of St. Paul was such a tremendous landmark in the history of the Church and exercised such far-reaching influence on the conversion of the Gentiles and the subsequent growth of Christianity that it is marked by a special feast. The grace of God with which He co-operated wholeheartedly, once his mind was convinced of the truth of Christ's teachings, changed this physically weak man into the magnificent apostle, the indefatigable missionary, the courageous confessor, and the unwavering martyr. Appropriately, therefore, is this a feast on which God's grace triumphs.

In our lives, also, the grace of God, always available to us in the holy sacrifice of the Mass and in the sacraments and sacramentals, requires our co-operation if we are to remain faithful to our baptismal promises and attain our eternal goal. May St. Paul with his instantaneous "Lord, what wilt thou have me to do?" (Acts 9:6) be both our example and our intercessor.

THE PURIFICATION OF THE BLESSED VIRGIN MARY, February 2: Since this feast is closely associated with

Christmas, it is considered in the section dealing with that season, on page 98.

Sᴛ. Bʟᴀɪsᴇ, February 3: The saintly bishop Blaise, who died about 317 as a martyr, was a great worker of miracles. The best known of these is the cure of the boy who was at the point of death because a fishbone had lodged in his throat. The liturgical blessing of St. Blaise originated through this miracle. It is given on this feast with two candles blessed for the occasion and a prayer for protection against diseases of the throat. The prayer reads:

> Through the intercession of the holy bishop and martyr Blaise, may God protect you from every disease of throat and from every other evil. In the name of the Father, and of the Son, and of the Holy Ghost. Amen.[22]

St. Blaise is one of the fourteen *auxiliary saints;* his help is also invoked in times of great distress of soul arising from having concealed grievous sins.

Sᴛ. Aɢᴀᴛʜᴀ, February 5: St. Agatha, whose name is the Greek word for *good,* was born of noble parentage in Sicily. During the persecution of Decius, about the year 250, she met a martyr's death with great fortitude after suffering many excruciating torments. She was highly honored in the early Church, especially because a relic of her veil had saved the city of Catania in Sicily on various occasions when it was seriously threatened by molten lava flowing from Mt. Etna. For this reason, St. Agatha is often invoked against

---

[22] For details about the candles used in this blessing, see the illustration on page 104.

the danger of fire. The breviary cites a beautiful saying of this brave virgin:

> I am the handmaid of Christ, therefore do I show myself outwardly as a servant; but this is the highest nobility, to be a servant of Christ.

Our highest nobility consists also in serving Christ our King, for "to serve God is to reign."

THE APPARITION OF OUR BLESSED LADY OF LOURDES, February 11: The Feast of the Apparition of Our Lady at Lourdes is a very recent one, for it was first prescribed for the universal Church by Pope Pius X on November 13, 1907. The occasion for introducing this feast was the apparition of the Immaculate Conception at the Grotto of Lourdes. There the Blessed Virgin appeared to a devout girl of a peasant family, Bernadette Soubirous, on February 11, 1858, just four years after the solemn pronouncement of the dogma of the Immaculate Conception. The many miracles that subsequently occurred at Lourdes, the place so marvelously favored by God's special graces, gave rise to the institution of this new feast which honors the Immaculate Conception anew, as the day's Oration clearly indicates:

> O God, who by the Immaculate Conception of the Virgin didst make ready a fitting dwelling place for Thy Son, very humbly do we who celebrate the feast of the apparition of the same Holy Virgin, put up to Thee our prayers for health both of body and soul.

God and our Blessed Mother have signally confirmed this dogma in a way, "through signs and wonders," which should convince us that the Church is constantly and infallibly guided by the Holy Spirit and should reawaken in us a loving confidence in the Immaculate Virgin Mother of God.

St. Matthias, Apostle, February 24:[28] St. Matthias does not belong to those disciples whom our Lord personally called to the apostolate. He was chosen by lot by the apostles, to take the place of the traitor Judas, when they were assembled in the upper room at Jerusalem after Christ's ascension (Acts 1:15 ff.). Through his constant fidelity to Christ and by his untiring zeal in preaching the gospel, he proved more than a worthy substitute for the misguided Judas. For over thirty years St. Matthias traveled as a missionary through Jewish and heathen lands, even into Ethiopia. He died a martyr, and his name appears in the Canon of the Mass after the Consecration.

According to Tradition, the greater part of the apostle's remains was transferred from Rome, about the year 325, to the old royal city of Trier. Here they were placed in a marble reliquary and are highly venerated even today.

Like all feasts of the apostles, this one also has a vigil.

St. Joseph, March 19: The harshness of Lent is somewhat softened by the celebration of the Feast of St. Joseph on March 19. We all know him, this beloved saint, pure spouse of the Mother of God and faithful foster father of the infant Jesus. God entrusted to his care the most sacred persons that ever lived on this earth. Both Jesus and Mary were united to Joseph with an intimate love; they obeyed him, they honored

---

[28] In leap year this feast falls on February 25.

and loved him. Not much is said about St. Joseph in the gospels, but what is said is sufficient to tell us how highly the gentle, humble carpenter of Nazareth was esteemed by God. We are told that he was "just," that he belonged to the royal house of David, that he was espoused to Mary, and that he knelt before the crib of the Christ-Child. He fled with his two precious charges into Egypt to escape the cruelty of Herod; later he returned to Nazareth with them and worked there with his own hands as a simple carpenter in order to earn the necessities of life for the Holy Family. He made a pilgrimage to Jerusalem with Mary and the twelve-year-old Jesus who, after teaching the doctors in the temple, went down to Nazareth "and was subject to them" (Luke 2:51). Tradition tells us, too, that he died in the arms of Jesus and Mary before the time of our Lord's public life.

St. Joseph is honored as the spouse of the Mother of God, as foster father of Christ and head of the Holy Family. This great saint, who had contemplated so long and so closely the humanity of the Divine Word on earth, is justly considered the patron and model of interior and contemplative souls. He is also a powerful intercessor before the throne of God. Therefore, in all our needs and cares the Church invites us to turn to St. Joseph for help. "Go to Joseph" (Gen. 41:55) was said of Joseph of Egypt with whom the liturgy compares St. Joseph.

"We beseech Thee, O Lord, that we may be assisted by the merits of the Spouse of Thy most holy mother that what of ourselves we are unable to obtain, may be given us by his intercession" (Oration of the feast).[24]

ST. BENEDICT, March 21: St. Benedict, whose name means *blessed* in Latin, is the founder of the Benedictine Order. The Rule which he wrote not only gradually superseded all previous rules for religious but also served as the basis for the rule of many

---

[24] The feasts of St. Joseph, St. Benedict, and the Annunciation often fall during Passiontide or Easter Week; in this case they are transferred to the week following Low Sunday.

During Easter time, on the third Wednesday after Easter, the Church celebrates another feast of St. Joseph, honoring him as the patron of the universal Church. For this feast see page 260.

modern orders and congregations. Hence, St. Benedict is called "the father of western monasticism."

Benedict was born about the year 480 in Nursia, a small town in southern Italy, son of a distinguished Roman family. He began to pursue his higher studies in Rome, but the scandalous lives of fellow students and the almost universal pagan spirit of immorality that prevailed led him to abandon his original purpose. Instead he fled into the solitude of Subiaco near Rome and spent almost three years in a cave in prayer and mortification with his whereabouts known only to one man, a monk of an adjacent monastery. Eventually he was discovered by shepherds, and the fame, of his sanctity spread. Other young men desired to profit by his example and instruction and became his pupils, making it necessary for Benedict to establish several houses or small monasteries. The most famous of these "schools for the Lord's service" was the Benedictine monastery of Monte Cassino, halfway between Naples and Rome; there he died on March 21 in 543 or 547.

The principal task St. Benedict gave his order was the fostering of the "Work of God," the liturgy, for he says in his holy Rule: "Nothing should be preferred to the Work of God" (Chap. 43). And the motto of the order is "That in all things God may be glorified" (Chap. 57). Truly no one ever promoted this "work of God" more zealously than did St. Benedict. The solemn service of God, the solemn High Mass, and solemn recitation of the Divine Office in choir are the principal duties of Benedictine religious. To St. Benedict the Church is indebted also for the present form of her official night prayer, Compline.

His *Rule for Monks* "has been characterized by St. Gregory the Great as 'distinguished for its discretion.' To Bossuet it appeared 'a summary of the Christian law, a learned and mysterious compendium of the doctrine of the Gospels, of the teaching of the Fathers, and of all the counsels of perfection.'"[25] It was the Benedictine Order that evangelized and Christianized the Germanic peoples of central and northern Europe. For centuries, its followers, numbered by the thousands, were the chief exponents of Christian culture in Europe. "Between the fall of the Roman empire and the rise of the culture of the Middle Ages, the Benedictines must be recognized as the saviours of the best in Greek and Roman tradition upon which the new European civilization could be erected."

St. Boniface, St. Columban, St. Gall, St. Ansgar, St. Willibrord, St. Willibald, St. Pirmin, and others, the best known missionaries of central and northern Europe, were Benedictine monks.

Even while he was still living St. Benedict performed many miracles. St. Gregory the Great, his biographer and the first of his monks to occupy the chair of St. Peter, has written about them. Many more miracles, however, took place after his death, and numerous are the extraordinary gifts and graces which God has bestowed upon the souls and bodies

---

[25] Cf. *Manual for Oblates of St. Benedict,* by Rt. Rev. Alcuin Deutsch, O.S.B., Second ed. (Collegeville, Minn.: St. John's Abbey Press, 1944).

of those who have sought his intercession or worn his medal.[26]

AVE GRATIA PLENA

THE ANNUNCIATION, March 25: The Feast of the Annunciation is one of the greatest feasts of the Blessed Virgin, intimately connected as it is with our

---

[26] Anyone interested in the efficacy of the Benedictine medal and the indulgences which can be gained by its use may obtain full information about it by writing to a Benedictine monastery, or by consulting the *Manual for Oblates of St. Benedict*, cited above.

redemption. Sent by God, the Archangel Gabriel came to Mary to announce that she was to become the mother of the Messias, the mother of the Son of God. After being informed that the Holy Spirit would work this amazing miracle in her, the pure and humble Virgin immediately expressed her willingness to co-operate with God's plan: "Behold the handmaid of the Lord; be it done to me according to thy word" (Luke 1:38).[27] With the consent of the Blessed Virgin, man's redemption began. Mary truly became the "Cause of our joy" when she became the "Mother most admirable" of the Christ-Child. Through her *fiat* Mary repaired what Eve had destroyed through her disobedience. Eve had been the mother of that curse, original sin, while Mary was decreed by God to be the mother of the Redeemer.

At the Annunciation, the Archangel Gabriel addressed our Lady for the first time with the opening lines of the Hail Mary.[28] This heavenly salutation admirably sums up all the tidings of God Himself to the most immaculate of virgins, and its sublime origin should surely prompt us to say it with truer fervor and more tender reverence.

St. Mark, the Evangelist, April 25:[29] St. Mark was the son of that Mary who appears in the Acts of the Apostles as the wife of the owner of the room in which Christ celebrated the last supper with His

---

[27] This first act in the mystery of the Incarnation is commemorated daily in the *Angelus*.

[28] Even the angel's tidings have been taken to indicate that Mary was destined to be the reverse of Eve, for the letters of the word EVA (the Latin for *Eve*) were reversed to form the word AVE.

[29] For the Major Rogation Day, celebrated on April 25 since the time of Gregory the Great, see page 157 ff.

apostles. Together with his cousin, St. Barnabas (Feast day: June 11), Mark was at first a co-worker of St. Paul whom he accompanied on his first great missionary journey and to whom he proved a great help during Paul's imprisonment in Rome from 61–63. After leaving Paul, Mark attended St. Peter as his disciple, companion, and interpreter. The gospel which he wrote in Greek about the year 58 at Rome was chiefly directed to the Romans and to those who had been recently converted from paganism. It is based primarily on the teachings of St. Peter, who influenced Mark greatly in its writing, and may have even supervised the entire piece of work.

Tradition tells us that St. Mark was the first bishop of Alexandria and that he died a martyr about 68. His relics were later transferred to Venice to the famous church which bears his name, where they are still highly venerated.[30]

THE SOLEMNITY OF ST. JOSEPH, third Wednesday after Easter: As he led and protected the Divine Child in Nazareth and provided for the Holy Family, so in heaven, as its powerful friend and protector, St. Joseph now guides the Church of Christ. In 1870 Pope Pius IX solemnly declared St. Joseph the patron of the universal Church,[31] and established this feast with an octave to honor him in that capacity.

On this solemn Wednesday (all Wednesdays are dedicated to St. Joseph), let us ask St. Joseph to be

---

[30] St. Mark's symbol, the lion, is explained on page 210.

[31] The Introit, Collect, Alleluia, and Offertory of this feast day's Mass refer to his guardianship of the Church (*ship*) whose head is Christ (the *Chi-rho* symbol as mast).

at all times to the entire Church, the pope, the bishops, the priests, and all the faithful, "helper and protector" (Introit), friend and guide, in life and death.

St. Philip and St. James, May 1: May begins with the feast of two apostles. Of these, Philip, like Peter and Andrew, was a native of Bethsaida and a fisherman on the sea of Galilee. He was one of the first disciples of Jesus. In his gospel (1:43 ff.) St. John

vividly describes Philip's call, his ready response, and
his invitation, in turn, to young Nathaniel whom
Christ hailed as the "true Israelite in whom there is
no guile" (*Ibid.*, 1:47). In several other places, as at
the miraculous multiplication of loaves (John 6:5 ff.),
Sacred Scripture speaks about Philip. For the rest
we have to depend on tradition which tells us that
the holy apostle preached the Gospel in Palestine and
in Asia Minor, and was persecuted by both Jews
and pagans. Because Philip refused to sacrifice to the
idols, he was scourged and then crucified like Peter,
with his head downward.

James, like his brother, Jude Thaddeus, was a
cousin of our Lord, since their father Alpheus (or
Cleophas) was married to Mary of Cleophas,[32] a close
relative of the Blessed Virgin. For that reason, according to Jewish custom, he was sometimes called
"the brother of the Lord." To distinguish this apostle
from St. James the Greater, whose feast occurs on
July 25, he is usually designated St. James the Less.
Among his fellow apostles and even among the Jews,
James was highly esteemed because of his justice and
sanctity, his courageous and mortified life. After the
Ascension of our Lord he was chosen to be the first
bishop of Jerusalem. In the council of the apostles
(Acts 15:13 ff.) he had a decisive vote. In the year 62,
after thirty years of fruitful activity as bishop of
Jerusalem and at the advanced age of ninety-six,
James was cruelly martyred. Urged on by hateful

---

[32] Mary of Cleophas, one of the holy women in the Gospel, was
present on the way of the cross, at the foot of the cross, at the
burial of our Lord, and on Easter Sunday.

Pharisees, the Jews threw him down from the terrace of the Temple into the valley, stoned him as he lay dying and praying for his enemies, and finally crushed his head with a club.

In Sacred Scripture there is a short *letter* written by James the Less a few years before his death. It is addressed to the Christian Jews, fearlessly rebuking them for existing abuses such as heresies, inconstancy in faith and love, calumnies, and impatience in suffering and want. He arouses them to practical Christian living and urgently requests that the sick and dying receive the sacrament of Extreme Unction:

> Is any man sick among you? Let him bring in the priests of the church, and let them pray over him, anointing him with oil in the name of the Lord. And the prayer of faith shall save he sick man, and the Lord shall raise him up; and if he be in sins, they shall be forgiven him (James 5:14-15).

In our day much could be gained if we would but follow the urgings of this pastoral letter of the apostle which counsels an increase of the exterior and interior life of faith for the apostolate of real Catholic Action.

THE FINDING OF THE HOLY CROSS, May 3: The purpose of this feast is to commemorate the finding of the holy cross on which Christ completed the work of our redemption. With the fall of Jerusalem to the Romans in the year 70, the sacred places were destroyed to a great extent and the ruins covered with earth and debris. Hadrian, the pagan emperor, tried his utmost to make the holy places unrecognizable, profaning even the hill of Calvary with the erection of a statue of Jupiter and a temple to the goddess

Venus. Such wanton destruction brought about the
loss of the holy cross and other relics of the Passion
which were not recovered until some three centuries
later.

In the lessons of the breviary for this feast, the story
of the finding is briefly told: In 312, the emperor
Constantine, through the power of the cross which
he saw in the heavens before the battle, won a decisive
triumph over his enemy, Maxentius. The saintly
empress Helena, mother of Constantine, was urged
shortly afterward in a dream to search for the true
cross of Christ. With the aid of her son, sometime
between the years 320 and 345, she had the pagan
temple on Calvary razed to the ground and the rub-
bish cleared away. After long and diligent search,
three crosses were discovered, deep in the earth, with
the nails and the inscription which had once been
fastened to the true cross.

The problem then was to distinguish the cross of
Christ from the two others found with it. An ancient
legend relates that all three crosses were touched to
a woman who was seriously ill, and that when she

came in contact with the third cross she was instantly cured. Through this same cross a dead person was brought back to life, by a miracle which dispelled all doubts as to the identity of the sacred tree. The veneration of the true cross can be dated from this time.

One part of the cross was deposited in Rome in the church which was thereafter called "Holy Cross in Jerusalem"; another was sent by St. Helena to her son in Constantinople. The larger remaining portion was encased in silver and sent to Jerusalem to be kept there. Constantine then had a beautiful church erected over the holy sepulcher in which this relic of the true cross was preserved. Later, when the veneration of relics became a more genera practice, particles of the true cross were distributed throughout the entire world and exposed for veneration.

The Feast of the Finding of the Holy Cross is very ancient. Of all relics, the cross on which the Saviour redeemed us deserves the highest veneration. Now during the Easter season the cross is no longer recognized chiefly as the wood of martyrdom, but rather as a sign of victory. The cross and the resurrection, Good Friday and Easter, the grave and eternal life are all interrelated. This fact is brought home through the celebration of this feast during the Easter season, and through *the prayer of the Holy Cross,* recited daily at Vespers and Lauds for this time, except on days when a major feast occurs.

Let us all venerate the cross of Christ as a sign of our redemption and our triumph. Let us salute it whenever we meet it, in churches and chapels, on the streets and in the fields. *Ave crux, spes unica!* Hail holy cross, sole hope of our release!

ST. BARNABAS, June 11: Barnabas, whose surname means "son of consolation," is one of the seventy-two disciples of our Lord. His original name was Joseph. Born on the island of Cyprus of the tribe of Levi (cf. Acts 4:36), he was one of the first and most faithful Christians of the first parish of Jerusalem. Later he also became the friend and trustworthy companion of the new convert, St. Paul. Recognizing his capabilities, the great Apostle of the Gentiles took Barnabas with him to Antioch to help organize the flourishing Christian parish there. In that city both received consecration as bishops at the hands of the apostles. During the years 45–48, Barnabas and Paul made a long missionary journey together to Asia Minor (Acts 13–14); in the year 50, they attended the council of the apostles at Jerusalem (Acts 15). With the evangelist Mark as his companion, Barnabas then continued his travels to spread the Gospel of Christ to the whole world and went to his home on the island of Cyprus. Around the year 70, according to tradition, he was stoned to death outside Salamis by his own people. Barnabas gave his life for the faith which he labored so zealously to spread. As early as the first century he was honored with the name "apostle," although he was not one of the twelve whom our Lord had chosen for this office. His name was also used in the first centuries in the Canon of the Mass in the commemoration of the saints which follows the Consecration.

St. Aloysius Gonzaga, June 21: Aloysius was the son of a rich margrave, born March 9, 1568, at the beautiful castle of Castiglione near Mantua in upper Italy. A great future was predicted for this gifted, manly, and energetic lad. Sparing nothing to prepare him for a brilliant career in the world, his father had him educated at the court of the princes in Florence, Mantua, and Madrid, where his exceptional talents were quickly recognized. But Aloysius centered his thoughts on higher things than a worldly career. All the world had to offer — love, pleasure, fortune, honor — all these the high-minded boy despised. He chose instead a life of self-denial and poverty, of obedience and seclusion, a life of purity and humility, filled with sacrifices for God and his fellow men. He had no desire to serve the world; rather, he pledged himself to serve Christ the King and the least of his brethren, the poor and the sick. He himself said that he left the world to enter the Jesuit Order not because he did not love his parents or his home, but because he loved God more. With admirable effort and perseverance he fought against his inherited characteristics, especially pride and self-will, and against the lure of freedom and independence. By strict control of his inclinations and emotions he preserved his first innocence so faithfully amid the dangers and corruptions of his environment, that he seemed confirmed in grace. He co-operated with divine grace by long hours spent in prayer and by the frequent reception of the sacraments, and thus, despite his youth, attained great sanctity and became the model and patron of the young. Aloysius died at the early age of twenty-three, while voluntarily caring for the sick during a time of pestilence.

Let us imitate him in persevering and devout prayer, in fervent devotion to Mary, and in a firmly rooted love for our Saviour. Then shall we also remain pure in the midst of impurity, kind in the midst of unkindness, truthful in the midst of lies, loyally brave in the face of cowardice.

A powerful means of advancing in holiness and of securing the unceasing protection of St. Aloysius is the observance of the *six Aloysian Sundays,* a practice strongly recommended by the popes and endowed with many indulgences.[33] By this means many have been strengthened in virtue or preserved from sin; others during these weeks of grace have received their vocation to the priesthood or to the religious life.

St. John the Baptist — *His Nativity,* June 24; *His Beheading,* August 29: After the Blessed Mother, perhaps the greatest of the saints is John the Baptist. He was the precursor of the Redeemer, of whom it was said in the Old Testament, "Behold I send my angel before thy face, who shall prepare the way before thee" (Mark 1:2).

Announcing his birth, the Archangel Gabriel said,

---

[33] The faithful who, on any of the six Sundays immediately preceding the Feast of St. Aloysius Gonzaga, or on any of six consecutive Sundays that they may choose during the year, spend some time in devout meditation or prayers, or who perform some other exercises of devotion in honor of the same Saint, are granted a plenary indulgence on the usual conditions (S. C. Ind., Dec. 11, 1739 and Jan. 7, 1740). *The Raccolta,* the Rev. Joseph P. Christopher, Ph.D., and the Rev. Charles E. Spence, M.A. (New York, N. Y.: Benziger Brothers, 1943).

". . . and many shall rejoice in his nativity. For he shall be great before the Lord . . . and shall be filled with the Holy Ghost . . . and he shall convert many of the children of Israel to the Lord their God.

And he shall go before him (the Saviour) in the spirit and power of Elias . . . to prepare unto the Lord a perfect people" (Luke 1:14 ff.). At John's birth, his father Zachary was inspired by the Holy Spirit to exclaim, "And thou, child, shalt be called the prophet of the Highest, for thou shalt go before the face of the Lord to prepare his ways . . ." (Luke 1:76). Finally, Christ Himself said of John, "Amen, I say to you, there hath not risen among them that are born of women a greater than John the Baptist" (Matt. 11:11).

Influenced by these passages in Sacred Scripture, the

ST. JOHN BAPTIST

liturgy distinguishes and honors St. John the Baptist
in a special way. Only for Christ Himself, for Mary,
His Mother, and for St. John the Baptist does the
Church celebrate the day of birth, on December 25,
September 8, and June 24, respectively.[34] In the case

[34] See page 290, Feast of the Nativity of the Blessed Virgin
Mary.

of all the other saints, she celebrates only the day of their death as their birthday into heaven.[35]

The Feast of the Nativity of St. John the Baptist, June 24, is a first-class feast with a vigil and an octave. It is sometimes referred to as the "Summer Christmas," and occurs at the time of the summer solstice. The ancient pagans took occasion, by lighting bonfires during the solstices, to honor the sun as the source of light. These rites were Christianized by the Church who considers them a symbol of St. John who was "a burning and shining lamb" (cf. John 5:35).

A separate feast on August 29 commemorates the saint's death. John died a martyr's death, beheaded at the order of the cruel Herod, to please the revengeful Herodias, the tyrant's unlawful wife (Matt. 14:1 ff.; Mark 6:14 ff.).

ST. PETER AND ST. PAUL, June 29: The events commemorated on this great day are clearly expressed in the words of the breviary,

> This day Simon Peter ascended the agonizing cross, Alleluia. This day the keeper of the keys of heaven went on his way to Christ with joy. This day the Apostle Paul, the light of the world, laying down his life for the name of Christ, was crowned with martyrdom. Alleluia." (*Magnificat* Antiphon for Second Vespers).

This is the first and highest feast of an apostle, and has, therefore, both a vigil and an octave. It is one of the oldest feasts in the Church, being recorded as early as 336. As it was customary in the early Chris-

---

[35] St. Agnes seems to be an exception to this rule, for the second feast in her honor, on January 28, is originally the ancient celebration of her birthday. See page 249.

tian centuries to celebrate the anniversary of the death
of a martyr at his grave, there were at first two solemn
services on June 29, one over the tomb of St. Peter in
the present church of St. Peter in Rome, the other
over the tomb of St. Paul in the splendid church outside the walls of Rome. Later, on account of the great
distance which separates the two churches, the festival
was lengthened to two days, with St. Peter receiving
special honors on June 29, and St. Paul on June 30.

Before his vocation to the apostleship, *St. Peter* was
known as Simon. He was a simple fisherman, like his
brother Andrew, on the shores of the Sea of Galilee.
From the beginning of his apostleship, however, he
was distinguished among the apostles. Together with
James and John, he was permitted to witness extraordinary events in the life of our Lord, such as the
Transfiguration on Mount Tabor and the agony in
the Garden of Olives. More than once his stormy, all
too self-reliant nature led to inconsiderate words and
rash deeds, the worst of which was his triple denial
of Christ in the court of the high priest. But his re-
pentance was sincere and humble, and never, after
that, did he allow anyone to outstrip him in fidelity
to his Divine Master. He became the firm "man of
rock" on whom Christ conferred the office of supreme
teacher, priest, and pastor when, after the Resurrection, He appeared to the disciples at the Sea of
Tiberias (John 21:15-17). In this capacity, St. Peter
governed the Church after the first Pentecost. He
undertook various missionary journeys, on one of
which he came to Rome, founded a Christian community, and became its first bishop. In the year 67 he

died a martyr's death on the cross, having his head downward at his own request. In the place where Peter shed his blood rises the mighty cupola of the largest and most impressive dome in Christendom today. It is the church of St. Peter in Rome.

Let us bestow generous and faithful love upon this church, upon our holy Catholic faith, and upon the servant of God, our Holy Father the Pope, successor of St. Peter.

St. Paul, by birth a Jew and a Roman citizen, was named Saul before his miraculous conversion. He was a strong Pharisee, educated first in his father's house at Tarsus, and later at Jerusalem, where he sat at the feet of the learned doctor of the law, Gamaliel. His original profession was that of tentmaking. As a convinced and zealous Pharisee with a very emotional character, he hated and persecuted Christianity with all the energy of a religious fanatic. He took part in the stoning of the first martyr, St. Stephen, and was also active in the fierce persecution of the Christians that followed Stephen's death. But by the grace of God, he was literally struck down while on a journey to Damascus,[36] and the former persecutor became a fiery, enthusiastic apostle, utterly fearless of persecution and death itself. His tireless labors brought marvelous fruit for the kingdom of God During the years 44–58, this indefatigable apostle undertook three long missionary journeys, full of privations and dangers and covering virtually the entire known world. In the year 67 Paul was beheaded at Rome.

His fourteen letters, addressed to various Christian

---

[36] See the Feast of the Conversion of St. Paul, page 250.

communities and to individual disciples, are still today a testimony to his great learning, his untiring and intelligent zeal for souls, and his constant self-sacrifice. The Church has used his Epistles extensively as a powerful instrument in her apostolate.

THE MOST PRECIOUS BLOOD OF OUR LORD JESUS CHRIST, July 1: It is through the blood of Christ that we were redeemed. So the heavenly Father wished it; so the only-begotten Son of God accomplished it. The

Circumcision, the agony in the garden, the scourging, the crowning with thorns, the way of the cross, the piercing of the most Sacred Heart: these are all specific instances when the Precious Blood flowed as the price of our redemption. The altar of our churches is the place where it still flows; it is a laver unto the sanctification and salvation of the souls of men.

The feasts of Good Friday, of Corpus Christi, of the Precious Blood, and two feasts of the Holy Cross, all together, did not yet furnish the Church and her faithful opportunity enough to celebrate the value of the Blood of our Redeemer. Nor were they sufficient thanks to the Triune God for the redemption accomplished through this Precious Blood. Consequently, popular devotion has dedicated the whole month of July to the praise of the Blood of Christ. The first day of the month, the Feast of the Most Precious Blood, is the fit introduction for these sentiments of praise and thanksgiving.

> Thou hast redeemed us, O Lord, in Thy blood, out of every tribe, and tongue, and people and nation, and hast made us to our God a kingdom (Introit).
>
> O almighty and everlasting God, who hast sent us Thine only-begotten Son to be the Redeemer of the world, and hast willed to be appeased by His Blood: grant unto us, we beseech Thee, in such wise, with solemn worship to reverence the price of our salvation, and in its might to find our defense against the evils of this life, that we may attain in heaven to the everlasting happiness it has brought for us (Oration).

The liturgy now sets up types of the Redeemer and His Blood for our contemplation. Abel, the paschal lamb of the Jews, and other bloody sacrifices of the Old Testament are such types. The feast itself was instituted as late as 1849 by Pope Pius IX as an expression of gratitude to God for saving the Church from a calamity.[37]

FOUNTAIN OF LIFE

THE VISITATION OF THE BLESSED VIRGIN MARY, July 2: The visit which the Blessed Virgin paid her cousin Elizabeth is one of the most charming events in the life of our Blessed Mother. The Archangel Gabriel, when he announced to Mary that she was chosen by the Eternal Father to be the mother of the Redeemer, told her that her cousin Elizabeth was also expecting the arrival of a child blessed by heaven. Faithful concern for relatives, deep humility and modesty, true charity, sympathy with and joy in Elizabeth's happiness, and not least of all, her own joy at being chosen to become the Mother of God: all these motives in-

[37] This was the revolution which drove the Holy Father from Rome. In 1849 the French army conquered the revolutionaries and the Pope returned from Gaeta. Pope Pius XI made the feast a double of the first class in 1934.

duced Mary to make the long and weary journey from Nazareth to the hill country near Jerusalem where Zachary and Elizabeth lived. The first act of Mary, after she had conceived of the Holy Spirit, was a mission of charity and benediction into the world, a pilgrimage of service to Elizabeth and John. To bless and sanctify the world and sinners is Mary's

BLESSED AMONG BLESSED FRUIT OF — ART THOU WOMEN IS THE THY WOMB

vocation as Mother of God and as co-redeemer and mediatrix of all graces. She fulfills this calling for the first time in the house of Elizabeth and Zachary. As Christ-bearer and Christ-giver she arrives at their house. Her intention is to fulfill the duties of a maid servant — to work, to help, to serve, to make others happy, and to be immensely joyful in doing so.

Enlightened by the Holy Spirit, Elizabeth greets Mary with "Blessed art thou amongst women, and blessed is the fruit of thy womb!" Thus she continued the greeting of the angel, and ever since, Catholics of the whole world continue to pray: "Hail, Mary, full of grace; the Lord is with thee; blessed art thou among women, and blessed is the fruit of thy womb,

Jesus." Elizabeth is the first one, after the Archangel Gabriel, to pay homage to God's Blessed Mother. She indicates the reason for honoring Mary — her dignity as mother of God, as mediatrix of all graces, and the most blessed among women.

But the humble handmaid of the Lord renders all this glory to the goodness and mercy of almighty God. She attributes all her blessedness to Him and His dispensation, to His infinite holiness and condescension. To Him she likewise attributes the creation, redemption, and sanctification of the whole world. She praises and glorifies and thanks Him in the wonderful canticle of the *Magnificat:* "My soul magnifies the Lord, and my spirit rejoices in God my Saviour . . ." (Luke 1:46-47).

This touching song, which praises the Incarnation and extols the goodness and greatness of God, was prayed and sung by Mary under the inspiration of the Holy Spirit. Now it has a prominent place in the liturgy of the Church. It forms the climax of daily Vespers as an expression of thanksgiving to God for redemption and as a hymn of praise to Mary.

Let us pray with deep and fervent devotion both the *Magnificat,* canticle of love to Mary, and the *Ave Maria,* the angelic salutation, favorite prayer of the children of Mary. Let ours be the same spirit of devotion, humble love, sincere gratitude, and complete self-immolation to God as was that with which Mary and Elizabeth prayed. Each time we receive Holy Communion, let us say in the spirit of Elizabeth: "How have I deserved that my Lord and God should come to me?" And with Mary, let us humbly confess that "he that is mighty hath done great things to me, and holy is his name" (Luke 1:49).

The entire *Magnificat* can be used appropriately as an act of thanksgiving after Holy Communion. And it should be our constant intention to venerate Mary faithfully and heartily as the Mother of God, the mediatrix of graces, as the Christ-bearer and Christ-giver, as the humble handmaid of the Lord, and as the one "blessed amongst women." Then we will belong to those happy chosen ones of whom Mary herself prophesied in the *Magnificat:* ". . . behold, from henceforth all generations shall call me blessed" (Luke 1:48).

St. MARY MAGDALEN, July 22, and St. MARTHA, July 29: According to an old Christian tradition, both Mary Magdalen and Martha were sisters of Lazarus of Bethany. This distinguished family frequently received our Lord as a beloved friend and guest. For the sake of the two sisters our Lord worked a great miracle, calling Lazarus back to life when he was already in the grave four days.

Mary Magdalen, called "the penitent" in the liturgy, fell into evil ways in her youth; but, moved by the personality and preaching of our Lord, she underwent a complete conversion, did public penance, and became a faithful follower of Christ. With His mother and a few other devoted women, she followed Him on the way of the cross and stood beneath it during His last agony. According to the gospel account she was the first to witness His resurrection on Easter morning, and was the messenger who announced the good tidings to the apostles. She is therefore called *apostola apostolorum,* the Apostle of the Apostles. On her feast the *Credo* is said, as in Masses of the apostles and of the Blessed Virgin.

Martha, Magdalen's sister, is remembered as the anxious and overzealous hostess of Christ at Bethany, who once pointed out to her that Mary, in sitting at His feet and providing nourishment for her soul, had chosen the better part. "Active life with all its labors and fatigues endured for the sake of Christ whom we serve in our neighbor, is very meritorious; contemplative life, however, which puts souls in direct contact with Christ, assures their personal sanctification more fully and obtains more efficaciously the graces by which a Christian apostleship becomes fruitful. Let us esteem at its just value the position that Jesus reserves to Mary, and if He calls us to share in Martha's solicitude, let us endeavor, like the saints, to make up by the spirit of prayer for what is wanting in the active life."[38]

St. Anne, July 26, and St. Joachim, August 16: St. Anne and St. Joachim were the parents of the Blessed Virgin Mary. It is not difficult to see why the Church celebrates the feast of this "most blessed couple," for as parents of Jesus' mother, they were by nature grandparents of the Christ-Child. Nothing is said about either of them in Sacred Scripture, but tradition tells us that they lived devout lives, were generous to the poor and the sick, and brought Mary up in the fear and love of God. At an early age they consecrated her to the service of God and sent her to the

---

[38] *St. Andrew's Missal,* Second Edition, 1927, p. 1533.

temple school to be educated in wisdom, piety, and virtue.

In some rites, the Benedictine, for example, the feasts of St. Joachim and St. Anne are celebrated on the same day, July 26, but in the Roman rite the Feast of St. Anne is observed on July 26 and that of St. Joachim on August 16.

Good Christian parents honor St. Joachim and St. Anne devoutly, and pray to them in behalf of their own children that they may be preserved in goodness, uprightness, and purity like Mary, the blessed daughter of these happy parents.

ST. PETER's CHAINS, August 1: The Feast of St. Peter's Chains commemorates the imprisonment and miraculous liberation of St. Peter, prince of the apostles. It also reminds us of the dedication of the Church of St. Peter's Chains in Rome in the fifth century. In this church are kept, according to tradition, the chains with which St. Peter was bound after he had been condemned, and from which he was miraculously set free by an angel. The event is strikingly described at length in the Acts of the Apostles (12:1–19).

On the same day the Church honors the courageous *Machabees,* both the brothers and their heroic mother, who all died a martyr's death under Antiochus Epiphanes (2 Mach. 7:1–4). Their relics are preserved in the Church of St. Peter's Chains in Rome. The feast is very old and liturgically significant in that it is one of the very few to honor Old Testament saints.

OUR LADY OF THE SNOW, August 5: In the missal

this feast is called, "The Dedication of the Church of Our Lady of the Snow." Further light on this feast, which commemorates the dedication of the largest and most important church of the Blessed Virgin in Rome (St. Mary Major), can be found in the section on the Dedication of a Church, page 315 ff.

THE TRANSFIGURATION OF OUR LORD JESUS CHRIST, August 6: Already in the fifth century, the Feast of the Transfiguration of Our Lord was regarded by the eastern Church as a feast in honor of the kingship of Christ. Sacred Scripture vividly describes God's glorification of His Son on Mount Thabor; the first three evangelists tell the story in detail (Matt. 17:1-8; Mark 9:1-7; Luke 1:28-36), and St. Peter refers to it in his second letter (1:16). Peter himself, and James and John "had been eye witnesses of His grandeur."

The feast was instituted for the western Church by Pope Calixtus III in the year 1457, after the brilliant victory of St. John Capistran (March 28) over the Turks near Belgrade, a victory which assured the triumph of the cross over the crescent.

Today we should dwell, not only on the wonderful event which happened on Mt. Thabor two thousand years ago, but also on a fact with which we are seldom impressed: we ourselves are destined one day to be transfigured in heaven. This transfiguration, however, will only come about if during our life we keep our bodies and souls pure and holy, and if, through loyalty to God and His commandments and frequent and worthy reception of Holy Communion which is the sacrament of glorification, we make ourselves more pleasing to God.

ST. LAWRENCE, August 10: The youthful, saintly deacon Lawrence, who acted so courageously during the persecution of the Christians under the emperor Valerian (253–260), was already highly venerated in the early Church. Second only to that of the princes of the apostles, St. Peter and St. Paul, his feast was celebrated with great solemnity

While his teacher and friend, the holy martyr-pope Sixtus II (August 6), was being led to death, Lawrence was disconsolate because he could not die with him. But as Sixtus had predicted, his wish was soon to be fulfilled. The pagan prefect of Rome asked Lawrence to deliver to him the treasures of the Church, but the young deacon brought the poor and the sick who were in his care, saying, "These are the real treasures of the Church by the inestimable gift of their faith, and because they convert our alms into imperishable treasures for us." Thrown into prison, the saint worked many miracles and induced some of the Roman soldiers to become Christians. He was scourged; his entire body was burned with red-hot plates. Finally, he was laid on an iron bed, having the shape of a gridiron, beneath which were placed hot coals to prolong his painful torture. His heroism throughout his excruciating sufferings is evidenced by the fact that Lawrence jested with his executioners, saying, "Now I am roasted on that side; you may turn me over." What a bright flame of divine love must have burned in his youthful heart! He died in 258, and his name is mentioned in the Canon of the Mass among the Roman martyrs.

Soon after Lawrence's death one of the most venerable and most frequented churches of Rome was built over his tomb. With St. John Lateran, St. Peter's, St. Mary Major, and St. Paul's Without-the-Walls, the basilica of St. Lawrence Without-the-Walls is one of the five major basilicas in Rome.

May the young hero-saint obtain for all of us a generous, self-sacrificing love of Christ and the courage to confess our faith at all times and under all circumstances.

THE ASSUMPTION OF THE BLESSED VIRGIN MARY, August 15: "Let us all rejoice in the Lord, whilst celebrating this festival day in honor of the Blessed Virgin Mary: in whose Assumption the angels rejoice and give praise to the Son of God" (Introit).

The Assumption of the Blessed Virgin is indeed an ancient and solemn feast of Mary. It dates from the sixth century in the West, and was observed still earlier in the East. It has a vigil and an octave. On this day of our Lady, the Church unites several solemnities into one:

1. *The day of the death of the Mother of God as the great harvest festival in her life.* Heaven is the glorious reward of Mary's faithful service as "the handmaid of the Lord." Mary's death was not the consequence of original sin, for she had been preserved from it. Rather, the mother of Christ died because of an unbearable longing to be reunited to her Divine Son.

2. *The glorious Assumption of Mary's body and soul into heaven.* It is a common and sacred belief in the Church since ancient times that together with her soul, the body of the Immaculate Virgin, which

had given human nature to the Son of God, was also lifted up to a glorified life in heaven. The liturgy pictures this entrance into heaven as a true march of triumph.

3. *The crowning of Mary as Queen of Heaven and of All the Saints.* The humble "handmaid of the Lord," the Mother of Sorrows, obtained the most precious crown of heaven; she ascended to a throne of honor beside the Blessed Trinity.

The time and place of Mary's death are unknown. It is probable that she died in Jerusalem after living with St. John at Ephesus for a long time. A legend tells how the apostles found fragrant flowers, instead of Mary's body, in the tomb. With this legend is connected the annual *blessing of herbs and flowers* which in many places occurs on August 15. The Epistle, too, compares Mary to beautiful trees and flowers and fragrant herbs. But it may be that with this blessing, as she did so frequently, the Church was merely Christianizing a pagan custom, that of gathering herbs for medicine at this time of the year. The prayer used in the blessing of flowers and herbs contains petitions for the welfare of both body and soul and for protection against all harmful influences; it also thanks God for the harvest that has just been gathered. For us, though, Mary's ruling in heaven as Queen of All Saints will always be the most glorious fruit of the redemption, and she the most noble servant of the Church.

If we follow the sublime example of virtue which Mary gave throughout her life, we shall also one day be privileged to celebrate a joyful assumption into heaven. Let us remain true to our heavenly Queen, for faithful children of Mary will not be lost eternally.

THE IMMACULATE HEART OF MARY, August 22: Earliest traces of liturgical devotion to the heart of the Blessed Virgin can be found among the Church Fathers in what they teach us concerning the spouse in the Canticle of Canticles. Many saints, both men and women, especially in the Middle Ages and the centuries which followed, have helped much to foster this liturgical cult. Already in the beginning of the nineteenth century, Pope Pius VII instituted the *Feast of the Most Pure Heart of Mary*. Approval for its celebration, which was fixed for the Sunday after the Octave of the Assumption, was not yet extended to the Universal Church but limited to those dioceses and religious institutions that had asked the necessary permission. About the middle of the same century, however, the feast had attained to such universal popularity and acclaim that Pope Pius IX endowed it with an appropriate Divine Office and Mass of its own.

The *lily blossom* and the *buds* in the illustration above form the letter *M*, the initial for the name of the most pure Virgin Mary. It springs from the root of Jesse (Isa. 11:10), indicating Mary's ancestry. The *roses* in the heart of the lily symbolize the love of God with which our Lady's heart was filled. The *triangle,* symbol of the Triune God, constitutes an essentia part of the design. It both supports and is supported by the lily, indicating thereby, that through the divine power Mary became the Christ-bearer, the Mother of God.

Devotion to the Immaculate Heart of Mary continued to spread. Under the gracious impetus and inspiration of the maternal heart of Mary, extraordinary and singular sanctity blossomed forth in many

souls, a more ardent love for God and His divine
Son flourished with renewed life, and a more generous and sincere reverence began to influence and
even characterize the relations between men,
redeemed as they are through the shedding of the
Precious Blood. Zeal inflaming the hearts of pastors
and the faithful nurtured the desire that a feast
in honor of the heart of Mary be extended to the
Universal Church.

Although the Church and the whole human race
had already been dedicated by Pope Leo XIII to
the Most Sacred Heart of Jesus, Pope Pius XII, in
1942, at the conclusion of the jubilee celebration
honoring the apparition of the Blessed Virgin at
Fatima, Portugal, and on December 8 of the same
year, deemed it opportune to consecrate them also
to the Immaculate Heart of Mary with great
solemnity.

This was a call for humanity, in a world stunned
and prostrate before the impact of international
carnage and destruction, to enlist the intercession of
the Queen of Peace, so that, through her, peace might
again return to the war-weary nations, liberty might
again be enjoyed by the Church of Christ, sinners
might abandon their evil ways, and all the faithful
might unite in a common love, an esteem and
reverence for purity, and the cultivation of virtuous
lives.

In order that the memory of this consecration
might be observed annually by the universal Church,
Pope Pius XII instituted the *Feast of the Immaculate
Heart of Mary* as a double of the second class with

an appropriate Divine Office and Mass and fixed the date for its celebration on the octave day of the Feast of the Assumption. Let us join the Church as she prays in the Oration of this feast: "Almighty and everlasting God, who in the heart of the blessed Virgin Mary didst prepare a dwelling worthy of the Holy Ghost; grant in Thy mercy, that we who with devout minds celebrate the festiva of that Immaculate Heart, may be able to live according to Thine own heart."

ST. BARTHOLOMEW, THE APOSTLE, August 24: The apostle Bartholomew, also called Nathanael, was one of the first disciples chosen by our Lord. Even at that time, Christ recognized his innocence and spoke of him as "a true Israelite, in whom there is no guile" (John 1:47). What glorious testimony! What a tribute to his straightforward, honest character!

Shortly after the first Pentecost and the council of Jerusalem, Bartholomew went on a missionary journey into India and Mesopotamia. Later he preached the Gospel in Armenia, converting the king and many other pagans. The pagan priests, however, and the king's brother fiercely persecuted his courageous messenger of the faith. They seized him, fastened him to a post, flayed him alive, and finally beheaded him. He died, a martyr, about the year 71. His body is venerated at Rome in the Church of St. Bartholomew which is built on an island in the Tiber.

Like all feasts of apostles, this one has a vigil. The Mass for the vigil of an apostle takes precedence over all the others in the "Common of the Saints," for it is very ancient and commemorates the apostles as friends of Christ and princes of the Church. It draws our attention to their dignity, and to the duties which led them ultimately to suffer martyrdom for Christ.

The Beheading of St. John the Baptist, August 29: See page 270.

THE NATIVITY OF THE BLESSED VIRGIN MARY, September 8, and THE MOST HOLY NAME OF MARY, September 12: These feasts of Mary are closely related, but, liturgically, Mary's birthday is of greater importance. Both are beautiful feasts for every Catholic family, but especially for the thousands of loyal children of Mary, who celebrate with unusual joy the birthday and the name day of their beloved and faithful Mother. Usually, only the day of a saint's death is celebrated, as the day of completion, the day of recompense, the day of birth into eternal bliss. Excepting our Blessed Lord Himself, only the Blessed Mother and St. John the Baptist have feasts in memory of their birthdays.

Chosen by God from all eternity to be the Mother of the Messias, Mary was conceived without the stain of original sin.[39] From the very first moment of its existence, her soul shone with an incomparable beauty. The liturgy often compares Mary to the aurora which precedes the rising sun. On her birthday the dawn of redemption appeared. For this reason the Church exults in the Mass, "Hail, Holy Mother, who in thy child-bearing didst bring forth the King who rules heaven and earth, world without end." The breviary tells us, too, "Thy nativity, O Virgin Mother of God,

---

[39] St. John the Baptist also was born into this world free from original sin. He was purified before his birth, when Mary came to visit Elizabeth, his mother. See page 276 ff.

was the herald of joy to the whole world, because from thee arose the Sun of Justice, Christ our God, who destroyed the curse, bestowed the blessing, confounded death, and gave eternal life" (*Magnificat* Antiphon).

THE HOLY NAME OF MARY, which means *Lady,* has always been honored, loved, and esteemed. It is pronounced with reverence by Christians, especially by children of Mary. Since the first centuries of the Christian era, it has been considered a privilege to receive the name of Mary at Baptism. To be her child is an honor, but it also entails the obligation of leading a good, Christian life.

The Feast of the Holy Name of Mary received unusual distinction on account of the glorious victory of the Christian armies under John Sobieski, king of Poland, over the Turks on September 12, 1683. By this victory, which the Mother of God had gained for them, the siege of Vienna ended and central Europe was saved. In thanksgiving, Pope Innocent XI extended this feast to the universal Church. It had been celebrated as early as 1513 in Spain.

Let us keep both these feasts of Mary, according to the mind of the Church, by thanking God for such a holy and powerful mother. A family rejoices and feasts on a mother's birthday and honors her on Mother's Day. So does the universal Church unite in paying joyful homage to its Mother Mary on her birthday and her name day.

Theologians say that faithful children of Mary will never be lost. Let us pray with the great St. Bernard, "Remember, O most gracious Virgin Mary, that never was it known that anyone who fled to thy protection, implored thy help, and sought thy intercession, was left unaided. . . ."

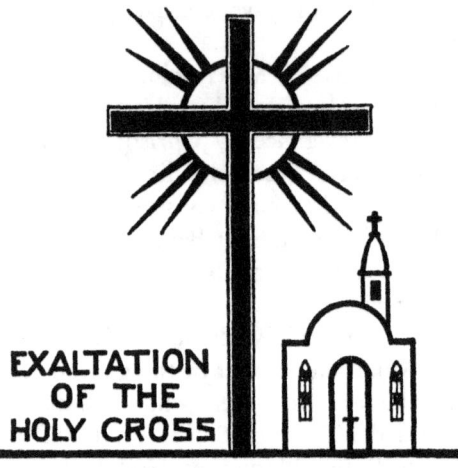

EXALTATION
OF THE
HOLY CROSS

This illustration shows the Holy Cross as the glorified symbol of victory. The Church of the Holy Sepulcher in Jerusalem was dedicated on this day, in 335.

THE EXALTATION OF THE HOLY CROSS, September 14: On May 3 the Church celebrates the finding of the Holy Cross by the Empress Helena in the fourth century. Today's feast commemorates the recovery of this precious relic which the Persians had carried away with them when they captured Jerusalem in 614. Fourteen years later the Christian Emperor Heraclius defeated the Persians, demanded the return of the cross, and brought it back himself in solemn procession to Jerusalem.

The fact that this feast occurs in autumn is significant. Now that the liturgy speaks so much of harvest, death, judgment, and eternity, we ought to turn our eyes to the cross of Jesus Christ, the sign of the victory of our redemption, the pledge of Christian hope, the remembrance of divine love and mercy. The Mass of the feast continually reminds us that in the cross of Christ "is our salvation, life, and resurrection." The cross is "our protection against the wiles of our enemies."[40]

THE SEVEN SORROWS OF THE BLESSED VIRGIN MARY, September 15: On Friday of Passion Week the Church commemorates Mary's Seven Sorrows (see page 121), recalling annually not only the sufferings of Christ but those of His Blessed Mother as well. At that time, however, she dwells particularly on the last three of Mary's Sorrows: her sufferings on the way to Calvary, at the death of Christ, and at His burial. With the Feast of the Exaltation of the Holy Cross still fresh in mind, the Church now commemorates all seven of these Sorrows by a devotion already celebrated in the seventeenth century by the Servites, whose special object was to venerate the Sorrowful Mother.

Today's feast was extended to the universal Church in 1817 by Pope Pius VII to commemorate his release from captivity under Napoleon.

Christians have always honored Mary, the Mother of Sorrows. Representations of the Sorrowful Mother are among the earliest pictures of Mary. Let us also have a childlike recourse to her under this title, espe-

---

[40] Thoughts suggested by the Preface of the Cross are presented in the discussion on Passion Sunday, page 119 ff.

cially when crosses burden us. She knows how to comfort us and help us carry each cross.

THE SEVEN SORROWS OF THE BLESSED VIRGIN MARY

The following are the Sorrows indicated in the illustration above: (1) the prophecy of Simeon; (2) the flight to Egypt; (3) the seeking of the boy Jesus for three days; (4) the meeting on the way of the cross; (5) the sight of her crucified Son and His death; (6) the body of Jesus placed in her arms; (7) the burial of Jesus.

St. Matthew, Apostle and Evangelist, September 21: Before his election by Christ, St. Matthew's name was Levi. He belonged to the class of publicans, a group of men, hateful to the Jews, who collected taxes and duties from their countrymen for the Roman oppressors. Matthew himself tells us the story of his call to the apostleship (Matt. 9:9 ff.). It is related also in the other synoptic gospels (Mark 2:14 ff.; Luke 5:27 ff.). Matthew wrote his gospel in Palestine about the year 50 and addressed it to Jewish Christians. He seeks above all to prove to his countrymen that Jesus Christ is truly the promised Messias and that the Church instituted by Christ is the true Messianic kingdom outside of which there is no salvation.

According to tradition, Matthew preached the Gospel in Persia where he was attacked while offering the holy sacrifice of the Mass. Pierced by a lance, he died a martyr's death. His remains rest in the Church of St. Matthew in Salerno, Italy.[41]

The Dedication of St. Michael, the Archangel, September 29. See page 204.

The Holy Guardian Angels, October 2. See page 207.

THE MOST HOLY ROSARY, October 7: This feast is above all one of thanksgiving for all the benefits and graces granted in the course of time to the entire Church through the rosary.

According to legend, Mary herself taught St. Dominic (feast day: August 4) this beautiful prayer and recommended its use in the fight against the various heresies of his day. At any event, the Order of Preachers was its chief promoter and founded the Confraternity of the Holy Rosary in 1470 at Douai, France. Pope St. Pius V, a Dominican (feast day: May 5), summoned the Confraternity of the Holy Rosary and all Christendom to prayer, when the Turkish hordes threatened to overrun the country, and ascribed the decisive victory over the Turks, at Lepanto on October 7, 1571, to the intercession of

---

[41] For the evangelical symbol of St. Matthew, see page 210.

Mary as "Queen of the most Holy Rosary." Accordingly he ordered a feast of thanksgiving to her as "Mary of Victory." In 1573 Pope Gregory XIII ap-

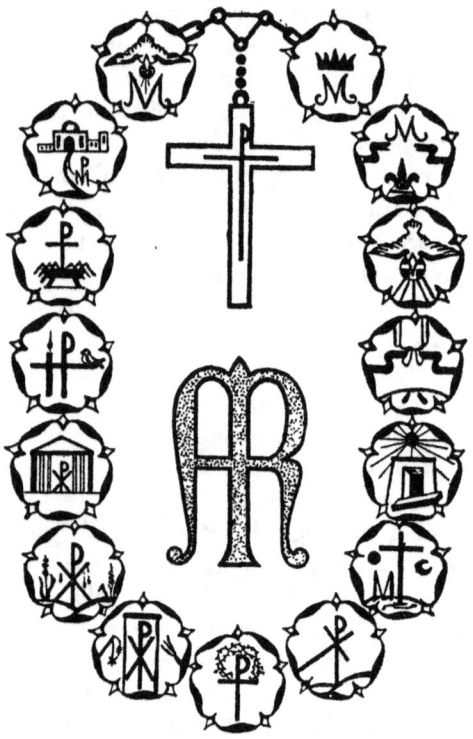

pointed the first Sunday in October as the Feast of the Rosary. Another victory, that of Prince Eugene at Peterwardein on August 5, 1716, led Pope Clement XI to extend the feast to the universal Church. Pope Leo XIII also did much for its spread; he gave it a new Office and Mass, and fixed the day of its celebration on October 7, in memory of the victory at Lepanto.

While the rosary is not a liturgical prayer in the strict sense, it is nonetheless approved and recommended and enjoys many indulgences. Anyone who says that the prayers of the rosary are tedious and spiritless simply indicates that he has not prayed it thoughtfully or that he has little love for prayer. The rosary honors Christ and His Blessed Mother. Its prayers have their origin, directly or indirectly, in heaven. Christ Himself taught us the Our Father; the Angel Gabriel and Elizabeth gave us the Hail Mary. If we say these prayers devoutly, reflecting at the same time on the mysteries of our redemption, from Gabriel's startling announcement to Mary that she was to become the Mother of God to her glorious Assumption into heaven, we will surely not deviate from the spirit of the liturgy.

When we pray the rosary we are in the best of company, for great men of all ages have been ardently devoted to this prayer. Among the popes who prayed it daily are Pius V, Pius VII, Pius IX, Leo XIII, Pius X, and Pius XI; our own holy Father, Pius XII, continues the beautiful example of his predecessors. Among the princes of this world who were specially devoted to it were Charles V of Spain and Alphonsus V of Portugal; among theologians, St. Thomas Aquinas and St. Albert the Great; among musicians, Haydn and Gluck; among field marshals, Count Tilly, Prince Eugene, and Radetzky; and among other great men were St. Thomas More, Windhorst, Ketteler, Seipel, and Dollfuss.

Through seven hundred years of history this prayer has been a gauge of the strength of faith. When faith weakened, the rosary was being neglected; but with each period of religious revival it came again into its own.

Let us learn to pray the rosary devoutly, meditating deeply on its mysteries, so that our faith may increase, our hope grow strong, and our love for Jesus and Mary become more ardent. Let us live with the rosary and die with it. Then the Queen of the Most Holy Rosary will attend to our future in heaven with her.

THE MATERNITY OF THE BLESSED VIRGIN, October 11: In the fourth century a heretic, named Nestorius, asserted that Mary was the mother of the *man,* Jesus, but not the mother of the *Son of God,* and that, therefore, she could not be recognized as the Mother of God. The bishops and faithful of the Church rose resolutely against this false teaching which tried to rob Mary of her greatest prerogative. In 431 the ecumenical council of Ephesus condemned the heresy of Nestorius and solemnly declared that Jesus Christ is true God and that the Blessed Virgin Mary, of whom He was born, is truly the mother of God.

Mary's dignity as Mother of God is, as a matter of fact, commemorated in all her feasts. This is especially true of Christmas when we see her before the crib, contemplating this great mystery as she adores her Divine Son. In some places a separate feast of Mary's maternity was observed in connection with the Feast of the Annunciation. Pius III (431–440), who became pope shortly after the council of Ephesus, had the oldest church of Mary in Rome, St. Mary Major, decorated with wonderful pictures to perpetuate the dogma of Christ's Incarnation and Mary's motherhood of God. On the 15th centenary of the council

of Ephesus, in 1931, Pope Pius XI had these pictures restored and extended the Feast of the Maternity to the universal Church. The pope called the attention of Christians, by an encyclical on this occasion, to the unusual privileges Mary enjoyed as a result of her divine maternity. He alluded especially to her life as a mother, to her resignation to God's will, to her selfless offering, and to her faithful devotion to the Holy Family at Nazareth. He admonished the whole Catholic world to celebrate this new liturgical Mother's Day with a true love for the mother of God, who is also our mother, and to give due regard to the dignity of motherhood. Because of Mary, let us obey, love, and honor our own mothers, and also learn something about a true Christian family spirit from Mary's example.

St. Luke, the Evangelist, October 18: St. Luke was a gentile by birth (Col. 4:10–24). He was a physician in Antioch, the capital of Syria. When he became a Christian is a matter of uncertainty, though his conversion may have occurred shortly after the stoning of St. Stephen. Because of persecution, the Christians fled from Jerusalem and its environs to Antioch and other cities, where they gradually built up Christian communities and were often visited by the apostles and their disciples. This gifted young man soon became the friend and faithful fellow laborer of St. Paul. He accompanied him on his second and third missionary journeys and remained with him during his captivity at Caesarea and Rome. According to tradition, St. Luke died a martyr at the age of eighty, in Greece. His remains were translated to Constantinople in 357 and later removed to Padua.

St. Luke left two important works, his *Gospel* and the *Acts of the Apostles*. One eminent scholar says of St. Luke's Gospel, "It is called the most beautiful of all books, and very truly so. It is the gospel of the Lord who in merciful love seeks to bring sinful mankind to Himself. The master hand of the evangelist pictures the Man of Nazareth as the merciful healer and Saviour in incomparably fervent language." It is St. Luke who tells of the nativity and childhood of Jesus and charmingly characterizes the Blessed Virgin and St. John. Legends about St. Luke claim that he was a painter and that he sketched the first picture of the Blessed Virgin. In his Gospel he has given us three beautiful canticles of the New Testament: the *Benedictus* (Luke 1:68 ff.), the *Magnificat* (1:46 ff.), and Simeon's *Nunc dimittis* (2:19 ff.), as well as the inimitable parables of the prodigal son (15:11 ff.) and the good samaritan (10:30 ff.), and the priceless stories of the conversion of Mary Magdalen (7:36 ff.) and of the repentant thief (23:39 ff.).

Together with the apostolic epistles, the Acts of the Apostles forms one of the most important documents of the history of the primitive Church. St. Luke probably wrote his Gospel about the year 62, and in 63 he wrote the Acts to prove to the Gentile converts that the teachings of Christ are true.

St. Luke is symbolized by the ox, the animal of sacrifice,[42] because he begins his Gospel with the sacrifice of Zachary in the temple, and because he emphasizes the universal priesthood of Christ. Ancient writers add that as an ox has two horns and four hoofs so St. Luke united the two testaments, the Old and the New, and the four gospels in himself and his books.

St. Raphael the Archangel, October 24: See page 206.
ST. SIMON AND ST. JUDE, APOSTLES October 28: The

---

[42] See illustration, page 210.

apostle Simon had the surname *Zelotes* because before his conversion he belonged to the Jewish party known as the Zealots, so called for its zeal in defending the faith. The party hated the Romans intensely and wanted to establish the promised Messianic kingdom by force of arms. After his conversion, Simon preached the Gospel of Christ, the true Messias, at first to his compatriots, the Jews, then to the Gentiles. In Persia he met and worked with the apostle Jude Thaddeus. Their great success aroused the enmity of the pagan priests who sought to kill them. St. Simon is said to have been cut in two by a huge saw and is usually pictured with a saw.

Jude was surnamed Thaddeus, which means "the courageous or valiant one." He was related to Mary and Joseph and hence is spoken of as "a brother of the Lord," an expression which at that time was used to refer to a near relative, as for instance, a cousin. The apostle James the Less was a brother of Jude; both brothers were called to the apostleship at the same time. St. Jude labored first in Judea. Then he went to Syria and Persia where he died a martyr with Simon about the year 72.

St. Jude wrote a short but important epistle between the years 62 and 67. In it he warns the Christian Communities against the doings of the schismatics within the Church. When he speaks of seducers and instigators, his words have a very modern tone: "These are murmurers, full of complaints, walking according to their own desires, and their mouth speaketh proud things, admiring persons for gain's sake" (Jude 16). "But you, my beloved," he earnestly admonishes the faithful, "building yourselves upon your most holy faith, praying in the Holy Ghost, keep yourselves in the love of God, waiting for the mercy of our Lord Jesus Christ, unto life everlasting" (20:21). The apostle Jude is honored as the helper of those who are in desperate need.

OUR LORD JESUS CHRIST THE KING, the last Sunday of October: In the early centuries and through the Middle Ages, Christians were well aware that Christ is the King of kings, the Lord of heaven and earth and of all nations, and that each man must admit and respect His universal kingship. Christ was pictured as a triumphant King even on the cross where he wore, not a diadem of thorns, but a kingly crown; for in the crucified Saviour they saw above all the Messias-King, victorious in death, who bought His kingdom of redeemed souls by shedding His blood on the cross. For this reason, the early Church often depicted him in paintings and in altarpieces as a triumphant King, clothed in gorgeous robes of gold.

Only after the Crusades did Christians begin to look at their crucified Saviour from a more human, subjective point of view. Gradually, the picture of the Crucified lost its royal robes and crown; now Jesus bows His tired head, weighed down by a crown of thorns. No longer is Christ triumphant on the cross as a divine King; He is the Man of Sorrows; He dies in pain and agony. The jeweled cross, *crux gemmata,* set with precious stones and ivory, gives way to one of cold bare wood on which the Son of God hangs dying, robbed of His clothes, crowned with thorns, pierced with nails, His body bruised and bent.

The Church has always clung fast in the liturgical texts to the ancient concept of Christ triumphant on the cross, though she has yielded to the human concept of the crucifixion to the extent of using that type of cross on her altars. But even there, as she honors Christ, the Man of Sorrows, she sees in the cross, not the wood of disgrace and humiliation, but the glorious and victorious sign of our redemption. And in Christ on the cross she sees the divine Redeemer, the royal King of eternal glory. Loudly she proclaims His kingly dignity and affirms His universal rights.

Many people today no longer concede to Christ His inalienable right to kingship. More and more have individual men, states, and nations separated themselves from Christ the King and refused to recognize His sovereignty. To counteract this spirit, Pius XI, in 1925, instituted the Feast of Christ the King with a beautiful Mass and Office. In an encyclical letter he stated clearly that he was establishing the feast to lead the entire human race back to Christ, the king of heaven and earth, who, as divine victor and sovereign, is enthroned at the right hand of the Father and will one day return "with great power and glory to judge the living and the dead."

Christ, the Son of the eternal God, is king and sovereign of every human being. He is king of man's intellect, for He is infinite wisdom and truth. He is king of man's will, for He is infinite holiness. He is king of man's heart, for He is infinite goodness and love. He is king of man's body, for to Him alone and to the faithful observance of His commandments should all the faculties of our body be directed that they serve only for the sanctification and perfection of this temple of the Holy Spirit.

THE REALM OF PEACE AND TRUTH

This illustration shows the royal *crown* imposed on the symbol for Christ, the *Chi-Rho*, with the inscription *Filius Dei*, the Son of God. The *two letters* are the first and last letters of the Greek alphabet, frequently used on altars, vestments and sacred utensils; they symbolize the words of the Lord, God, ' I am the Alpha and the Omega, the beginning and the end" (Apoc. 1:8). The words *"The realm of peace and truth"* are taken from the Preface of the feast. This same thought is expressed in the inscription of the jeweled cross: Christ is our king (*Rex*), law (*Lex*), light (*Lux*), and peace (*Pax*).

All Saints, November 1: It would be difficult for the Church to commemorate solemnly, or even to mention, in her liturgical year, all the saints whom she has ever canonized. Already in the fourth century a feast was instituted to celebrate the memory of all the martyrs. The *Pantheon* was a pagan temple erected by Agrippa in 273 B.C. in honor of all the pagan divinities of Rome; in 610 Pope Boniface IV had it transformed into a Christian church. He transferred to it a great number of relics from the catacombs, and then consecrated it as a Christian basilica in honor of the Mother of God and all the martyrs. It still stands today. In 835 Pope Gregory IV changed its feast of dedication to November 1, fixed it as a permanent date on which to honor all the saints, and extended the feast to the entire Church.

According to the mind of the Church, the Feast of All Saints is pre-eminently a day of thanksgiving, especially to God, the Holy Spirit, for the innumerable graces He has given to so many million souls. All Saints' Day celebrates the triumph of Christ over pagan deities; it is the triumph of grace over human nature. Above all, it bears witness to the efficacy of the Church's work for souls. It illustrates in a concrete way the results of her teaching and her sanctifying powers. Especially does it show that by means of the Holy Eucharist, which is both sacrifice and sacrament, sinners have become saints and an uncounted multitude has gained strength to walk the way of the ten commandments and the eight beatitudes.

All Saints Day honors all those who have attained heaven. "Blessed are ye, . . . be glad and rejoice, for your reward is very great in heaven" (Matt. 5:11–12). There they constitute the glorious following of Christ the King whom the Church counsels us to praise on this feast with the following words: "Come, let us adore the King of kings, for He Himself is the crown of all the saints." The newly instituted Feast of Christ the King, on the Sunday immediately preceding this feast, pictures Him as King of heaven and earth. Surrounded by all the saints, He is enthroned in heaven and will come again one day as judge of the world.

This illustration, "Jesus, Crown of all Saints," represents all the saints (apostles, martyrs, confessors, virgins, and holy women) in symbols. The Gospel of the feast speaks of eight crowns of saints, reminding us of the eight beatitudes, which are the steps to heaven. This sketch pictures *eight crowns,* all directed toward Christ, who calls men to sanctity and provides the grace for attaining it.

This feast day should be one of joy for us. By its position at the end of the liturgical year it is intended to arouse in us a longing for heaven, which is also our goal, and confidence in the helping grace of the Holy Spirit and the intercession of our brothers and sisters who are already there. The lessons of Matins during the octave express these thoughts again and again. We learn who the saints are. All classes, of every age and sex, are represented. They were people like us, but they took the ten commandments seriously and faithfully performed the duties of their state of life for the love of God. Many of them had been great sinners; but once they had allowed the illuminating grace of the Holy Spirit to shine in their souls, they renounced their sinful ways and were conscientious in the pursuit of sanctity. They allowed nothing — not earthly goods, nor money, nor honors, nor temptations — to divert them from their upward climb. They gave up even life itself rather than take the risk of losing sanctifying grace, and with it, the sonship and friendship of God. These weak and erring men, by their co-operation with divine grace, became champions of the love of God and neighbor, and even faithful counterparts of Christ Himself.

St. Augustine tells us what our mental attitude must be if we would become saints. "If these were able to accomplish it, why should I not be able to become a saint also?" To honor the saints, he says, means primarily to imitate them. "You, Christian, are a poor and effeminate soldier," says St. John Chrysostom, "if you imagine that you can be victorious without a battle or triumph (over the devil) without a struggle. Therefore develop your strength, fight bravely, and struggle perseveringly in this war." The imitation of the saints means being faithful to our holy Church, faithful to her teaching, to her ministers, to her holy sacrifice, to her holy sacraments. Then we shall be on the sure way to heaven, our eternal home.

THE COMMEMORATION OF ALL THE FAITHFUL DEPARTED, November 2: "On this day, the commemoration of all the faithful departed, Mother Church endeavors to come to the help of all those who are still held in purgatory, and through her powerful intercession to her Lord and bridegroom Christ, she prays that they soon may be joined to the company of the blessed in heaven." With these words the Martyrology proclaims the purpose of this day.[43] It is a day of the Church's loving care for the dead, a day of compassion and of action, of prayer and atonement for sin.

The saints whom we honored yesterday are at home in their heavenly Father's house. We, who sojourn here on earth, are still on our way home. We can still pray, work, fight, sacrifice, and merit. We can and should always become better, always strive for higher, spiritual things. God's grace is ever at our disposal and we can obtain it without great effort. But we have brothers and sisters in eternity who have not yet reached the goal, who are not yet at home. They are the poor souls, who can no longer do anything for themselves in the way of prayer or merit; they can only suffer and atone. Because of temporal punishment due to sins for which they have not yet offered sufficient satisfaction, they are deprived of eternal bliss, of the vision of God, and are detained in a place of pain and suffering. They, who for a brief moment

---

[43] The Roman Martyrology "gives in brief, for each day of the year, the names and main biographical facts of all the saints that are honored in different parts of the Catholic world" — Dom Virgil Michel, *The Liturgy of the Church* (New York, N. Y.: Macmillan, 1937), p. 15.

saw God, now long for Him, for their home in heaven, for the place of comfort, light, and peace. They love God with all the power of their souls. They long for Him alone, but they cannot yet see and possess Him; they cannot rest in Him. Because of the heinousness of their sins which they now understand and regret, they are separated from eternal Love and

Goodness, from "eternal joys in the land of the living." But all their desires, their longing and petitions are of no avail for themselves. "The night when no one can work" (John 9:4) has come upon them. They are dependent on our sympathy and help.

The Church knows the sufferings and the need of her children in purgatory, and prays for them today. From her altar of sacrifice rich graces stream into all the regions of purgatory. And the Church asks each one of us to be generous in helping the poor souls through prayer and sacrifice. Today she shares with us her inexhaustible treasury of graces in the *toties quoties* indulgence.[44] This is a most efficacious way of helping the dead. We can help them, too, by other prayers, by mortification, work, and suffering.

God indeed frequently demands and counsels prayer and sacrifice for the poor souls. "Blessed are the merciful, for they shall obtain mercy" (Matt. 5:7). And the poor souls whom we free from purgatory by our prayers and sacrifices will be thankful, faithful friends and powerful intercessors on our behalf.

All Souls' Day, in its present form, goes back to the famous Benedictine abbot, Odilo of Cluny (d. 1048), who, in 998, ordered that in all the monasteries under his rule the Office of the Dead be said after the Vespers of All Saints, and that on November 2, holy Masses be offered for all the departed. This salutary practice was soon imitated elsewhere. Pope Pius X earnestly promoted the feast, and Pope Benedict XV, in 1915, granted to every priest the privilege of offering three Masses on this day. Beautiful new Mass prayers, together with a revised Preface of the Dead, were introduced; these and the Sequence *Dies Irae* are rich in meaning.

On the feasts of All Saints and All Souls we are impressed with the consoling doctrine of the *Communion of Saints*. It includes the *Church triumphant*, the saints in heaven, the *Church suffering*, the poor souls in purgatory, and the *Church militant*, the faith-

---

[44] The Holy See grants a plenary indulgence, under the usual conditions, applicable to the Poor Souls, for each visit to a church from noon of All Saints' Day to midnight of All Souls'. At each visit six Our Fathers, six Hail Marys, and six Glorys are to be said according to the intention of the Holy Father; we may *not* substitute other prayers for this indulgence.

ful still on earth. Together they form one body, one family, one Church, the Mystical Body of Christ. We are called upon to help one another in a spirit of love so that we may all reach our eternal goal. We here on earth are helpers of the poor souls, as are the saints in heaven who intercede for them. To the extent that we are united and help one another in love and union with Christ, we ourselves will become more holy.

Dedication of the Basilica of our Saviour in Rome, November 9. See page 320.

ST. MARTIN, November 12: The Feast of St. Martin, bishop, is one of the oldest feasts of a saint who was not a martyr. It was celebrated by the Church as early as the fifth century.

St. Martin, born about 316 in Hungary, was a Roman soldier who abandoned the rough military profession to consecrate his life to God in a monastery in France. Here in 371 he was chosen bishop of Tours, much against his will. Even as bishop he lived a poor and simple life in a monastery founded by himself. Rare holiness and some wonderful miracles made him famous far beyond France. He died in the year 397 at an advanced age, and was soon venerated as one of the first of the confessors.

Because St. Martin was so much venerated in the early centuries of the Church, he is frequently represented in pictures. Usually he is portrayed as a Roman soldier riding a horse and dividing his mantle into two parts with the sword in order to share it with a destitute beggar, thus illustrating an incident recorded in his life. Sometimes he is represented as a bishop with a goose. This concept of the saintly bishop owes its origin to an old custom of eating a roasted goose on the Feast of St. Martin, shortly before entering upon the Advent fast, which was much longer and more severe in past ages than it is now.

DEDICATION OF THE BASILICAS OF ST. PETER AND ST. PAUL IN ROME, November 18:[45] St. Paul's basilica Outside-the-Walls had to be rebuilt because the old church was destroyed in 1823 by a disastrous fire. On December 10, 1854, on the occasion of the promulgation of the dogma of the Immaculate Conception of Mary, the solemn dedication of the splendid new church was made by Pope Pius IX. The remembrance of this dedication is celebrated throughout the universal Church, together with that of St. Peter's, on November 18.

PRESENTATION OF THE BLESSED VIRGIN MARY, November 21: There is nothing in Sacred Scripture about the event which occasioned the institution of this lovely feast of Mary. But tradition and legend relate that the saintly parents, Joachim and Anne, brought their God-given child, Mary, as a little girl to the temple in Jerusalem, in order to dedicate her to God and to have her reared with the temple virgins in quiet seclusion and deep piety. Her childhood years as well as her entire life were to belong wholly to God.

The eastern Church celebrated this feast ("Solemn Entrance of the Mother of God into the Temple") in the sixth century; in the eleventh the feast was celebrated in England; Pope Sixtus IV prescribed it for

---

[45] See the section on the dedication of a church, page 321.

the whole Church in 1472; and Pope Sixtus V confirmed this extension in 1585.

Christian parents should learn from the saintly
Joachim and Anne to care for their children as gifts
of God, to rear them in piety and godly fear.

**THE PRESENTATION OF THE
BLESSED VIRGIN MARY**

St. Cecilia, November 22: St. Cecilia was born of
a noble Roman family. As a faithful Christian she
sought to convert the young people of the pagan nobility to the faith of Christ. Her husband, Valerian,
and his brother, Tiburtius, both became Christians
and later suffered martyrdom. Cecilia was finally ar-
rested for being a Christian and died as a martyr
about the year 230. Already in the fourth century a
church in Rome was built in her honor. In 1599 her
body was found to be still incorrupt.

Cecilia is one of the earliest and most venerated virgin martyrs of the early church. Her name is men-

tioned daily in the Canon of the Mass in the prayer, *Nobis quoque peccatoribus.*

Since the Middle Ages, St. Cecilia has been honored as the patron of sacred music and the chant of the Church. She is usually represented, therefore, with a lyre or an organ. "At the sound of musical instruments," says the first response at the Matins of her feast, "the virgin Cecilia sang to God in her heart." Very beautiful are the chants and lessons of the breviary for this feast, a further indication of the great esteem and honor in which St. Cecilia has always been held.

DEDICATION OF THE CHURCHES: The Church celebrates in her liturgy each year the dedication feasts of her consecrated churches. It is the joyful memorial day of their solemn consecration by the bishop. After consecration, each church can truly be called "the house of God." There we are surrounded by holy quiet and can regain our peace of soul and fortitude to continue, with the grace of God, on the way to our heavenly home.

The impressive ceremonies of the consecration of a church arouse a new awareness of its significance as "the house of God." But human nature is quick to forget. To keep this tremendous and solemn meaning before us constantly, the Church celebrates various dedication feasts in the course of a year. They are:

1. The dedication day of the parish church, if it has been consecrated;

2. The dedication day of the bishop's cathedral, if it has been consecrated;

3. The dedication days of the four principal

MY HOUSE IS
A HOUSE OF PRAYER

This illustration brings to the foreground the liturgical thought behind the blessing of a church. We see a parish church, a cathedral, and St. Peter's in Rome, all mounted by the cross, the symbol of salvation. They are made one in Christ, the heavenly head, the founder of the holy Catholic Church, whom we love and by whose commandments we wish to live.

churches of Rome because they are the mother churches of Christendom, and because in some of them, as in St. Peter's and in St. Paul's, the bodies of the princes of the apostles rest.

Dedication feasts of churches are mentioned early in the history of the liturgy. It is evident that such feasts as the *Exaltation of the Holy Cross,* September 14; *Our Lady of the Snow,* August 5; *St. Michael,* September 29; and *St. Peter in Chains* originally commemorated dedications, and only later were declared feasts of the whole Church.

1. *The Dedication of the Parish Church* (if consecrated): This anniversary of the dedication of the parish church should be a joyous feast for all the children of the parish. The church is the house of God where Jesus lives among us to bless each family and each individual. Grandparents and great-grandparents, perhaps for many generations, have gone there to ask for courage and strength, blessing and grace, and help in every need. They came together there to praise God, to thank Him, and to beg His assistance. There also those who come after us will go to "render to God the things that are God's" (Matt. 22:21).

The dedication feast of our parish should remind us of all the many and great benefits which it brings. It calls us to the most important work in our lives, the care of our immortal souls. The church steeple points upward like a mighty finger and counsels us, *Sursum corda,* "Lift up your hearts to heaven." The bells call out often during the day: "Man, forget not your God, your home in heaven, your immortal soul." When the church bells ring for the last time for us, when our bodies are laid to rest, we hope that then our souls will have arrived safely in heaven. The altar, the sanctuary lamp, and the communion rail remind us of the presence of Christ in His churches. The way of the cross and the crucifix teach us how to carry the crosses and sorrows of life. The confessional tells us where we can always find forgiveness for our sins. The pulpit counsels us to hear and follow the word of God. The pictures of the saints tell us of the brave soldiers of Christ, each of whom was richly rewarded for his love of God and is willing to help us by his intercession and example to gain the same crown of victory.

The feast of the dedication also urges us to love especially our own parish church. It has a greater personal meaning for us than any other in the world. Here by Baptism we became children of God. Here we confessed our sins for the first time. Here we stood with lighted candles and hearts aglow with love, filled with many good resolutions, about to receive our first Holy Communion and Confirmation. Here we pledged eternal faithfulness to Jesus and His Church in the presence of all the people. Here our grandparents and parents were united in holy wedlock. Indeed, the most beautiful, the holiest hours of our lives were spent in our parish church. In our most difficult moments we found comfort and strength from our Lord and we still find them there.

Let us, therefore, love our parish church and support it bounteously. Let us be faithful Christians, coming every Sunday without fail to holy Mass, and as often as possible on weekdays. We know the proverb: "As your Sunday, so will be the day of your death." Or, "He who prays well, lives well; he who lives well, dies well; he who dies well, has a safe journey into eternity." Let us also conduct ourselves reverently in church, for God, our Redeemer, our King, and our Judge, dwells there. It is a fact of experience that as long as people love their church, value what takes place there, and show their appreciation by offerings according to their ability, so long do they prosper.

The dedication feast of the parish church is a first-class feast with an octave.

2. *The Dedication of the Bishop's Church:* All parishes celebrate the anniversary of the dedication of the cathedral[46] or bishop's church, if it has been consecrated. As each parish is made up of families over whom the pastor presides, so all the parishes of a diocese form a body whose head is the bishop, the successor of the apostles, the leader and father of all the priests and faithful in his diocese.

3. *The Dedication of the Four Principal Churches of Rome:* We belong not only to a parish and a diocese, but also to the great body of the holy Catholic Church, headed by our holy father, the pope. The parish church, the diocesan cathedral, the universal church — these are the widening circles of an ever increasing body into which we were born through the holy waters of Baptism. It is this mounting progression from the parish to the cathedral, from the

---

[46] The word *cathedral* comes from the Greek word *cathedra* which means *chair* or *throne*. Such a chair is found in a bishop's church.

cathedral to Rome, that we celebrate with the Church in her liturgy. So, having celebrated the dedication of our parish church and of our diocesan cathedral, we turn to the churches of Rome and their dedication feasts. The principal ones are:

a) *Dedication of the Basilica of our Saviour,* November 9: This church was built by the emperor Constantine near his own great Lateran palace, exactly on the spot where he was baptized by Pope Sylvester (314–335), after he had proclaimed freedom of religious worship in 313 and brought the period of bloody persecution to an end. The Basilica of our Saviour was first consecrated to our Lord; later in the twelfth century, to His precursor, St. John the Baptist. For this reason it is called the *Basilica of Our Saviour* or *The Church of St. John Lateran.* It is the pope's own church, his cathedral. Later the church of St. Peter became the papal cathedral.

In former times the pope lived near the Basilica of Our Saviour in the Lateran palace on the Coelian hill. The palace had belonged to Fausta, wife of Constantine. After his conversion, the emperor gave it to the pope as his residence. It was the first papal church and carried this proud inscription over its entrance: "Mother and Mistress of all Churches." It is the old parish and baptismal church of the city of Rome. Even today it is one of the most beautiful churches of the eternal city, and the scene of many liturgical feasts. During the period of a thousand years one hundred and sixty-one popes lived in the Lateran, of whom forty-seven are canonized saints. Twenty-three popes have been buried there. Until the sixteenth century, more than twenty-five councils were held in this basilica, five of which were great ecumenical councils. There is ample reason, therefore, for the whole of Christendom to celebrate the dedication feast of this first papal cathedral on November 9.

b) Dedication of the Basilicas of St. Peter and of St. Paul, November 18: Since the apostles Peter and Paul are commemorated together on June 29, the dedication of their churches is also commemorated on one and the same day, November 18.

Both churches, like the Basilica of Our Saviour, owe their construction to the emperor Constantine, for he had a church built over the tomb of each apostle. The original edifices do not exist today; in their stead stand two of the most magnificent basilicas of Rome.

The Basilica of St. Peter is the largest church in the world. One hundred and twenty years were spent on its construction by the most renowned architects of the time. Among them were Bramante, who built the cupola, and the great artist, Michelangelo. On November 18, 1626, it was solemnly consecrated by Pope Urban VIII. The Basilica of St. Peter is now the cathedral church of the pope. Beside it is located the Vatican palace in which the holy father resides at present. The magnificent courtyard in front can accommodate more than 150,000 persons at one time and is perhaps the most beautiful place in the world. In the great vault under St. Peter's are the tombs of many popes. The tomb of St. Peter is under the beautiful high altar above which rises the famous cupola.

St. Paul's Outside-the-Walls had to be rebuilt in the nineteenth century because the old church was destroyed by a disastrous fire in 1823. On December 10, 1854, the splendid new basilica was solemnly consecrated by Pope Pius IX.

c) Dedication of the Church of our Lady of the Snow, August 5: The Basilica "St. Mary of the Snow," more generally known as the Church of St. Mary Major, was built in the fourth century and is the largest church in Rome dedicated to our Lady. According to a legend, Mary herself indicated the place of construction through a miraculous snowfall. On one of the hottest days of summer, snow fell in Rome. In a vision, witnessed by Pope Liberius († 366) and a princely, childless couple who wished to give their temporal wealth to honor the Mother of God, it was revealed that on the place where the snow fell a church should be built and dedicated to Mary. From this incident comes the name of the feast as well as the name of the church.[47]

Most of the dedication feasts are celebrated in the autumn of the Church year and for good reasons. The Church is for us "the house of God and the gate of heaven." It is the home of our souls on earth, the type of our everlasting home, the heavenly Jerusalem, as the liturgy says. By studying the prayers of the Mass of dedication, we shall see how all these feasts, directing our attention to our eternal goal, fit so appropriately into the Church's autumnal season.

---

[47] The great nave of this patriarchial basilica is formed by two rows of forty-eight white marble columns. The ceiling is covered with the first gold brought from America.

INDEX

www.ingramcontent.com/pod-product-compliance
Lightning Source LLC
Chambersburg PA
CBHW070903120626
46546CB00001B/112